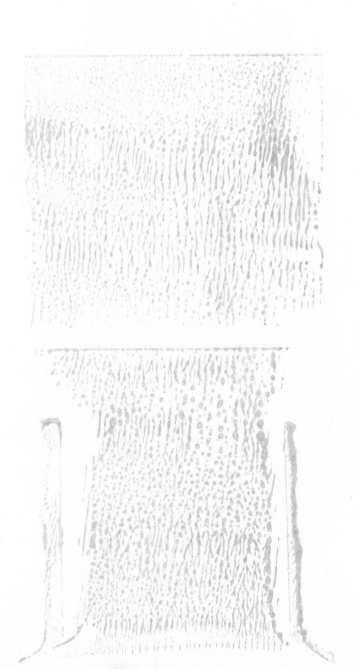

The Role of
Place in Literature

The Role of
Place in Literature

LEONARD LUTWACK

SYRACUSE UNIVERSITY PRESS   1984

Copyright © 1984 by SYRACUSE UNIVERSITY PRESS
Syracuse, New York 13210

Library of Congress Cataloging in Publication Data

Lutwack, Leonard.
  The role of place in literature.

  Includes bibliographical references and index.
  1. Setting (Literature) I. Title. II. Title: Place
in literature.
PN56.S48L8   1984   809'.922   83-24264
ISBN 0-8156-2305-4

Manufactured in the United States of America

CONTENTS

PREFACE

THE ROLE OF PLACE IN LITERATURE is a topic of ancient lineage in the history of literary criticism, and yet no one has treated it at length. Prescriptive critics made rules for the use of place in drama, rhetoricians identified some place types such as the pleasant place *(locus amoenus),* and biographers have shown the significance of geographical places in the careers and works of a few writers. But no one has examined in a single study more than one or two aspects of the subject, perhaps because it appears presumptuous and foolhardy to encompass an element of literature that is so ubiquitous. Yet looking at the whole extent of an immense amount of material may have some results that a complete mastery of an isolated part of it cannot produce. That, at least, is the hope of this study.

The focus of the book necessarily shifts from very broad considerations to more limited ones. This is particularly the case with Chapter 1 which introduces the thematic and formal interests pursued throughout the book. It raises some philosophical issues regarding attitudes toward mankind's home, the earth, the ultimate ground on which the literary theme of place is based; then it turns briefly to examples of the formal uses of place in a literary work. Chapter 2 is a classification of the physical properties of place as they are rendered in literature, and Chapter 3 narrows the focus to the functioning of a single place metaphor, the analogy of place and the human body. I see these two chapters as a beginning model for a rhetoric in which the many uses of place in literature are classified and exemplified. In the last three chapters the primary emphasis is shifted from place to three literary matrices employing place for their special purposes: an author—Herman Melville, a national literature—American, and a period of writing—the twentieth century.

It will be noted that these widely various topics, while they are deemed pertinent to the subject, are not drawn together by an over-all theory of place in literature. My method has been, rather, the accumulation of numerous and, I hope, telling examples of place usage, principally from American and British literature and the discrete evaluation of these in terms of the social attitudes giving rise to them and the manner in which they contribute meaning, form, and psychological effect to literary works. Although the primary responsibility I have taken upon myself is the description of a common literary element, the book ultimately finds its motive in the unique twentieth-century anxiety over the condition of mankind's total environment, the earth-as-place, and my conviction that literature has a part to play in addressing itself to that grave concern.

In the long pursuit of so broad a subject I have become indebted to colleagues and students, whose suggestions I profited from in the search for materials, and to the General Research Board of the Graduate School, University of Maryland, whose summer grants provided me with free time for research and writing. For these my deepest gratitude.

College Park, Maryland   LL
Spring 1983

The Role of
Place in Literature

1

THE NEW CONCERN FOR PLACE

LITERARY CRITICISM may not be said to progress as science presumably does, but at least a sense of progress can be gained from the fact that the preoccupations of one age of critics seldom fail to appear as trivial to a later age, which then flatters itself upon discovering matters neglected by an earlier age. Critical concerns move in and out of focus, but no concern is ever wholly overlooked or lost. All that was once thought to be worth saying about the role of time in literature used to come under the heading of unity of time in drama. Not too long ago it was hardly credible that the unity of time exercised critics from the Renaissance to the nineteenth century, when, after the affair of Hugo's *Hernani* in 1830, it finally became a dead issue. Yet in the twentieth century time has again become an important subject for criticism, except that now it is time in the novel rather than time in the drama that fascinates critics. It is a further irony in the history of literary criticism that while no one considered time of any consequence in such a loose form as the epic, now it turns out that its successor, the novel, employs the most subtle and most controlled uses of time never before suspected to be possible in the art of narrative.

Criticism may not progress, but it sometimes discovers literary elements that are exposed to view whenever the style of writing changes or whenever society changes so radically that new perspectives are forced upon the attention. The violence of literary change and experiment in the twentieth century has presented criticism with the opportunity to make an unprecedented examination of literary phenomena now suddenly laid bare. With the recession or mangling of traditional centers of meaning—plot, character, theme, and style— criticism is forced to uncover literary elements that have either escaped notice or assert themselves in newly important ways. Time is one of these old elements in new guises; it has received such intensive

1

treatment in the writing and criticism of twentieth-century fiction that it is now possible for a critic to assert that "the novel . . . may be thought of as an attempt to come to terms with Time."[1] As interest in the social and intellectual contexts suffers from the general disorientation of our time and as the kind of reductionism long practiced in science becomes more popular in the humanities, we can expect criticism to look more closely at the physical contexts within a literary work, specifically its rendering of space, motion, things, processes, and places. Denis Donoghue calls for this very emphatically:

> History and time are dangerous concepts because they seem to identify meaning with teleology and they lead the poet to fancy that he sees the spirit of the age by reading its signs in history. Eliot, Pound, Yeats, Wyndham Lewis: political messes, historical delusions. Poets would do better to turn away from time toward space, from history toward geography, topography, landscape, place.[2]

In addition to a new interest in place as a formal element in literature, the twentieth century evidences a new interest in place as an important issue in general. This is a result of widespread public recognition that earth as a place, or the total environment, is being radically changed and perhaps rendered uninhabitable by more and more pervasive and powerful technologies. Science, ironically, creates the technologies and posts the warnings. Terrible anxiety, surpassing the apocalyptic fears of earlier times, is the emotional result for people all over the world. Accommodation to man-made changes in the environment would alone be a serious enough challenge, but now little doubt exists that the issue is the survival of mankind. There is a growing conviction that man's use of the earth's resources, his alteration of places in every corner of the globe, must proceed now with a view not only to present profit and pleasure but to the survival of the very next generation. The great question is whether man can change his perception of himself in relation to his surroundings in such a way as to achieve this end. An increased sensitivity to place seems to be required, a sensitivity inspired by aesthetic as well as ecological values, imaginative as well as functional needs. In so far as the representation of place in literature has an important influence on how people regard individual places and the whole world as a place, it may be concluded that literature must now be seen in terms of the contemporary concern for survival.

Awareness of ecology, like the Christian dogma of the Fall,

creates a feeling of guilt over man's mistreatment of earth. The sin against earth may be absolved not by transcending this life but by practicing an earth ethic calculated to restore the earthly paradise. The distinguished ecologist René Dubos writes: "An ethical attitude in the scientific study of nature readily leads to a theology of earth."[3] The space scientist, on the other hand, sees in the exploration of outer space a hope of man's expansion in the universe, the possibility that he may break out of earth's environment and use extra-terrestrial space to enhance earth's capabilities if not to serve as a totally new habitat for mankind. Between them ecology and space science thus reflect new emphases of old Christian views of earth, ecology believing in earth before the Fall and space science believing in a leap beyond earth after the Fall; one takes a conservative position—strangely enough winning the assent of intellectuals—while the other hopes for a radical break with earth, promising to obtain with technology what Christians once took on faith. Norman Mailer states the opposed views in this way: "Perhaps we live on the edge of a great divide in history and so are divided ourselves between the desire for a gracious, intimate, detailed and highly particular landscape and an urge less articulate to voyage out on explorations not yet made."[4]

The dilemma posed by Mailer—"caught between our desire to cling to the earth and to explore the stars"—is nothing new but rather the age-old ambivalence of man's view of his earthly abode. Two opposed ideas about earth have always competed for man's assent: one, that earth is a hostile, alien place, keeping man from a human potential that can only be realized by transcending earth; and the other, that earth is man's true home, his only possible environment, which he must adapt to and control in order to fulfill himself. Judeo-Christian religious thought casts earth into a minor role in a narrative governed by time rather than place, the redemption of mankind being a terminal point, whereas science, committing itself to space and matter, makes earth an object worthy of its understanding and control. Religion accords no honor to gods who have had the misfortune of visiting earth and remaining imprisoned there, chained to a rock, like Prometheus, or buried under a mountain, like Enceladus. Satan's ignoble punishment is to remain fixed at earth's center, and Jesus may return to heaven only when the rock before his earthly tomb is miraculousiy rolled away. The Shekinah, or actual presence of God in Judaic belief, never occupies an earthly place but hovers ten hand-breadths above the ground; being placeless, God is therefore illimitable as well as invisible. Of earth-bound gods Prometheus is the most exceptional because he is content with earth and helps man accommodate himself to earth through technology, like the scientist; Enceladus is the most godlike because he absolutely refuses to accept the condition of earth-boundedness—the earth "chained for a ball to drag at his o'erfreighted feet," writes Melville in *Pierre;* and Christ lies somewhere between, visiting earth to redeem mankind but finally escaping earth to dwell in heaven; upon his second coming earth will cease to exist. Being made in God's image, man is to that extent homeless upon earth. Christ may be speaking for man as well as for himself when he says in Matthew 8.20: "The foxes have holes, and the birds of the air have nests; but the Son of man hath not where to lay his head." The earth is a home for animals but not for men.

The modern age has seen a curious reversal of religious and scientific attitudes toward earth. With the prodding of science and the Enlightenment, Christianity in the last two centuries has learned to entertain the possibility of transforming a fallen world into a happy place, and it is science that now is time-ridden and full of dire warnings of earth's demise through technological and ecological disaster. Science, too, now seeks for ways to make earth superfluous, either by sealing up man in a totally artificial environment or by giving him the means to leave the planet altogether and inhabit space or another planet, where his intelligence, like the soul of the Christian, can fulfill its potential by mastering the mysteries of the universe beyond earth.

In expressing the need both to embrace and to escape earth, religion and science reflect, in specialized ways, the common experience of the race. The association of earth with the human body that is so pronounced in a primitive condition weakens as mankind becomes civilized. A concern for time rather than place is the mark of civilization. As Wordsworth, and later Jung, so well understood, the maturation of an individual is a process of growing away from nature. The difference between archaic man and modern man, Mircea Eliade points out, "lies in the fact that the former feels himself indissolubly connected with the Cosmos and the cosmic rhythms, whereas the latter insists that he is connected only with History."[5] Only upon the special pleading of sophisticated theory can man be made to feel close kinship with nature, for this requires the surrender of some measure of humanity to accomplish. Contemporary ecology continues the romantic idea of man's harmony with nature, but its scientific underpinning does not make it any more palatable. Critics of the artificial environment of our times forget that man's alienation from earth is probably more natural than his close association with it and cannot be attributed solely to the Judeo-Christian tradition or modern finance capitalism. Humanity seems permanently disposed to waver between acceptance and tran-

scendence of earth, between kinship with earth and revulsion against
the environmental dependence that must be suffered equally with
animal and vegetable forms of life. The ultimate cause of this ambivalence is the knowledge that earth is both the source of life and the
condition of death, a place where life begins and ends. Though born of
earth, man is reluctant to return to earth, to surrender possibility and
accept known limitation.

To discover a stay against death and dissolution on earth is the
ambition of literature as well as religion and science. The imagination
of the poet is his means to celebrate earth, but it is also his means to
escape earth in a "flight" to a realm where he can dispose of things
without reference to their limitations in nature. Thus both ecstatic
identification with earth and horror of earth compete for expression.
The drag of earth toward death is rendered in place terms by Edgar
Allan Poe in a remarkable passage from "The Colloquy of Monos and
Una": "The consciousness of *being* had grown hourly more indistinct,
and that of mere *locality* had, in great measure, usurped its position.
The idea of entity was becoming merged in that of *place*. The narrow
space immediately surrounding what had been the body, was now
growing to be the body itself." For Poe the horror of dying is that place
and the body are joined to usurp consciousness. The pantheistic,
Wordsworthian program of William Cullen Bryant's "Thanatopsis"
calls for the identification of soul with earth ("To mix for ever with the
elements,/To be a brother to the insensible rock"), but Bryant cannot
leave it at that and closes with the more traditional figure of the soul
lying down to rest in a "chamber in the silent halls of death." As
Thoreau so knowingly puts it, the Indian is Nature's "inhabitant and
not her guest, and wears her easily and gracefully. But the civilized
man has the habits of the house."[6] The fear of earth is often on the pen
of William Faulkner, who writes, on the occasion of Mink Snopes's
death in *The Mansion:*

> Because a man had to spend not just all his life but all the time
> of Man too guarding against it; even back when they said man lived
> in caves, he would raise up a bank of dirt to at least keep him that
> far off the ground while he slept, until he invented wood floors to
> protect him and at last beds too, raising the floors storey by storey
> until they would be laying a hundred and even a thousand feet up in
> the air to be safe from the earth.[7]

There is also in Faulkner an appreciation of the life-giving power
of earth, but it is not transcendent: "the earth dont want to just keep

things, hoard them; it wants to use them again. Look at the seed, the
acorns, at what happens even to carrion when you try to bury it: it
refuses too, seethes and struggles too until it reaches light and air
again, hunting the sun still."[8] Cleanth Brooks labors to prove that there
is a strong Wordsworthian strain in Faulkner, but he must conclude
that in the final analysis there is "no easy subsidence into nature" for
Faulkner: "But love nature though man should, and respect it though
he must, he is alienated from nature and must never presume upon an
easy union with it if he wishes to call himself a man."[9] John Gardner's
novels preserve a balance between the gravity of earth and man's
efforts to escape gravity. Like Faulkner's Mink Snopes, James Page, in
October Light, is a mean, adamantly earth-bound man:

> He was a man who worked with objects, lifting things, setting
> them down again—bales of hay, feedbags, milkcans, calves—and
> one of his first-class opinions was this: All life—man, animal, bird,
> or flower—is a brief and hopeless struggle against the pull of earth.
> The creature gets sick, his weight grows heavier, he has moments
> when he finds himself too weary to go on; yet on he goes, as long as
> he lives, on until the end—and it *is* a bitter one, for no matter how
> gallantly the poor beast struggles, it's a tragic and hopeless task.
> The body bends lower, wilting like a daisy, and finally the pull of
> the earth is the beast's sunken grave.[10]

To this man, escape from earth's gravity is but "the illusion of freedom
and ascent," a false vision from the Devil, "all dazzle and no lift, mere
counterfeit escape, the lightness of a puffball—flesh without nu-
trients—the lightness of a fart, a tale without substance, escape from
the world of hard troubles and grief in a spaceship." But by the end of
the book Page reaches a reconciliation with his sister, who represents
the spirit of ascent that he had reviled. In Gardner's *The Sunlight
Dialogues,* Fred Clumly also finds a position between the two poles,
this time represented by the earth-loving Mesopotamians, on the one
hand, and the transcendent, duty-bound Jews, on the other.

The opposing views of earth get translated into literary terms
through various genres and literary movements. The pastoral, from
ancient times to its modern adaptations, presents man in ideal harmony
with a natural environment only improved by the arts of civilization. In
this setting the country swain is a permanent inhabitant, content with
land, animals, and people; his city cousin is an occasional visitor, who
finds in the country a temporary relief from the excessively artificial
life in the city. These are degrees of control and adaptation: Utopia

asserts the triumph of the distinctively human spirit over environment, while the pastoral Arcadia prizes accommodation to a natural environment.[11] The tragic and epic genres, on the other hand, show man asserting his will over nature in a struggle that often results in the hero's fall and nature's damage.[12]

Robinson Crusoe is true to the spirit of eighteenth-century rationalism in attempting to strike a balance between the comic and tragic response to the problem of man's occupancy of earth. The island he is shipwrecked on is Crusoe's world, and the narrative traces his reluctant acceptance of its limitations. Having been conditioned by the amenities of a civilized society, he views the island, a natural place, as a fallen Eden, God's harsh judgment for his sins. He sees his situation as entirely tragic: the island is a prison, an "Island of Despair," indeed "the most miserable condition that mankind could be in." The only good thing about it is that it is better than death. His first act on the island is not to explore the place for the life-supports it may have to offer but to defend himself against the perils he imagines it harbors, principally attacks from cannibalistic savages. Like Kafka's mole he is obsessed with building an impregnable hideout, which he calls his castle—he never needs to use it. But as well as scaring himself with unnecessary anxieties, Crusoe also applies himself realistically to the problems of survival, and after twenty-three years he is completely "naturalized to the place" and can even find reasons for its superiority over civilized places. It is typical of his lingering civilization, however, his basic unsuitableness as an inhabitant of a primitive island, that he keeps up his morale by imagining himself the emperor of his domain, miserable though it is, and dreams of enslaving captured savages to do his bidding. Only the fear of death continues to bind him to the place, for when he attempts to sail away, a day spent on the shoreless sea is enough to convince him that the island is preferable to the terrors of the open sea: "Now I looked back upon my desolate, solitary island, as the most pleasant place in the world." Nevertheless, when Crusoe is finally taken off the island in a safe manner, he does not regret leaving his home of twenty-eight years. He bequeaths it to three mutineers on the principle that men who face hanging in England ought to be thankful to shift for themselves on a primitive island.

Romantic poetry expresses a more passionate acceptance and rejection of earth than Defoe could muster. It lends itself to the scientist's view of environment by adding to the factualism of science an emotional identification with places and things. As Wordsworth notes in his preface to the Lyrical Ballads, the poet's passions, thoughts, and feelings are connected "with the operations of the elements, and the appearances of the visible universe; with storm and sunshine, with the revolutions of the seasons, with cold and heat." The excitement over new-found places in the Age of Exploration was rather abstract, when it was not given over to fantasy, and needed the romantic insistence on fact as well as feeling to complete it. The Renaissance exploration of the world had to be repeated by romantic poets in order to teach people how to experience places intimately. To romantic literature, which owes so much to the inspiration of travel, belongs the credit of changing our sensibility of geographical place from ignorant supposition and curiosity in the bizarre to sentimental valuation. Because of the romantic revolution in feeling, Western man cannot regard the earth and its places quite as he did before.

The most extreme expression of the romantic esteem for earth is the mystical identification of the poet with earth and its elements. Walt Whitman, for example, adapts a common metaphor when he celebrates his origin in earth ("Long I was hugg'd close—long and long") and his return to earth upon dying when he surrenders his body to air ("It coaxes me to the vapor and the dusk"), to water ("I effuse my flesh in eddies"), and to soil ("I bequeath myself to the dirt to grow from the grass I love"). This exceeds Shelley's identification of poetry with the elements ("a wave, a leaf, a cloud") in "Ode to the West Wind." But no one has gone to the extremes of a certain Walter Whiter, who wrote four volumes to prove that all language derives from earth terms, specifically from the consonantal cluster RTH in the word *earth*— Emerson and Thoreau were impressed by the theory.[13] Melville was more cautious in accepting the idea of earth identification. In a letter to Hawthorne in June, 1851, he interpreted Goethe's "Live in the all" to be an invitation to "spread and expand yourself, and bring to yourself the tinglings of life that are felt in the flowers and the woods, that are felt in the planets Saturn and Venus, and the Fixed Stars." As a universal precept this was nonsense, but as "a temporary feeling" Melville could not deny the experience: "You must often have felt it, lying on the grass on a warm summer's day. Your legs seem to send out shoots into the earth. Your hair feels like leaves upon your head. This is the *all* feeling."

The same power of imagination that enables the poet to identify with earth also may be used to give him wings to escape earth. Such, at least, is the long-standing conviction of literary criticism—of Sir Philip Sidney, who insists in *An Apologie for Poetrie* that the poet is not subject to nature, "not inclosed within the narrow warrant of her guifts, but freely ranging only within the Zodiack of his owne wit"; of Andrew Marvell in "The Garden":

> The mind . . . creates, transcending these,
> Far other worlds and other seas,
> Annihilating all that's made . . . ;

of Emerson on the poet in *Nature:*

> By a few strokes he delineates—as on air—the sun, the mountain,
> the camp, the city, the hero, the maiden, not different from what
> we know them, but only lifted from the ground and afloat before
> the eye. He unfixes the land and the sea, makes them revolve
> around the axis of his primary thought and disposes them anew.

Shakespeare is Emerson's prime example: "His imperial muse tosses
the creation like a bauble from hand to hand, and uses it to embody any
caprice of thought that is uppermost in his mind." The image is similar
to one in Act I of Goethe's *Prometheus:*

> Könnt ihr den weiten Raum
> Des Himmels und der Erde
> Mir ballen in meine Faust?

Speculating on the possibility that the stone he uses to build a wall may
be a fallen meteorite, Robert Frost writes in "A Star in a Stone-Boat":

> Such as it is, it promises the prize
> Of the one world complete in any size
> That I am like to compass, fool or wise.

For all its feeling for place and for all its respect for real places,
romanticism yet seeks to transcend earth through flight or motion and
find fulfillment beyond earth. Wordsworth's two skylark poems illustrate the romantic ambivalence in accepting and transcending earth.
The bird in his 1825 poem returns to his nest from the "privacy of
glorious light" in the sky; he may "soar but never roam," and he remains "True to the kindred points of Heaven and Home." In the poem
of 1805 a more typically romantic skylark escapes earth altogether to a
"banqueting place in the sky," a place which is no place at all because it
is free of all places. Beyond the real places they loved to return to for
renewal of the man, romantic poets cherished the unearthly visionary

place where spirit alone may abide—Shelley's "Eden of the purple East" in *Epipsychidion* and the "circumscribed Eden" of Poe's dreams. The earth-bound Whitman, especially in his later poetry, also happily yearns for the identification of his soul with extra-terrestrial entities in "Passage to India":

> Thou matest Time, smilest content at Death,
> And fillest, swellest full the vastnesses of Space.

Again, in "Darest Thou Now O Soul," the journey of the soul into "the unknown region" is welcomed:

> Till when the ties loosen,
> All but the ties eternal, Time and Space.

The temporal ties are those binding the soul to the body, and when these are loosened in death, the body reverts to earth, to place, and the soul to motion.

The romantic writer lends himself both to the joy of place and the exhilaration of free flight in space. His is an ambivalent view of earth, best expressed in lyrical poetry but also in characterizations such as Faust or opposed heroes like Ahab and Ishmael. Ahab is intent on smashing all creation to satisfy his Enceladean outrage against the limitations imposed on man, but Ishmael lovingly assimilates all the details of creation in both scientific catalogues and in frequent trance-like moments of complete identification with the cosmos. The persona Thoreau creates for himself is both naturalistic and transcendental: his devotion to the facts of the natural environment is just short of scientific precision, but he never fails to remember that man is "but a sojourner in nature" and must not try to establish himself there. In one sense *Walden* may be an ecological primer on the orientation of man in nature, yet it also fulfills the function of all good literature in separating man from nature: "The best works of art are the expression of man's struggle to free himself from this condition."[14] Faced with the ultimate substance of earth, matter, Thoreau is revolted; the rocky heights of Mount Katahdin appall him in *Maine Woods:* "This was that Earth of which we have heard, made out of Chaos and Old Night."[15] It is a little surprising to hear Thoreau repeating the pre-romantic horror of mountains, but a rock is the ultimate form of unhumanized earth, and a mountain is a fearsome collection of rocks. Even a mountain lover like James Ramsey Ullman can be struck by the "immense vista of ruin and decay" that the Swiss Alps present to the eye in *The White Tower;* and the mountains are emblematic of earth: "It was as if the structure of the earth itself were slowly and inexorably converging, carrying the whole vast tattered fabric of peaks and wasteland with it into one distant ultimate node of sterility and nothingness."[16] A mountain is the most insistent of places, blotting out time itself: "It was the next rock, the next step, the next breath." But both views of man's environment, as horror and splendor, must be experienced. Once Ullman's mountain climber has come to know the mountain through scaling it, he knows the condition of man in the world: "It was as if slowly, as he climbed, one veil after another were being withdrawn from between him and the apprehensible world."

The Industrial Revolution made the romantic love affair with earth untenable. The effects of industrialism on the countryside, which it despoiled and abandoned, and on the cities, which it crowded and polluted with unmanageable masses of people, were deplored by romantic writers; but these conditions became the stock-in-trade of naturalists. Drawing on romanticism's attachment to place and its respect for the facts of place, naturalism developed the techniques of detailed and cumulative description of environment to reveal the horrors of town and city, farm and factory, thus extending the range of places treated in literature and reversing the romantic feeling of endearment to one of revulsion. Without the fund of sentiment for places accumulated by romantic writing, the naturalistic reaction would not have been so strong: if there had not been so great an exhilaration over nature and its power of uplift, despair over the victimization of man by his environment would not have been so deep; if landscape had not played so great a role as a consolator of man in romantic poetry, landscape would not have become so fierce an "assailant" in the writing of the twentieth century. Naturalism made capital out of the clash between a beautiful earth and an ugly earth, between nature and city, between a happy adjustment to surroundings and entrapment.

The ultimate result of a century or more of naturalistic writing has been that the sense of place inherited from Renaissance exploration and romantic identification has yielded in the twentieth century to a sense of place-loss and a sense of placelessness. This will be discussed at length in the last chapter dealing with literature of the last one hundred years. The point to be made here is that literature always reflects ambivalent attitudes toward earth and its constituent places. Plotting the history of attitudes would result perhaps in a bell curve: alienation and fear in man's earliest history yield in the late eighteenth and early nineteenth centuries to intense celebration of earth, but this feeling soon wanes and fear, now touched with despair, again asserts

itself. The curve may reflect either a cyclical or linear reality, a renewal
or final demise of earth, but at any point along the curve, literature is
capable of expressing both dread and joy of earth, escape and union.

PLACE AND FORM

Place gets into literature in two ways, as idea and form: as attitudes
about places and classes of places that the writer picks up from his
social and intellectual milieu and from his personal experiences, and as
materials for the forms he uses to render events, characters, and
themes. While there is no lack of scholarship on attitudes about place
and the influence of place on authors' lives and works, critical consideration of the formal use of place in literature has only recently gone
very far beyond the traditional unity of place in drama. There are
studies on the use of place by particular writers—the houses of Henry
James, for instance—and there is a long tradition of investigating the
influence of landscape painting on poetry and the novel.[17] There are
also many place typologies, or studies of the use of certain kinds of
places in specific periods of literary history, such as A. Bartlett
Giamatti's review of the earthly paradise in Renaissance epic, Bernard
Blackstone's analysis of the favorite places of six romantic poets,
Joseph Warren Beach's unfinished study of the obsessive place imagery of poets between 1930 and 1950, W. H. Auden's little book on
the sea in romantic poetry, and Richard Gill's history of the role of the
country house in English fiction.[18] The ideas people have about places
make up the material for works like Marjorie Nicolson's history of the
revolution of thought about mountains and Henry Nash Smith's discussion of the American's view of the West.[19]

Still, there is lacking a theory of the formal use of place in literature. One would have to agree with Alexander Gelley that "we have
barely begun to construct a rhetoric of fiction dealing primarily with the
scenic aspect of the novel."[20]

Place and Genre

Unity of place in the drama was for many centuries the only category under which literary criticism treated the role of place in literature. An offspring of the unity of time—"From the narrow limitation of

time necessarily arises the contraction of place," declared Dr. Johnson—unity of place was always a more troublesome matter; for time,
as Johnson further observed, is "most obsequious to the imagination,"
while place is not so easily assimilated to the requirements of dramatic
action. Since plays are presented in plain view of an audience, the
dramatist must reckon with both the place where the actors are imaginatively supposed to be, as represented by the stage setting, and the
place where they actually are, the theatre. The theatre may be dimmed
when the lights go down, but the theatre room continues to impose
conditions of space and light in the staging of a play. The construction
and changing of stage settings naturally restrict the number and kind of
places at the disposal of playwrights. More important, the stage setting
constitutes such an insistent physical presence that it may beguile and
distract the attention, verbalization being at a disadvantage when it is
in close competition with visualization. It was this consideration that
induced Aristotle to rate stage setting as the least important of the six
elements of tragedy because it was the work of the carpenter rather
than the poet and could create "an emotional attraction of its own"
apart from the more essential business of the play.

Through verbal clues in conjunction with unobtrusive settings, the
good dramatist manages to incorporate place without jeopardizing dramatic force. An acceptable way to evoke off-stage places is through the
cumulative effect of references in the dialogue of characters. Shakespeare does this effectively in eight of his comedies, which, though
limited to a single stage setting, still present the impression of a second
place through the introduction of characters from that place. "The
action," writes Clifford Leech, "depends primarily on the impact of the
strangers (who generally bring with them a sense of another locality,
which is not presented on the stage) on the normal inhabitants of the
locality."[21] Shakespeare thus plays off the staged place against the
unseen place, the wild island of the New World against over-civilized
Italy and its warring principalities. The same is done in Chekhov's *The
Cherry Orchard* in which the normal course of dialogue provides us
with a vivid picture of the orchard as it was in the old days, as it is now,
and as it will be when it is subdivided; or in Ibsen's *The Master Builder*
in which a hundred stylistic nuances give us a sense of contrast between the crumbling foundation of the present life of Solness and his
aspiration to ascend to great heights in the future, culminating in the
reported off-stage scene when he climbs and falls from the tower of the
new house. Regardless of these successful representations of place, it
still must remain an incontrovertible principle that in dramatic art a
character is better displayed by his responses to other characters in

present circumstances than by his responses to places, either present
or remembered.

To avert altogether the problem of place in the drama, the purist
would limit stage setting to a "platform in space"; the realist, on the
other hand, would make more use of modern technology to create the
illusion of actual places on the stage. With the development of cinema
the debate between the purist and realist is less crucial because the
ability of the camera to literalize setting gives the realist fuller scope for
his requirements than the stage can ever afford, leaving the purist his
bare boards, his "lieu théatral." The camera, of course, may choose
not to use its literal powers and may instead assert its ability to distort
places with expressionistic filming; but more often the use of the camera is bound to result in more detailed and more numerous scenes than
the stage can possibly achieve. No matter what technology may be able
to do with settings, however, there remains in all dramatic production,
whether on stage or film, a clear necessity to hold in check the strong
pull of place-setting away from dramatic interest toward spectacle or
the simply pictorial. Dramatic force can be dissipated by unrestrained
use of the camera as well as by intrusive stage setting.

The poet is also restricted in his use of place. Place is only part of
the phenomenal world at his disposal, and if he exploits it for its own
sake his writing sinks to the rather insignificant sub-genre Dr. Johnson
called "local poetry" or place-poetry, the kind of "itinerary" poems
that Wordsworth wrote to honor places he visited on his travels in
England, Scotland, and the continent. A place may inspire, but a balance must be maintained between the place that inspires and the poet
who is inspired, between object and subject. In the relationship between place and person, the person cannot come off second best, for
what counts is the subjective flow set in motion by the place, the
amount and intensity of inwardness that external stimuli can arouse. In
his best work Wordsworth understood this, and for this reason it is
possible for one of his readers to say that Wordsworth "responds to
landscape rather than observes it; he feels it, almost, rather than sees
it"; and for another reader to say that Wordsworth's encounter with
landscape was significant because of "the poet's reflection upon its
effect upon his mind."[22] This compares with what has been said about
William Carlos Williams, for whom writing had to make contact with
the actual, "but having made contact, his preoccupation was with the
use of it; for he did want to use it, not just look at it and record it."[23] In
another discussion of Williams the principle at stake here is evolved:
"The poet must transcend the limitations of logical, visual, or geo-

graphical space in order to bring into existence the new poetry of multiple elements in fluid intimacy."[24]

Wordsworth recognized two dangers in the association of the poet with landscape: if landscape is viewed too objectively, mind is threatened; if the poet identifies too closely with landscape, he may lose himself in narcissistic solipsism. In a poem such as "Tintern Abbey" the balance between place and subjective experiences associated with place is maintained with only twenty lines to set the scene at the beginning of this long poem and two lines to return us to the scene at the end. Similarly, T. S. Eliot's "Burnt Norton" begins *Four Quartets* with a fairly steady focus on a rose-garden and closes with a fleeting reiteration of that place in the lines

> There rises the hidden laughter
> Of children in the foliage.

The same garden is also found at the very end of *Four Quartets,* completing, as M. H. Abrams points out, the circuitous journey of the whole poem.[25] In both the Wordsworth and Eliot poems places are used as frames within which the poet ranges freely in pursuit of a chain of reflections that spring from associations with places but ultimately transcend place in order to use it as a symbol for a variety of ideas—freedom, faith, divinity. Concentration on a single place makes possible a greater range and intensity of reflection. In the fusion of mind and nature that constitutes art for Coleridge, the poet inclines toward the excitements of the mind, with a consequent dilution of nature. Coleridge's emphasis on imagination is confirmed by poets in all ages. It is the frequently reiterated point of a good deal of Wallace Stevens's poetry: "seemings" or "the way things look" are what the poet deals with, and "seeming is description without place"; indeed, the poet has his origin in the fact that he inhabits an alien world:

> From this the poem springs: that we live in a place
> That is not our own and, much more, not ourselves. . . .[26]

It is not knowing the place that counts, however, but knowing oneself or finding the truth about oneself in a place. "This was the place!" exclaims the knight in Browning's "Childe Roland to the Dark Tower Came," but it is not the discovery of "the round squat turret" that matters to him but the sudden understanding of his destiny. Robert Langbaum's insistence on the indestructible lyrical element in dramatic monologues like "Childe Roland" and "The Love Song of J. Alfred Prufrock" is pertinent here since place is part of the dramatic situation:

> The result is to make the outward movement of the poem a device for returning inward, to make the dramatic situation the occasion for lyric expression; so that in effect the speaker directs his address outward in order to address himself, and makes an objective discovery in order to discover himself. . . . he rather makes the circumstances a part of himself as he develops inward toward an intenser manifestation of his own nature.[27]

The action of poetry, writes Glauco Cambon, "inevitably, extends to all space, all space, namely, takes place in 'space-time'—in a contemporaneity made perceptual."[28] Thus in Eliot's *Four Quartets* places matter less than the discovery of the poet that he is no longer bound by place and time. The remembrance of a place has for Eliot, as for romantic poets before him, a magical power of leading him to knowledge; there must be "the right time and the right place." But finally, as the poet learns in "East Coker," "Here and there does not matter"; and in "Burnt Norton," "I can only say, *there* we have been: but I cannot say where."

The tendency of Eliot's entire poetic production is to transcend place, to move away from realistic places—city streets and rooms—toward traditional places representing stages in contemporary man's spiritual journey from despair to faith: the desert of Bible tradition, the staircase of St. John of the Cross, the garden of Dante. These places become more allegorical and less substantial as Eliot exchanges the naturalist's factualism for the poet's symbolism. The attenuation of place in *Four Quartets* may be found in even greater degree in Crane's *The Bridge* and Williams's *Paterson*. Although these long works are ostensibly about specific geographical sites, one looks in vain for substantiality of place in them, so dense is "the metaphysical fusion of thought and reality, of psychic and urban physiognomy."[29] *The Bridge* fails, according to Allen Tate, because of the "discrepancy between the sensuous fact, the perception, and its organizing symbol"; the city in *Paterson,* according to David Weimer, "never emerges in sufficient richness of detail to persuade us of its reality."[30] *Paterson* turns out to be just as unlocalized as Eliot's city. "Books Three and Four," continues Weimer, "are so tenuously located in time and space, furthermore, that they could be thought to repose almost any time and anywhere."

In remaining true to his craft, the poet must eventually prefer the inner to the outer landscape. The vividly realized Eden of *Paradise Lost* becomes "a paradise within thee, happier far" in the sequel: "For *Paradise Regained* takes place not in vast cosmic space but entirely in the fallen world of flesh: its internal and external landscapes are created by the limits and conditions of each character's perception."[31]

Drama must set limits on place in order to protect itself from non-dramatic distraction; poetry transforms place by making it serve subjective and imagistic needs. There is nothing in the art of narrative that makes place the troublesome problem it is in drama because, being verbalized only, place in narrative cannot have as insistent a presence as it has in stage settings. Thus, in a single passage, Homer can switch the attention of his readers from the plain outside of Troy where Achilles is dragging the body of Hector to a chamber in Troy where Andromache is preparing a robe and bath for her dear lord. Drama's immediacy of action cannot be matched in narrative, of course, but the accumulation and repetition of the details of the place in which action occurs can significantly qualify action in ways that drama cannot duplicate. Setting in fiction is more intimately related to character than it ever can be in drama because it functions as the detailed and continuous environment in which character is formed and to which character reacts over a long period of time. The storyteller may not transform place like the poet, nor lose sight of its concreteness, because place is too necessary in the rendering of action, which must have a specific locale to occur in, and of character, which cannot fully exist without an environment to which it owes its identity through consistent orientation. But these responsibilities do not forbid the storyteller from using place as imagistic material in the speech and consciousness of his characters as well as in authorial comment, and in these uses the narrator comes closest to the poet's fusion of mind with reality. Place for him, however, is not a mental event in his imaginative life but an event in the life of his characters. To do justice to his genre, the novelist, moving a giant step beyond the storyteller, must create a seemingly complete world for his characters. From its inception in the eighteenth century, the novel has been devoted to the history of character as it is formed by and reacts to a specific environment—"the genre of location and property, the literature whose form was primarily spatial and whose space was that of a map."[32]

The novelist enjoys a wide range of choice in the amount of emphasis he puts upon place in his work, from the barest suggestion of the scene of his action to the most detailed description, from geographical verisimilitude to symbolical reference. The novel may freely expand in time and space through the accumulation of innumerable details, or it may limit itself to a tiny fragment of time and space. Criticism has developed no restrictions on the use of time or place in the novel because there is no practical problem of scene-changing and no possibility that the setting will compete for attention in its own right as a spectacle without words. There are limits, of course, to what narrative can do with place or omit doing: a novel too exclusively concerned with the description of actual geographic places may become a travelogue or a history; a novel with too little attention to place may verge toward abstraction. Curiously, excessively minute attention to place detail may be self-defeating. In Robbe-Grillet's *Jealousy* language ultimately fails to convey the specificity the author wishes to get in his description of the setting and a plan of the house must be supplied. The novel, warns Wallace Stevens, is subject to "the fatality of seeing things too well."[33] Between the extremes of facticity and abstraction it is not profitable to discriminate further. Lawrence Durrell tries to be axiomatic: "What makes 'big' books is surely as much to do with their site as their character and incident."[34] Upon reflection, however, one could name many essentially siteless novels—*Tom Jones,* for example. Works with crucial sites form a special category, survival narratives, in which the exclusive interest is the desperate contest of people against places—an island in *Robinson Crusoe,* a mountain in James Ramsey Ullman's *The White Tower,* a river gorge in James Dickey's *Deliverance.* These are place-saturated books and measure their success by the close accommodation of human behavior to physical environment of the most demanding kind. The psychological novel, on the other hand, puts less emphasis on place than on subjective responses to place. Panoramic narrative moves in general terms over a wide range of places whereas the dramatic novel strives to develop a few settings intensively.

History of the Formal Use of Place in Literature

Just as asserted earlier that attitudes toward earth as the place of man's habitation are ambivalent and not progressive, so it can be concluded that the use of place as a formal element presents no single line of development over the course of literary history. Instead of a clear evolution in the treatment of place there appears to be a variety of formal uses coexisting in the writing of any single period and recurrences of earlier uses in later periods. In medieval romances, for example, place is merely an appropriate stereotyped backdrop for action, yet in *Beowulf* and *Gawain* place is specified quite literally and has atmospheric and symbolic uses of a sort associated with more modern writing. The naturalistic details of a city practically dominate the consciousness of Joyce's characters in *Ulysses,* while city dwellers in contemporary Kafka and Gertrude Stein are either absolutely oblivious of their surroundings or respond to them as allegorical reflections of the mind. It is sometimes said that not until the eighteenth century did fiction begin to develop the environment as a matrix in which character is formed. Thus the "blasted heath" where Macbeth hears the prophecy of his future is a symbolical backdrop only and has nothing to do with the formation of his character, whereas the provincial town of Yonville has everything to do with Madame Bovary's. Walter Allen, in his history of the English novel, claims that the Gothic novel, especially the version of Mrs. Radcliffe, was the first to establish "a peculiarly intense relationship between the characters and their immediate environments."[35] It might be objected that the romantic correspondence of feeling and place was more subtle than the rather mechanical Gothic nexus, though it is true that the romantic feeling did not get itself represented in fiction until after the Gothic novel reached its peak. It goes without saying that the realistic novel demanded the close articulation of places and people. Balzac, writes Percy Lubbock, "cannot think of his people without the homes they inhabit; with Balzac to imagine a human being is to imagine a province, a city, a corner of the city, a building at a turn of the street, certain furnished rooms."[36] Ian Watt goes back to Defoe to find "the first of our writers who visualised the whole of his narrative as though it occurred in an actual physical environment"; Allen Tate goes forward to Flaubert, whom he credits with developing "a technique of putting man wholly into his physical setting."[37] But examples of the considerable importance of place in characterization are not difficult to find throughout the entire history of literature. The contrast of Achilles and Hector in the *Iliad,* for example, is helped by the association of Achilles with the plain and Hector with the walled city, and confrontation of the two heroes on the plain before the walls of Troy is artfully conceived by Homer to bring together the two places that conditioned their different lives. As the two warriors race around the walls, they pass

> the two sweet-running well-springs . . .
> where the wives of the Trojans and their lovely

daughters washed the clothes to shining, in the old days
when there was peace, before the coming of the sons of the Achaians.[38]

For a moment Homer evokes a domestic scene occurring at another, happier time on the very spot where now an act of terrible violence is about to be perpetrated. Through the juxtaposition of two contrasting aspects of the same place, the domestic and the military, the tragic end of Hector is thus thrown into remarkable perspective. Homer's method is essentially the same as Henry James's, two thousand years later, when he contrasts two gentlemen in terms of the apartments they inhabit in *The American*.

An excellent study of place in literature, Marjorie Nicolson's *Mountain Gloom and Mountain Glory,* is a history of only one kind of place, and many exceptions must be allowed, including *Beowulf* and *Gawain,* which are cited as not conforming to the "dominant tendency" toward "abstract and allegorical" scenery in medieval writing. Still, it is useful to observe tendencies and to make generalizations, for example, that before the eighteenth century literalism of place was infrequently used and symbolism of place was so prominent that it is possible to describe such diverse works as the *Odyssey,* the *Divine Comedy,* and the *Romance of the Rose* as allegories of place. A turning point occurred in the eighteenth century with two new interests in man's physical surroundings: the enthusiasm for the picturesque, or the aesthetics of landscape, and curiosity about the practical industrial processes and social organizations whereby society maintains itself. With the nineteenth century environment became so important to writers responding to theories of evolution that their detailed delineation of place and the deterministic construction they put upon it very nearly pushed fiction into historical and scientific documentation. It is this naturalistic extreme that twentieth-century fiction reacts against in eschewing detailed settings and cultivating the indirect presentation of place through dialogue and the consciousness of characters.

TWO EXAMPLES OF THE USE OF PLACE

A few practical exhibits may illustrate the varieties in the formal use of place in prose fiction over a period of a hundred and fifty years. For Henry Fielding it was sufficient to present places only in the most general terms. After announcing at the start of *Tom Jones* that the

Such reluctance to delineate the physical contexts of action and character is hardly to be found in Fielding's contemporary, Tobias Smollett, whose works are saturated with the details of places and the paraphernalia of journeys. This difference in the two writers may be accounted for in generic terms: Smollett moved toward the novel from a consuming interest in travel literature, Fielding from a delight in the comedy of manners. In both cases there is an imperfect assimilation of place to narrative. Fielding leaves the scene bare, but curiously enough Smollett's accumulations of details concerning a number of places have surprisingly little relation to the action in which his characters are involved. Place in Smollett bears a close, even documentary relation to actual places like Bath, but not by virtue of this fidelity to realism, nor by Fielding's ironic bow in the direction of landscape painting, does place become an integral element in fiction. A novelist's verisimilitude of place or painterly interest in place may support ancillary studies of the variety of raw materials that go into the novel, but cannot figure much in the critical appraisal of the role of place as a formal element in the art of fiction.

Almost any novel of Thomas Hardy could serve to illustrate the intensive use of place in fiction, none more decisively than *The Return of the Native*. Egdon Heath is both a symbol and an actual environment in which Clym Yeobright attempts to renew himself and from which Eustacia Vye attempts to flee in despair. A more easily managed example, however, is the journey of Gabriel Oak in *Far from the Madding Crowd*. A disappointed lover separated from his sweetheart, just like Tom Jones, Gabriel takes to the road and accidentally comes upon the trail of his estranged Bathsheba. To be nearer her, he sets out from Casterbridge at dusk, walks until it is black out, sleeps in an empty wagon, and wakes to find himself "being carried along the road at a rate rather considerable for a vehicle without springs." He determines the time by observing the stars ("Charles's Wain was getting towards a right angle with the Pole star") and estimates how far he has come. He leaves the wagon, and, seeing an unusual light, crosses a ploughed field and comes upon a fire in a rick-yard and helps to put it out. The farm is Bathsheba's and we are ready for the second encounter of the seemingly mismatched couple.

Gabriel, unlike Tom, does not abstractly travel post from Casterbridge to Weatherbury. Instead, he is in close physical contact with the land, knows its forms and conditions even in the dark, masters the fire with well-directed action. In subsequent episodes Gabriel proves again and again that he is the ideal rural man because of his knowledge of place and processes appropriate to certain places. His fellow countrymen recognize this at once, though Bathsheba does not, and Gabriel must repeat and expand his pastoral prowess before she learns to recognize his special merit and subsequently accept him as her husband. Gabriel's easy journey across the land stands in contrast to the hectic trip that Bathsheba makes by fast trotter and gig to join her lover in Bath, the fatal last journey of Fanny Robin, and the mysterious disappearance and miraculous reappearance of Sergeant Troy. It is a comment on Hardy's emergent anticipation of the twentieth-century sense of alienation from the land that Gabriel, the hero of one of his first novels, is a man truly in harmony with the land, that Clym Yeobright feebly attempts to adapt himself to the near-wasteland of Egdon Heath, and that poor Jude, Hardy's last hero, is altogether unable to thrive either on the land or in the city, which have become false places.

Place assumes so much importance in Hardy that the interest many readers may have in that aspect of literature begins and, unfortunately, ends with Hardy. His emphasis on place, perhaps too great, almost puts his work into the kind of place-saturated fiction which is expressly devoted to the assault upon a mountain or the survival in a forbidding place. Though one must agree with Dorothy Van Ghent that "Hardy is able to use setting and atmosphere for a symbolism that . . . is blunt and rudimentary,"[43] the question remains whether his use of place is both too blunt and too rudimentary.

Against Smollett's digressive prolixity of place detail and Hardy's obsessive place symbolism, let us set Henry James's strict economy. The city is James's ideal place, representing the ultimate in civilization, and Paris is his favorite city. In *The Ambassadors* the greatest effort is to create an impression of the city's enchantment, for it is the city, as well as Chad's new sophistication and Mme. de Vionnet's exquisite beauty and manners, that must be made to constitute for Strether the new world of wonderful possibilities. For this purpose James allows himself only a few Parisian places: Chad's third-floor apartment in Boulevard Malesherbes, the garden of Gloriani, the restaurant where Strether has lunch with Mme. de Vionnet, and that lady's drawing-room. Each of these places is done with the barest minimum of detail and the maximum of personal reflection on these details, for James is the most subtle materialist: what the eye perceives—a gesture, a movement, a mere finial—becomes the material for the most complex response imaginable. James pushes the art of synecdoche to its furthest extreme. Early in the book, Strether reconnoiters Chad's neighborhood and for three pages ponders the "continuous balcony" before the windows of Chad's apartment. The passage is a model of James's mature treatment of place as well as his own critical evaluation of the importance of place in fiction.

> Many things came over him here, and one. . . . was that the balcony in question didn't somehow show as a convenience easy to surrender. Poor Strether had at this very moment to recognise the truth that, wherever one paused in Paris, the imagination reacted before one could stop it. This perpetual reaction put a price, if one would, on pauses; but it piled up consequences till there was scarce room to pick one's steps among them. What call had he, at such a juncture, for example, to like Chad's very house? High broad clear—he was expert enough to make out in a moment that it was admirably built—it fairly embarrassed our friend by the quality that, as he would have said, it "sprang" on him. He had struck off the fancy that it might, as a preliminary, be of service to him to be seen, by a happy accident, from the third-story windows, which took all the March sun; but of what service was it to find himself making out after a moment that the quality "sprung," the quality produced by measure and balance, the fine relation of part to part and space to space, was probably—aided by the presence of ornament as positive as it was discreet, and by the complexion of the stone, a cold fair gray, warmed and polished a little by life— neither more nor less than a case of distinction, such a case as he could only feel, unexpectedly, as a sort of delivered challenge?[44]

The balcony, he goes on to say, "placed the whole case materially," that is, made it clear that Chad's life in Paris was worthwhile and had to be preferred to his own situation, represented at present by "the small, the admittedly secondary hotel on the by-street from the Rue de la Paix." Waymarsh, his American travelling companion, seems to Strether to be the alternative to the young man who had by this time appeared on the balcony. "When he [Strether] did move it was fairly to escape that alternative. Taking his way over the street at last and passing through the porte-cochère of the house was like consciously leaving Waymarsh out. However, he would tell him all about it."

Three months later, the cumulative force of Paris strikes Strether as he views the city from Chad's apartment: "the great flare of the lighted city, rising high, spending itself afar, played up from the Boulevard and, through the vague vista of the successive rooms, brought objects into view and added to their dignity" (281). Now things speak to him in a different voice, "which he took as the proof of all the change in himself." From the perspective of the apartment the significance of Chad's new life and of Paris combine for Strether in a strange experience of freedom, "the freedom that most brought him round again to the youth of his own that he had long ago missed." For a revelatory moment the place he is in "represented the substance of his loss, put it within reach, within touch, made it, to a degree it had never been, an affair of the senses. . . . a queer concrete presence, full of mystery, yet full of reality." (The essence of James's realistic aesthetic is in this, and much of the Proustian belief in the evocative, almost mystical, power of the sense of place and things.) There follows on the balcony a conversation in which Strether and Chad move closer to a resolution of their differing postures toward the possibilities of the fully realized life, which lies symbolically before them in the city of Paris. "It was," writes James, "as if their high place really represented some moral elevation from which they could look down on their recent past" (284).

Here, finally, we have woven together place in its literalness, a character's response to this place in both its concreteness and its symbolical relation to his life, and an important action transpiring in this place. This is a proper use of place in a measure not too meager to do justice to the importance of place in narrative nor so concrete as to overwhelm with fact the imaginative power in the art of fiction.

2

A RHETORIC OF PLACE I
The Properties and
Uses of Place in Literature

REAL AND SYMBOLICAL PLACES

To REPRESENT THE CLASS of phenomena under investigation, the term *place* seems more satisfactory than any other. It is more comprehensive than *scene, setting,* or *landscape;* and it is more appropriate than *space,* a category of philosophical and scientific inquiry that is too far removed from sensory and imaginative experience to be of much value in literary studies. Whereas the philosopher Whitehead, for example, must regard mere location as a "simplification of nature," the literary critic sees place in its natural, physical, and readily perceived quality as the very stuff of literature.[1] In Cassirer's distinction between "the space of sense perception and the space of pure cognition,"[2] the poet would have to be identified with the first term and the philosopher and scientist with the second. The crucial difference is that the poet's space must be capable of arousing feelings and becoming the vehicle of meanings. It is as the friend of poets that Gaston Bachelard affirms the superiority of perceived space: "Inhabited space transcends geometrical space."[3] "Psychological space" is the term Richard Neutra uses to counter the "impoverishment" of Euclidean and Newtonian space.[4] From the geographer Yi-Fu Tuan we have this fine humanistic distinction: "Enclosed and humanized space is place. Compared to space, place is a calm center of established values."[5]

For literary purposes, then, place is inhabitable space, "lived space" or *erlebter Raum.*[6] Even objects—an automobile, a box, an old boiler—may be considered as places as long as they are susceptible of human occupation, either actual or imagined. Through imaginative identification with a bird, the poet may see a bird's nest as equivalent to a house, and in the next step "a dreamer might say that the world is the nest of mankind.["]7 This is precisely what Emerson does when he calls nature "my gentle nest," in his essay *Nature*. The reverse of this, making an unhabitable place habitable, is Whitman's imagining the sea as the cradle of his youth in "Out of the Cradle Endlessly Rocking."

Though sometimes borrowed by critics of fiction—Lubbock, for example—*scene* is properly a term of dramatic criticism and includes both the stage setting and the whole business transacted in a particular stretch of dialogue and action. *Setting* denotes a place of action in both narrative as well as drama and to that extent is an important category of place in literature, but *setting* is not adequate to describe the use of places unrelated to action, such as metaphors or evocations of places in the speeches or consciousness of characters. In the phrase "porches of the ears" Shakespeare makes a specific analogy between an architectural place and a part of the body; in a few lines at the opening of *Paradise Lost* Milton evokes three mountains by simply naming them. The mere sight of a stranger carrying a rucksack triggers, in the mind of Mann's Aschenbach, a strong desire to visit "a landscape, a tropical marshland"; and to a character in Flaubert's *Sentimental Education,* upon seeing a Swiss girl dancing, "horizons of tranquil voluptuousness in a chalet at the side of a lake opened out under the footsteps." Within a single moment there flashes across the consciousness of Bloom in *Ulysses* numerous places he has seen, heard about, or imagined, yet in none of these is setting properly involved. Setting is a dramatic scene of action, a concentrated and persisting occurrence of place in literature, whereas place imagery and place allusions are ubiquitous and fleeting, though they may have a powerful cumulative effect.

The term *landscape* once referred to all that could be seen of the earth's surface from a single vantage point, but now has been extended to include unseen things, such as a configuration of ideas or a set of conditions, or the psychological make-up of an individual *(le paysage intérieur)*. Literary criticism has customarily used the term to mean a special ordering of topography, vegetation, animals, and man-made constructions in a limited area of the earth's surface. It is useful to preserve the principle that landscape, as distinguished from natural landforms, is artfully arranged topography, or a grouping of objects with qualities in common with paintings. Painterly landscapes in literature must be considered as places, of course, and when writing consciously imitates painting, they are very important places. But it is an unnecessary limitation upon literary study to consider landscape in this sense to be the only kind of place worth noticing, for there are literary representations of places that neither conform to any aesthetic norm for painting nor incorporate topographical features. The problem literary criticism has with literary landscapes is that they may be cherished for their own sake as verbal substitutes for paintings quite independently of the works in which they appear. One does not quite know what to do with collections of landscape sketches gleaned from an author's works and offered for our separate enjoyment, such as may be found in Richard Aldington's *The Spirit of Place,* a selection of places described by D. H. Lawrence, and Dorothy Brewster's *Virginia Woolf's London.* Writing that celebrates places for their own sake falls into the minor category of travel literature.

A similar problem lies in the use of the term *geographical.* Just as literary landscapes must conform to painterly norms, so the representation of real places in literature must satisfy standards of verisimilitude. "To name a place, in fiction, is to pretend in some degree to represent it," warns Henry James in the preface to *Roderick Hudson.* Realistic writing is philosophically committed to the faithful rendering of actual places in order to qualify as realism, and certainly regionalism is bound by definition to do justice to the geographical particularities of a specific area. It must be remembered, though, that place does not have to figure prominently in all regional writing, which has at its disposal a good many other features to characterize a region: local manners, speech, folklore, and history. On a less programmatic level of writing, specific geographical sites become associated with certain themes through custom or fashion: adventure stories and detective stories are commonly played out against the backdrops of foreign scenes because actual places impart a sense of reality to compensate for the extravagant action of such plots and intense action seems to be helped by unfamiliar scenes for its enactment. Africa has been a favorite place for primitivistic adventure—though this is bound to change with the growing Westernization of the African continent; the northern shore of the Mediterranean is the location for romantic entanglements and disentanglements, for "running away . . . from bad love," as it is said in John Knowles's *Morning in Antibes;* Paris, the prime expatriate place; North Africa, Mexico, India, and the lands of dark-skinned natives, the places where despairing Europeans are marooned in their search for pelf or spiritual rebirth.

There is no question that a good part of the attraction of realistic writing consists in the pleasure of recognizing in their verbal form places already familiar to the reader through personal experience and discovering new places whose descriptions carry the authenticity of actual geographical sites. Having made these concessions, however, we must return to the axiom that fidelity to geographical realism and painterly beauty finally exact a price that the writer cannot afford to pay. When their power to attract grows primarily out of extra-literary satisfactions, landscape and geography cannot be wholly assimilated to the texts in which they appear. Conversely, the more successfully places are integrated with other literary elements in a text, the less suited they are to be considered as separable verbal paintings and mimetic records of places. Francis Palgrave recognized this in doing his anthology *Landscape in Poetry* when he took for his standard of inclusion not the function of a place description within the work but its fidelity to an actual place and the feeling that place aroused, "the perfect truth of the painting"; consequently he had to reject those passages in the *Aeneid* "brought in as background to the human figures."[8] Henry James, on the other hand, learned to avoid the danger of committing himself to the representation of a place with the "systematic closeness" and "density" of Balzac.[9] In doing the shop in the opening of *The Golden Bowl* he realized that it must be "but a shop of the mind, of the author's projected world, in which objects are primarily related to each other, and therefore not 'taken from' a particular establishment anywhere, only an image distilled and intensified, as it were, from a drop of the essence of such establishments in general." With respect to "romantic and historic sites," James warns that they "offer the artist a questionable aid to concentration when they themselves are not to be the subject of it. They are too rich in their own life and too charged with their own meanings merely to help him out with a lame phrase; they draw him away from his small question to their own greater ones." James is being falsely modest here about the importance of art. He continues: "Venice doesn't borrow, she but all magnificently gives. We profit by that enormously, but to do so we must either be quite off duty or be on it in her service alone."

With unfailing literary instinct James knew that even in fiction having a high degree of verisimilitude settings must only seem to be modelled on actual places, or otherwise the writer's freedom is impaired. Speaking of the island home of Queequeg in *Moby-Dick*, Melville writes: "It is not down in any map; true places never are." The fact of a place does not in itself constitute literary value; getting the reader to accept the illusion of a place's facticity does. What matters in literature is the affective power of the writer's representation of the physical properties of places, and it is of little consequence whether these properties belong to actual places. Each of the sections of Eliot's *Four Quartets* has a geographical starting point that is presented with such precision that one is teased into identifying the originals; but this is impossible unless the reader has access to extra-textual information, and so he must finally accept the four settings as generic places used symbolically—a garden, a village, a seacoast, and a ruined chapel. Denis Donoghue tells us that the garden in "Burnt Norton" was a real enough garden Eliot visited in Gloucestershire and it even "played some part in the imaginative process which led to the composition," but "Eliot is not interested in making the reader see the rose-garden, he is using language in such a manner that things are recognized, by its means, rather than seen."[10] The same process may occur even when the place in question is readily identifiable as a public or historic site: in spite of the literal detail Thackeray accumulates concerning Brussels in *Vanity Fair,* it is after all a city on the edge of a war, like the mythical Troy.

As with all literary materials, place has a literal and a symbolical value, a function serving both geographical and metaphorical ends. But the literal and geographic aspect of place is always under the strain that all literature feels to attain the condition of poetry, of symbol, and it is difficult to avoid the proposition that in the final analysis all places in literature are used for symbolical purposes even though in their descriptiveness they may be rooted in fact. Repeated association of some generic places with certain experiences and values has resulted in what amounts almost to a system of archetypal place symbolism. Thus, mountains have come to represent aspiration and trial; forests and swamps, peril and entrapment; valleys and gardens, pleasure and well-being; deserts, deprivation; houses, stability and community; roads or paths, adventure and change. From these basically concrete associations more specialized meanings are generated to form materials for literary genres like the pastoral, medieval romance, and Gothic novel, in which there is a steady relationship between settings and literary form. Allegories such as *The Divine Comedy, The Faerie Queene,* and *Pilgrim's Progress,* depend upon a conventional stereotypy of place to advance their elaborate ideologies. Although figurative correspondence rather than mimetic fidelity is the objective in this kind of writing, places in allegories always retain some degree of specificity, much more in Spenser, certainly, than in Malory or Bunyan. But even if they do not, they have a literary function to perform and it is a mistake to discount them, as some historians of ideas have done, because they lack naturalistic detail. Camelot is not Bridgeport, Connecticut, but it has a real enough presence in the dream-life of the Boss in Twain's *Connecticut Yankee in the Court of King Arthur.* It is the use to which a place is put that counts, not the historical mode dictating its form. An allegorical place may have a more effective role if it is tied in with the meaning of a work than a mimetic representation of a place that is not related to anything else in the work. Moreover, the symbolical use of

place is less open to error than the realistic: the means Dos Passos
employs to create the impression of a real city in *Manhattan Transfer*
can be appreciated by all readers alike, but the correspondence of this
impression with New York City is a subject for debate among ur-
banologists.

All places, whether drawn from geographical reality or fantasy,
from literature or actual life, serve figurative ends and thereby sacrifice
part of their concreteness as they cater to some human desire or crav-
ing beyond present reality. The mind almost automatically picks out
homes in the strange landscape flashing by in the car or train window,
and with a little effort it is capable of transforming all but the most
forbidding environments into glowing utopias. As Gaston Bachelard so
well demonstrates in *The Poetics of Space,* the imagination draws its
"primal image" from such physical properties of space as verticality
but soon transcends them in a dream-life that is almost independent of
reality. "A house that has been experienced is not an inert box," he
writes, but "apprehended in its dream potentiality, becomes a nest in
the world, and we shall live there in complete confidence if, in our
dreams, we really participate in the sense of security of our first home"
(47, 103). Paradise begins as a place of pleasure and comfort *(locus
amoenus)* and ends up as an abstract idea of the perfection of man's
spiritual condition. For Milton paradise regained is Christian virtue
regained. Even for modern realists there is sometimes a curious removal from the physicality of place to the realm of spirit. Willa
Cather's American West, in the final analysis, becomes a testing
ground for the moral stamina of her characters; regional realist though
she is, full of the sights and sounds of the prairie, Cather ultimately
falls back on a conception of the New World very close to that of the
Pilgrims. In his last moments the Hemingway hero struggles to gain
control over himself, not his surroundings.

A kind of moral geography springs from man's ability to adapt
himself to hostile environments. Mountains, observes Roland Barthes,
"seem to encourage a morality of effort and solitude."[11] The Puritans
almost welcomed the hardships of the American continent because it
constituted a new Sinai; they *"needed* a Wilderness to be voices in."[12]
The Puritan transvaluation of Christian holiness into virtue and power
emerges later in the middle-class ideal of a hero such as Robinson
Crusoe, who wins a moral victory for himself by making the best of
being shipwrecked on a deserted island. After he proves himself, the
only use the island has is to serve as the site where three more sinners
can improve their character. George Bernard Shaw sees moral geography as a product of Judeo-Christian civilization when, in *Man and*

Superman, he refers scornfully to the "pious English habit of regarding the world as a moral gymnasium built expressly to strengthen your character in." But the "landscape of difficulty" has always figured prominently in literature, from *Gilgamesh* to the latest thriller, and the temptation of remaining in a congenial environment is as much eschewed by the pagan Odysseus as by the Christian Tommo in Melville's *Typee.* Even science takes a moral view of man's relationship to the earth when, in the science of ecology, it emphasizes what man must do to make amends for disrupting ecosystems.

A marvel of economy, the imagination may thrive on the most meagre materials to make a place meaningful. As Coleridge, in "This Lime-Tree Bower My Prison," expresses it:

> No plot so narrow, be but Nature there,
> No waste so vacant, but may well employ
> Each faculty of sense, and keep the heart
> Awake to Love and Beauty.

Emily Dickinson is even more to the point when she writes,

> To make a prairie it takes a clover and a bee,
> One clover, and a bee,
> And revery.
> The revery alone will do,
> If bees are few.

A true sister of hers is Miss Caroline Spencer, the heroine of Henry James's "Four Meetings," whose whole impression of Europe comes from thirteen hours spent waiting for someone in Le Havre. What to the narrator is "poor old prosaic shabby Havre . . . a place of transit" Miss Spencer sees with "freshness of perception" and accepts as an adequate representation of Europe. "It was not miserable," she insists. "It was delightful." In his essay "The Art of Fiction," James cites the case of an English novelist who comprehended "the nature and way of life of the French Protestant youth" merely by "having once, in Paris, as she ascended a staircase, passed an open door where, in the household of a *pasteur,* some of the young Protestants were seated at a table round a finished meal." It does not take many trees to make a forest, says Bachelard: "We do not have to be long in the woods to experience the always rather anxious impression of 'going deeper and deeper' into a limitless world" (185). Robert Frost was struck with the same truth, and in the very first poem of his first published volume of poetry, "Into My Own," he imagines a thin line of trees to be "the merest mark of doom" stretching into infinity, an idea that haunts his work throughout. Wallace Stevens loved Connecticut for its spareness: "The man who loves New England, and particularly Connecticut, loves it precisely because of the spare colors, the thin light, the delicacy and slightness and beauty of the place."[13]

It is up to the writer to manipulate the wide range of effects places may have. The physical qualities of place are expressive only as they are assimilated to the over-all literary complexion of the work. Like sounds in poetry, they must be made to seem appropriate and symbolic within the range of meaning prepared for them by the arts of language. The cliffside to which Edgar presumably leads his blind father in *King Lear* is no place at all but an opportunity to develop the imagery of falling, and the fear of falling is instinctive, not the place in which one falls, although in becoming associated with this fear the place is symbolic of falling. Gloucester's acceptance of a feigned place as real is the very essence of literary art in its treatment of place. (A comic treatment of the same idea, the suggestive power of the imagination, is Hamlet's cloud, which appears as both weasel and whale to Polonius.)

Each genre establishes for itself the proportions of literalism and symbolism in the treatment of places. The *Odyssey* is a work holding the literal and the symbolical in perfect balance. Telemachus visits real places and converses with real people, while Odysseus narrates his visits to marvelous fantasy places that nonetheless represent conditions in the life of Everyman that he must learn either to accept or avoid. A travelogue of real and allegorical places, the *Odyssey* lays the ground for the novel. In relating factual Dublin to both Telemachus's Greece and Odysseus's allegorical Mediterranean, Joyce in *Ulysses* accentuates the success the novel has had throughout its history in using real places for symbolical as well as representational purposes. The novel reverses the power of the romance, which attempts to make fantasy places seem real by their association with historical characters and events. Even in the most uncompromisingly realistic fiction, places may be forced to take on symbolic meaning as they become associated through emphasis and repetition with themes and tones. Such is the railroad station in *Anna Karenina,* the series of houses in *Portrait of a Lady,* the dry river bed observed by the narrator in *Farewell to Arms,* Polk Street in *McTeague,* the ash heaps in *Our Mutual Friend* and *The Great Gatsby*. At its furthest symbolic stretch a single place may represent the world-at-large: the ship in *Moby-Dick* or Katherine Anne Porter's *The Ship of Fools,* the island in *Penguin Island* or *South Wind.* At the other extreme, the "world" of a novel is understood to be the massive accumulation of literal details that altogether reconstitute the actual environment.

Places lend themselves readily to symbolical extension because there is so little that is inherently affective in their physical properties. Spatial dimensions and climatic conditions, for example, do not in themselves stimulate a constant emotional response; rather the qualities of places are determined by the subjective responses of people according to their cultural heritage, sex, occupation, and personal predicament.[14] Gibraltar is impregnable not because it is a rock but because people *think* a rock is impregnable. Thomas Pynchon, in his novel *V,* explains how the inhabitants of Malta survived the bombing in World War II in this way: "The same motives which cause us to populate a dream-street also cause us to apply to a rock human qualities like 'invincibility,' 'tenacity,' 'perseverance,' etc. More than metaphor, it is delusion. But on the strength of this delusion Malta survived" (305). The human will and imagination go the longest way in making places what they are for human beings, and the mood of a person has much to do with determining the quality of the places he is in. In his rage against God, Milton's Satan can "make a Heaven of Hell." To James's Isabel Archer, newly arrived in Europe, "the thick detail of London . . . loomed large and rich," but five years later, after her disappointment with her husband, "there was something terrible in an arrival in London. The dusky, smoky, far-arching vault of the station, the strange, livid light, the dense, dark, pushing crowd, filled her with nervous fear and made her put her arm into her friend's."[15] Social attitudes shape conceptions of places for masses of people: Indians, Spaniards, and Anglo-Americans had altogether different responses to the American Southwest; political ideology in the eighteenth century and racial prejudice in the twentieth century made the city appear as an evil place to millions of Americans.

With no inherent qualities to maintain fixed values, it is not surprising that traditions fail to assign constant emotional responses to certain physical properties and that ambiguity and change characterize the cultural inheritance. Places are neither good nor bad in themselves but in the values attached to them, and literature is one of the agencies involved in attaching values to places. Thus, spaciousness may elate or terrify; small enclosures may be sought-after refuges, wombs where the spirit may be reborn, or they may be prisons, the place of despair and death; a forest may be a sheltering grove or a dark wood to get lost in, a place of freedom or of horror; and a garden may harbor earth's delights or earth's poisons. It is simply not possible to assume a fixed relationship between places and their effects, as Joseph Addison did:

> The Mind of Man naturally hates every thing that looks like a Restraint upon it, and is apt to fancy it self under a sort of Confinement, when the Sight is pent up in a narrow compass, and shortened on every side by the Neighbourhood of Walls or Mountains. On the contrary, a spacious Horizon is an Image of Liberty.[16]

Maud Bodkin similarly errs when she assigns "steadfast relations" to heights and depths.[17] Absolutist psychologies do not work with places, which are always open to ambivalence. Byron's prisoner of Chillon learns from his incarceration to be indifferent to freedom and to love despair, but Camus's Meursault, in an age when one would least expect it, is led to "the brink of freedom" through the self-consciousness he develops in a prison cell: as his name suggests, he learns in prison to leap the wall that once separated him from mankind.[18]

The valuation of places changes. Paradise is the traditional type of the paramount good place, hell the unmitigated bad place, but the attributes of paradise and hell vary with the times. For centuries the garden, which in its earliest form was simply an oasis or a marked-off area in the wilderness, represented the paradisal place, while mountains, unhabitable and inaccessible, were considered blemishes on earth; but the romantic revolution created a positive feeling for mountains, for wild rather than cultivated places, for expanse rather than enclosure. Under the romantic spell American writers like Cooper came to regard the forest as Eden and the clearings or settlements as undesirable. Primitivists have sought the wilderness for purity and eschewed the garden because of its corruption. A society in which movement through space receives the highest priority discards the notion that paradise is a resting-place. The city ideal was once incorporated with the image of the garden; nothing seemed more reassuring than a system of enclosures that kept distances between man and nature and between man and man. Now the city is associated with inferno. The house once symbolized the established political order and family authority. The great hall in Ithaca had to be cleansed of suitors and sinners before Odysseus could rest assured in his kingship, and the monster Grendel had to be driven from Heorot to restore the kingdom of Hrothgar. Late eighteenth-century values saw the deterioration of the house from an Augustan mark of civilization and character, as in Pope, to the Gothic place of horror where the accumulated wrongs of the establishment festered in secret attics and dungeons until they threatened the present generation with insanity, sexual perversion, and destruction. The monster that had once penetrated the sacred space of the house from the outside became a permanent resident. Edwardian fiction attempted a revival of the country house as a symbol of civilized living, but the house is no longer a significant place in the writing of our time. Many mourn its passing, but, in spite of Gaston Bachelard's beautiful comments on the importance of the house in the development of the imagination in childhood—calling it "a nest in the world"—other places may satisfy the human need for security. A moving place—automobile, van, spacecraft—may be the nest for people of the twentieth and twenty-first centuries.

THE PHYSICAL PROPERTIES OF PLACES

For all its adaptability to symbolical ends, place imagery is more tenacious of concreteness and more impervious to attenuation than any other imagistic materials. The most elemental orientation of a reader to a narrative text is through its evocation of places. Setting is immediately positive and reassuring until action and character are gradually unfolded.

Place is part of the physical contexts of a literary work, if we take context to mean the reconstitution in words of those aspects of the actual environment that a writer puts together to make up the "world" in which his characters, events, and themes have their show of existence. The physical context consists of such elements as space, time, objects, and processes; it is to be distinguished from the intrapersonal relationships, customs, and values that go to make up the larger cultural and historical context. The distinction is a crucial one for the study of place in literature. A way of life by itself, without reference to the physical properties of the surroundings in which it occurs, is not germane to this study; nor is regional writing which depends only on local lore and local speech, nor a city novel that presents only the social, economic, and political aspects of urban existence. Augustine's city and More's Utopia, from this point of view, are less interesting than the London of Dickens because their settings have little relation to the social and spiritual forms that thrive there. Utopias are not places at all but social systems, just as the Fatherland is a political entity and not the land itself, which is better represented in the image Mother Nature.[19] Journeys from one place to another do not adequately involve either motion or place if there is no attempt to suggest the sensation of body movement and the perception of and interaction with surroundings. The considerable traveling in *Don Quixote* and *Tom Jones,* for example, furnishes occasions to experience new predicaments in the plot, not new places; the heroes are moved around, but with little sense of motion. The speed of a horse-drawn coach, writes DeQuincey in "The English Mail-Coach," may be actually exceeded by newer and faster vehicles but not the sensation of speed: "They boast of more velocity—not, however, as a consciousness, but as a fact of our lifeless knowledge."

To recognize these differences is not to condemn writing that does not emphasize place as part of the environment but merely to remind ourselves that in some writing the physical context may be minimal or may not have a sufficiently important influence on the chief interest of the work to merit our attention. Place simply may not be one of the facts of man's condition that informs a writer's imagination or contributes anything to his objectives. It is for the writer to decide the extent to which place will figure in his work, and his decision will be determined by his conception of the work he is creating. Fielding's Tom Jones is not at all influenced in his behavior by the places he happens to be in, whereas Meursault in *The Stranger* is moved to murder a man as a direct result of the assault upon his senses of the sun and the heat in North Africa.

Extent

An obvious property of a place is its size or extension in space. Beyond the planets of our solar system and the visible stars, place is unimaginable, Milton's "vast vacuity." Stars and planets, however, play an important role because they mark the border between outer space and the habitable world; they may be the source of divine influences and the sites of future worlds. No matter how inaccessible practically, they are imaginatively inhabitable and are thus places in our sense of the word. Within the limits of the universe there is a series of places of diminishing size: earth, continents, regions, landscapes, dwellings, the interiors of dwellings, areas within touching distance, and finally spaces too small for human occupation except by imaginative extension.

Not all of the places in this hierarchy of size and volume are equally perceivable by the senses. The universe, earth, continents, and regions may be comprehended only partially, and the idea one has of them must be filled out by the extension of available sense data. Synecdoche and analogy are the means literature adopts to give form to places we cannot fully perceive. The world is thus represented by Homer by a description of the design on the shield of Achilles; the city in naturalistic fiction is most often rendered by an account of the activities of a single street. The analogy of microcosm to macrocosm permits writers to include in their repertoire of settings places either too small or too extensive or remote for human occupation. By the imaginative reduction in the size of human beings Rabelais populates the mouth of a giant; Isaac Asimov, the science-fiction writer, sends a team of doctors on a journey through the bloodstream of a heart patient in *Fantastic Voyage;* the movie *TRON* has people in the inside of a computer; Robert Louis Stevenson's bed-ridden child creates "The Land of Counterpane" from the folds of his bed-clothes.

Verticality

A number of place attributes depend on the relative position of a place in relation to other places—whether a place is high, low, central, or apart. Ancient cosmologies commonly identified three levels—upper, middle, and lower—a distinction that encouraged polarization of the extremes and ambivalence of the area between. Differentiation of levels inevitably leads to a hierarchy of values. Thus in the Christian cosmology heaven and hell are absolutely opposed while earth has the qualities of both, the rarefication of air and the grossness of matter. Christianity associated the high place with good and the low with evil, although pre-Christian concepts made no regular distinction of that sort and romanticism later restored respect for the lower world in its fondness for the imagery of underground rivers, caves, and sea depths. Great depths as well as great heights are often held sacred, for there the middle place, earth, is intersected by realms inhabited by gods, and there the extraordinary man may be favored spiritually, as Moses on Sinai and Aeneas in Dis. A mountain, like the one Gilgamesh encounters, may touch both the heavenly realm above and the world below. Northrop Frye calls this "the point of epiphany" and supplies examples in the mountain-tops, towers, and staircases of the Bible, Dante, Yeats, and Eliot.[20] In connecting places on different levels stairs symbolically afford a passage from one mode of existence to another. The soul thus ascends to God on the ten steps of the ladder of love of Saint John of the Cross, or, in the secular life, the individual may ascend the ladder of fortune. From the works of Dostoevsky, Donald Fanger claims, "one could . . . deduce a whole 'poetics of the staircase.' "[21]

The high place inspires feelings of elation, domination, tran-

scendence; it is the traditional home of poetry, whose function, writes
Frost in "New Hampshire," is

> To tap the upper sky and draw a flow
> Of frosty night air on the vale below.

Bachelard goes so far as to claim that verticality in houses has a strong
appeal to the consciousness and that there is something wanting in the
imagination of people who have had the misfortune of being brought up
in Paris, where houses do not have the "polarity of attic and cellar."
Views from heights draw all into comprehensible focus. The temptation of Christ by Satan occurs on a mountain top, a scene adopted by
Henry James in the so-genteel *The Wings of the Dove* when Milly
Theale, seated on "the dizzy edge" of an Alpine peak and "looking
down on the kingdoms of the earth," finds herself "in a state of uplifted
and unlimited possession."[22] In *Paradise Lost* the angel Michael takes
Adam to the highest hill in paradise to see the whole world revealed in
space and time, its total geography and history. The rationality of the
eighteenth century was frequently expressed in the image of the "prospect" a high place offered of the well-ordered English countryside, as
in Thomson's "A goodly prospect of hills, and dales, and woods, and
lawns, and spires."

Scaling heights is a test of character, and the conflict of adver-
saries is accentuated when it occurs in a high place, a device used in
the commonest melodrama as well as in the subtle confrontations of
The Magic Mountain. The promise of greatness in a high place, however, may turn into disaster, for under Mount Etna yawns the volcano.
Competing with man's desire to escape gravitational pull is his instinctive fear of falling, the severest loss of orientation in space. Consequently, verticality elicits responses that vary with different
individuals and cultures. It is a laughable skeleton that climbs the stairs
from cellar to attic in Frost's "Witch of Coos," but there is no denying
the terror inspired by inhabitants of top floors in Gothic novels.

Horizontality

Lacking the unknown potential of heights and depths, flat places
are safe, restful, reassuring. In *Modern Painters* John Ruskin assem-
bles a whole page of references testifying to mankind's acceptance of
the "general principle of flatness."[23] But other examples may be

gathered supporting the opposite principle that predominantly horizontal places are uninspiring and dull, while, as Roland Barthes puts it, "the picturesque is found any time the ground is uneven."[24] Flatness pervades naturalistic novels in which things are found side by side in tedious juxtaposition, whereas romantic writing offers abrupt changes of plane that betoken danger as well as discovery and relieve the sameness of the scene with privileged looks into adjoining places. Chateaubriand found it most fitting, in Book IV of *The Genius of Christianity,* that the spires of Christian churches pointed heavenward while Greek temples remained "horizontal," and Rousseau, in Book IV of *Confessions,* expresses a preference for heights: "No flat country, however beautiful, has ever seemed so to my eyes. I must have mountain torrents, rocks, firs, dark forests, mountains, steep roads to climb or descend, precipices at my side to frighten me."

Levelness portends tragedy. In the Scriptures the sign of direst catastrophe is the levelling of high places, the hills and the towers. Wastelands are usually flat—"the lone and level sands" of Shelley's desert in "Ozymandias"; "the arid plain" stretching behind Eliot's Fisher King; "the gray plain all round" that the questing knight finds in Browning's "Childe Roland to the Dark Tower Came." Desperate, epoch-ending battles are fought on plains or the floors of valleys: the plains of Troy and Philippi; "the darkling plain/Where ignorant armies clash by night" in Arnold's "Dover Beach"; "the waste sand by the waste sea" where King Arthur's last battle is fought in Tennyson's *Idylls of the King.* World War I is associated with the plain in Hemingway's *Farewell to Arms;* his warrior-hero is wounded in "God-damn flat country" along the Piave River, and the ugly mood of the war is best caught in the description of the Italian retreat across the plains of the Tagliamento River. Hemingway's more exciting war in *For Whom the Bell Tolls* is fought in the hill country of Spain.

"Horizontal Is to Die" is the title of a chapter in one of Buckminster Fuller's books, and before that Richard Neutra had written, "To gain height against the eternal pull of gravity is the supreme triumph of the living; only the dead must lie level."[25] In ancient literature the land of the dead in the afterlife is flat, as is, ironically, the land of the living dead in modern literature. Holland is the "negative landscape" of the dead to Clamence in Camus's *The Fall:* "A soggy hell, indeed! Everything horizontal, no relief; space is colorless, and life dead. Is it not universal obliteration, everlasting nothingness made visible?"[26] Horizontality is the single dimension of Samuel Beckett's Trilogy, which is probably the most severe presentation of "a world collapsing" and an individual disintegrating that modern literature has to offer. "Molloy country" consists of bogland and tidal flats. In utter despair Molloy asks: "For what possible end to these wastes where true light never was, nor any upright thing, nor any true foundation, but only these leaning things, forever lapsing and crumbling away, beneath a sky without memory of morning or hope of night."[27] Robbe-Grillet's topography is similar to Camus's and Beckett's: "Flatness is the basic structural principle of Robbe-Grillet's world," concludes one critic.[28] Faulkner's rural wasteland, Yoknapatawpha County, is said to be named after "a Chickasaw Indian word meaning water runs slow through flat land."[29]

Centrality

To orient himself in the world man seems to require a sense of the deployment of persons, things, and places around a center, and this center thus acquires paramount importance over all around it. For groups of men such a place—a city, a temple—is sacralized, in the terms of Mircea Eliade, because at that spot there is a "break in plane" between heaven and earth; around it revolves the spiritual life of a traditionalist society.[30] In expressing alarm over "the desacralization of the cosmos accomplished by scientific thought," Eliade joins those who believe that tremendous disturbances in the spiritual history of the West were caused by the loss of earth's centrality in the Copernican astronomy. The secular view is that centrality is conferred by man on his surroundings, first with reference to his body, then by virtue of his needful works—his dwelling, his alteration of topography for agricultural and industrial purposes. Art, through the unity of its own components, creates a center for itself. Wallace Stevens proclaims the principle in "Anecdote of the Jar":

> I placed a jar in Tennessee,
> And round it was, upon a hill.
> It made the slovenly wilderness
> Surround that hill.
>
> The wilderness rose up to it,
> And sprawled around, no longer wild.

By an imaginative leap Stevens extends a principle that operates quite literally in the case of architecture and sculpture.[31]

The centrality of a place in a literary work is established by the frequency and importance of the transactions that occur in it, by its weight in the behavior of characters, and by the force of the imagery and style describing it. Centrality is associated with rest, certainty, wholeness—Matthew Arnold's glade and Eliot's "still point of the turning world." One of the most satisfying narrative motifs is the journey of the hero from a central place to a number of outlying places and from them back to the starting place. The peripheral places offer variety of action and scene but are kept within a unified field by the framing effect of the dominant central place. The hero's return to the center creates a feeling of stability and completion.

A central place, however, may be tragic if the hero is restricted to it or drawn to it in some self-destructive way. The classical unity of place, no matter what else it did, certainly helped to create the atmosphere of doom. The sense of tragedy is helped by binding the victim to a single place. Doomed Troy cannot be avoided either by Achilles, who is fatally drawn to the city from the outside, or by Hector, who cannot escape it from the inside. In *Wuthering Heights* and *The Return of the Native* characters are held within the severely limited world of the moors, just as in *The Scarlet Letter* Reverend Dimmesdale and his tormentor, Chillingworth, are attracted again and again to the scaffold in the center of the town until they perish there. Hester Prynne, not being marked for tragedy, escapes "that magic circle of ignominy" and is even able to contemplate an ocean voyage to complete freedom.

Very long narratives may be given concentration through a centralized setting. Faulkner's long series of Yoknapatawpha County novels turns on the central location of Jefferson, the county seat. As Gavin Stevens approaches the city from Seminary Hill in *The Town,* he sees the whole county radiating out from the center, a geographical area and also a metaphor for the literary creation of an author:

> And you stand suzerain and solitary above the whole sum of your life beneath that incessant ephemeral spangling. First is Jefferson, the center, radiating weakly its puny glow into space; beyond it, enclosing it, spreads the County, tied by the diverging roads to that center as is the rim to the hub by its spokes, yourself detached as God Himself for this moment above the cradle of your nativity and of the men and women who made you, the record and chronicle of your native land proffered for your perusal in ring by concentric ring like the ripples on living water above the dreamless slumber of your past; you to preside unanguished and immune above this miniature of man's passions and hopes and disasters. . . .[32]

In addition, each novel in the cycle has its own special center, usually a house: in *Light in August* Joanna Burden's house, from which paths radiate "like wheelspokes"; the Sutpen house in *Absalom! Absalom!;* the old Frenchman's place in *Sanctuary;* the Compson house in *The Sound and the Fury.* Another example of centralizing focus, less bombastic than Gavin Steven's reflection, is the vision Mrs. Armstid has of Frenchman's Bend when she confronts Flem Snopes on the gallery of Varner's store, the center of *The Hamlet:*

> After a time Mrs. Armstid raised her head and looked up the road where it went on, mild with spring dust, past Mrs. Littlejohn's, beginning to rise, on past the not-yet-bloomed (that would be in June) locust grove across the way, on past the schoolhouse, the weathered roof of which, rising beyond an orchard of peach and pear trees, resembled a hive swarmed about by a cloud of pink-and-white bees, ascending, mounting toward the crest of the hill where the church stood among its sparse gleam of marble head-stones in the sombre cedar grove where during the long afternoons of summer the constant mourning doves called back and forth.[33]

This has the economy of poetry comparable to the scene-setting lines of Frost's "Out, Out—":

> And from there those that lifted eyes could count
> Five mountain ranges one behind the other
> Under the sunset far into Vermont.

A-centrality

The opposite of the central place is the peripheral place, or the place removed from the center by distance or difficulty of access. As such it is a relatively strange place, and the objective of much narrative writing is to familiarize the reader with strange places by bringing them into relation with the known place. In the pastoral and utopian genres the unfamiliar setting affords the perspective of difference as a means of taking critical views of the familiar place. When a strange place may not be easily comprehended as part of the greater world, it is truly a place apart, such as uncharted islands, underground areas reached by hidden entrances, sequestered houses, secret rooms, valleys "surrounded by unscalable mountains and precipices," as Eldorado in *Candide.* Complete separation from the familiar world allows the suspension of the usual environmental conditions in these places and makes possible the purity of their essential nature: absolute good in paradise without even a variation of time or season, absolute evil in inferno, absolute perfection in utopia. The difficulty of reaching the outlying place without special effort has a compensation in the privileged experiences the hero may have there, such as conversing with the dead or discovering some magic object or profound understanding, which he may then carry back to the central place for its enrichment.

The peripheral place may be a refuge to which the hero repairs out of the workaday world to heal his wounds and renew his heroic dedication, like Lancelot being nursed back to health in his bower, Huck Finn loafing on the river between bouts with civilization on shore, Nick Adams making camp up in Michigan to compose himself after the war, Tom Joad hiding out in a culvert before taking the big step into labor agitation. From time to time the individual requires the reintegration that withdrawal to a special place affords; there, limited space helps to concentrate the ego and distinguish it from what is not ego. "Life on the border," a phrase used by Graham Greene and an important element in his work, gives the hero a vantage point from which to examine a role before coming to a decision to play a part in it.[34] It is thus a point in the transition of the hero from one stage in his career to another. The fact that border places are preferred by many modern heroes is an indication that confidence in central places, in certainties and hierarchical structure, has changed to distrust and that the only recourse is to a peripheral place where the hero's total commitment is not required. The American hero especially, according to Tony Tanner, needs to preserve his identity at some point between a flowing and structured existence; "edge city" is Ken Kesey's border place in Thomas Wolfe's novel about Kesey and his associates.[35] For purely dramatic purposes, a place apart serves to focus attention on the confrontation of characters in a climactic scene.

Exotic places harbor rare things and make possible a kind of experience not common at home. "The exotic and the erotic ideals go hand in hand," writes Mario Praz.[36] Exotic places inspire intense sexual feelings, probably because a change of customary place encourages a change of customary feeling. Lovers have trysts in unfrequented places; bridal pairs seek out a strange place to begin their love life, married couples to renew love. In the nineteenth century Europe became synonymous with sexual adventure for Englishmen and Americans living in a repressive Puritan culture. Henry James's travelling American is often a character in search of sexual experience denied to him at home. The objective is seldom achieved—by Isabel Archer or Strether—though the effort is always an interesting means of character development. (One success is Miss Jane in the short story "Europe"; of the three daughters held in check by their mother only one, Miss Jane, manages to escape to Europe, where she develops "a new character" and takes to "flirting.") In the twentieth century tourism feeds sexual desire as much as it feeds nostalgia and vanity.

Distance from the center is not always a feature of apartness. The worlds in fairy tales and science fiction sometimes lie right next to the ordinary world, but they must be reached by some mysterious passage—through a doorway or mirror, up a ladder, down a hole into the ground, under a floorboard. They defy natural law in being adjacent or parallel to the known world, though in themselves they are governed by a perfectly consistent system of laws.

The peripheral place may sometimes be distinguished by its formlessness. The earth's inhabitable surface has a relatively constant form because it is so well known, but the mountains, caves, and jungles appall because of their unfamiliarity and incapability to support human life. The imagination peoples them with monsters inimical to human kind. Mountains were unacceptable to Western man until eighteenth-century aesthetics, in the interest of provoking more intense feelings, placed a high premium on obscurity. As Edmund Burke maintained in his epochal essay on the sublime and the beautiful, "dark, confused, uncertain images have a greater power on the fancy to form the grander passions than those have which are more clear and determinate." Poe often repeated the idea in his pleas for "indefiniteness" and "indeterminate glimpses" in poetry. Romantic writers tamed the terror of obscurity in picturesque landscapes, although some of the old feeling lingered on, and we can find Wordsworth reporting in *The Prelude* of his childhood that there was a time when a huge black peak that he observed one night from a boat cast a "darkness" over his thoughts for many days:

> No familiar shapes
> Remained, no pleasant images of trees,
> Of sea or sky, no colours of green fields;
> But huge and mighty forms, that do not live
> Like living men, moved slowly through the mind
> By day, and were a trouble to my dreams. (I.395–400)

Even someone as late in the romantic tradition as Henry David Thoreau found it impossible to admit the mountain to the company of places he loved because it conformed to no conception of the earth he knew. His reaction is like Wordsworth's: "Here was no man's garden, but the unhandselled globe. It was not lawn, nor pasture, nor mead, nor woodland, nor lea, nor arable, nor waste-land. . . . It was Matter, vast, terrific."[37]

The underworld has an even richer heritage of terror than the mountain top, its formlessness being accentuated by darkness and the association with the ultimate loss of form, the death and dissolution of the body. From the depths autochthonous monsters arise to assault mankind on the surface. Grendel walks in shadows and inhabits the misty moors and misty hills *(mistige móras* and *mist hleoþum),* and his mother lives in the depths of the *caelda streamas.* The hero who can withstand the terror of the mountain and cave is the savior of mankind, Christ in the New Testament, Beowulf in the English wpic.

The sea's formlessness has always represented the ultimate disorder in man and universe. The sea is the least assimilable of all terrestrial places: in its depths human existence is impossible, on its surface no human trace remains. It is "the primordial undifferentiated flux," writes W. H. Auden in his book on romantic imagery, a "state of barbaric vagueness and disorder out of which civilization has emerged."[38] Thoreau observes that in all of man's history only the shore of the sea has been altered: "The ocean is a wilderness reaching round the globe, wilder than a Bengal jungle, and fuller of monsters, washing the very wharves of our cities and the gardens of our seaside residences. Serpents, bears, hyenas, tigers rapidly vanish as civilization advances, but the most populous and civilized city cannot scare a shark far from its wharves."[39] Peter Benchley's *Jaws* is presaged here. Outer space now vies with the sea as the favored place for uncommon adventures and strange monsters.

Place and Process

The character of a place is conditioned by the kind of human activity that is performed there. The sea in Stephen Crane's "The Open Boat" wears quite a different aspect to the men in the boat than it does to the vacationers on the shore. The sea as seen from the deck of the *Pequod* is not the same as the sea observed from Dover Beach. The *Pequod,* in turn, is a ship with a special quality as a place because of its association with the process of whaling. Further, the *Pequod* is distinct from other whalers because the equipment she carries is devoted to revenge on a particular whale. The land Hardy's Tess loved as a participant in dairy farming becomes intolerable when she has to work at large-scale harvesting. A place used in play is perceived to be altogether different from a place used in labor. Most shocking and ironical are the results of war in its transformation of familiar surroundings into places of horror. Homer observes that the place outside the walls of Troy where Achilles runs down Hector is much changed from that same place in peacetime when the Trojan women washed clothes there. Hemingway's and Pynchon's studies of war pay particular attention to the adjustments soldiers and lovers must attempt to make in places changed by war.

Place and Things

The relation of things to a place, writes Cassirer, is "never purely external and accidental; the place is itself a part of the thing's being, and the place confers very specific inner ties upon the thing."[40] Henry James would have liked this formulation since he was fascinated with the relation of things to places. In *The Spoils of Poynton* it is a matter of critical nicety whether things, specifically *objets d'art,* or the three houses where they may be displayed have a more important role. In his preface to the novel James selected things to be "the citadel of interest," an image that in itself, however, testifies to the powerful urge of the imagination to localize things, to compose them for their own benefit in a special area.

Vegetation has a most important influence on the quality of places. Vegetation is life, and its degree of density indicates the amount of life a place harbors. Places devoid of plant life are associated with deprivation and death, places of abundant vegetation are pleasant and erotic.[41] Deserts and mountain tops present the terrifying aspect of lifeless matter whereas the forest is life in an active, wild state. As a refuge from history and an opportunity for freedom, the forest restores man and consoles him. Without vegetation a city may fail to satisfy the need for life images in the environment, and thus the garden has been maintained in the heart of Babylon and New York. The garden, with its well-watered trees and pruned plants, represents the reassuring compromise of life contained—an oasis in the desert, a clearing in the forest, a sequestered spot in the city. It is a piece of the natural world which man encloses in order to hold out alien presences and to cultivate desirable plants.

Lack of vegetation is generally associated with sterility in the many literary wastelands of the twentieth century. As a symbol of the forlorn condition of the contemporary world, Hardy's Egdon Heath has been succeeded by Gide's deserts in North Africa, Eliot's "stony places," and the barren streets of numerous naturalistic city novels.

But excessive vegetation can be equally objectionable because it stifles the civilized man with too abundant life and too insistent sexuality. Hardy again points the way with Angel's distaste for the rank growth associated with Tess and with the life-smothering luxuriance of the forest in *The Woodlanders:* "huge lobes of fungi grew like lungs. . . . The leaf was deformed, the curve was crippled, the taper was interrupted, the lichen ate the vigour of the stalk, and the ivy slowly strangled to death the promising sapling."[42] In spite of the lush vegetation of Cayman Island, where "tree names, flower names . . . gainsay death's brittle crypt," Hart Crane, in "O Carib Isle," sees the place only in terms of his death both as writer and person:

> Under the poinciana, of a noon or afternoon
> Let fiery blossoms clot the light, render my ghost
> Sieved upward, white and black along the air
> Until it meets the blue's comedian host.

The delight a boy has climbing to the topmost branches of trees in Robert Frost's "Birches" is inspired by the desire to escape for a while the demands of life, which are imaged as noisome vegetation:

> And life is too much like a pathless wood
> Where your face burns and tickles with the cobwebs
> Broken across it, and one eye is weeping
> From a twig's having lashed across it open.

The twentieth-century male's rejection of female fecundity is often symbolized by his preference for places barren of vegetation. Thus, the contest between Marcel and his wife in Gide's *The Immoralist* is represented by his perverse liking for arid places and her attachment to "green Normandy." Eustacia Vye and Clym in Hardy's *The Return of the Native* are similarly divided over Egdon Heath, which she is desperate to flee, though not to seek fertility, and to which he returns for spiritual sustenance. The whole last third of Mailer's *The Naked and the Dead* is a counterpointing of female and male topography. The jungle is pictured as repulsively female; the passage of a squad of soldiers through it is accomplished by "cutting a trail" in the dense vegetation, "a tunnel whose walls were composed of foliage and whose roadbed was covered with slime. . . . They were engulfed in sounds and smells, absorbed in the fatty compacted marrows of the jungle. The moist ferny odors, the rot and ordure, the wet pungent smell of growing things, filled their senses and loosed a stifled horror, close to nausea."[43] Finally breaking out of the jungle, the men are born into a world of light and space, of sparse vegetation ("yellow hills covered only with kunai grass or an occasional grove of shrubbery")—all under the domination of the peak of Mount Anaka. Stripping landscape of vegetation is like the ravishment of the female; so it was in the colonial imagery of America as woman, and so it is in cynical anti-sexual expressions of the twentieth century: in Huxley's *Point Counter Point,* Spandrell enjoys knocking down "pleasingly phallic" foxgloves with a stick, and in Ford Madox Ford's *Some Do Not,* Tietjens uses his walking stick on yellow mulleins, "like a woman killed among crinolines."[44]

Heavily vegetated places are considered primeval; such is the heart of Africa where Kurtz is found, a place representing the condition of man "when vegetation rioted on the earth and the big trees were king."[45] Because the battle between man and vegetation was supposedly won in the prehistoric past, the decay of civilization may be effectively symbolized by the recrudescence of vegetation in civilized places, especially within houses and cities. Animism in plants, what Poe, in "The Fall of the House of Usher," terms "the sentience of all vegetable things," is particularly horrible when it destroys the works of man. The Gothic novel is rich in imagery of once-great houses being overrun by the neighboring forest, such as the castle in Ann Radcliffe's *The Mysteries of Udolpho;* well might the heroine be dismayed: "She looked fearfully on the almost roofless walls, green with damp, and on the gothic points of the windows, where the ivy and the briony had long supplied the place of glass, and ran mantling among the broken capitals of some columns, that had once supported the roof."[46] The idea of vegetative re-conquest is useful for writers who pursue the apocalyptic theme in contemporary science fiction: in Piers Anthony's *Omnivore* three people struggle to survive on a fungi-dominated planet, and in Brian Aldiss's *The Long Afternoon of Earth* the process of "devolution" has gone so far that mankind is being forced off of earth by the size and almost animal activity of plant life. A favorite touch in twentieth-century apocalyptic fiction is the encroachment of vegetation on the scene of the most advanced civilization, the city. The narrator of Walker Percy's *Love in the Ruins* observes that "The house next door has been abandoned, its slab cracked and reclaimed by the swamp, by creeper and anise with its star-shaped funky-smelling flower. Wild grape festoons the carport."[47] At the end of his losing battle against a dying civilization, he goes to live in a swamp, in the "misty green woods, and sleepy bayous," a place once inhabited by black slaves. In *The Tenants* Bernard Malamud pictures the ultimate demise of literature in the situation of two writers who try to compose in an abandoned apartment house in New York. The trees painted on the walls of one room are described as having "moved off the walls onto the dark floors in the flat. Taking root, they thickened there and spread into the hall and down the stairs, growing profusely amid huge ferns, saw-toothed cactus taller than men, putrefying omnivorous plants."[48] Bitter enemies—one a Jew, the other black—the would-be authors kill each other "in a grassy clearing in the bush. The night was moonless above the moss-dripping, rope-entwined trees. . . . Their metal glinted in hidden light, perhaps star-light filtering greenly through dense trees." In Vonnegut's latest version of post-apocalyptic America, *Slapstick* (1976), New York has become an "ailanthus jungle." An ultimate affront to the most advanced technology occurs in Thomas McGuane's *Ninety-Two in the Shade* in which the narrator inhabits the fuselage of a warplane: "a remnant of a crash-landed navy reconnaissance plane rested logically on a concrete form and had by now in the quick tropical growing season become impressively laced with strangler fig (a plant whose power was now slowly buckling the riveted aluminum panels)."[49]

For civilized man gods and *genii loci* are no longer identifiable with places, and it is not possible to accept Milton's notion in *Paradise Lost* of the generation of animals from earth at the Creation:

> The grassie Clods now Calv'd, now half appeer'd
> The Tawnie Lion, pawing to get free . . .
> . . . the swift Stag from under ground
> Bore up his branching head. . . . (VII:463–66)

But the identification of animals with places is still as active a force in literary imagery as animistic vegetation; the writer can get us to accept the association of near-mythical animals with certain kinds of places. The persistence of earth's primitive past is symbolized by the half-animal, half-human Caliban in *The Tempest* and the autochthonous monster in John Gardner's *Grendel*. Almost like Milton's stag, "a great buck" suddenly materializes from a cliffside in Robert Frost's "The Most of It," much to the consternation of the man who "thought he kept the universe alone." In Frost's "Two Look at Two," a pair of mountain climbers feel as though "a great wave" has passed over them when they are observed by a doe and a buck:

As if the earth in one unlooked-for favor
Had made them certain earth returned their love.

Old Ben, the bear in Faulkner's novel, is the animal deity reigning over the remnant wilderness in Mississippi. He appears magically like a god, "emerging suddenly into a little glen. . . . It was just there, immobile, fixed in the green and windless noon's hot dappling." The bear disappears just as mysteriously: "It didn't walk into the woods. It faded, sank back into the wilderness without motion as he had watched a fish, a huge old bass, sink back into the dark depths of its pool and vanish without even any movement of its fins."[50] A similar spectral appearance also occurs in Faulkner's short story "The Old People": "Then the buck was there. He did not come into sight; he was just there, looking not like a ghost but as if all of light were condensed in him and he were the source of it, not only moving in it but disseminating it." Faulkner's "huge old bass" reminds us of Melville's white whale sounding in the sea, "no bigger than a white weasel," though when it surfaces again "the glittering mouth yawned beneath the boat like an open-doored marble tomb."

Wild animals are thus identified with the two remaining wild places on earth, Old Ben with the forest and Moby Dick with the sea, and nothing man does can expunge their presence. The white whale and the sea live on after man's adventure on earth is finished—"the great shroud of the sea rolls on as it rolled five thousand years ago." Old Ben and the Mississippi forest do not survive but when the hunt is long since over and the woods are being logged, Ike encounters an animal survivor, a rattlesnake, "the old one, the ancient and accursed about the earth, fatal and solitary." Most earth-bound of creatures, yet moving in a miraculous way—"free of all laws of mass and balance"—the snake was in the unfallen garden in the beginning and is now the last denizen of the degraded forest. It was in this sense that Cooper in *The Pioneers* gave to the last survivor of the Mohican Indians the name Chingachgook, meaning Great Snake, "the last of his people who continued to inhabit this country." The same quintessential animal earth-spirit appears in a poem by D. H. Lawrence entitled "The Snake," in which an "earth-brown" snake issues "from the burning bowels of earth" to drink at the poet's water-trough:

Like a king in exile, uncrowned in the underworld,
Now due to be crowned again.

In Lawrence's *The Plumed Serpent,* the snake is the earth component of the god Quetzalcoatl.

Because the experience has become so rare for people living in a highly predictable machine environment, the appearance of a wild animal in a free state constitutes a dramatic reminder of the animate character of earth itself, its remnant wildness and mystery. Taming a wild animal is like possessing its habitat, and the returning of an animal to its home is a sign of deep respect for wilderness places. This is the motif of a growing number of animal stories such as Joy Adamson's *Born Free* and Marguerite Henry's *Misty of Chincoteague.*[51] Only seeing the wild animal is sufficient for some, like Frost and Lawrence; facing a lioness in a pen is required of the hero in Saul Bellow's *Henderson the Rain King,* stalking and killing animals is necessary for primitivists like Hemingway and Faulkner. In his *Meditations on Hunting* Ortega y Gasset also insists on the kill, disallowing art, specifically photography, as a means of making contact with wilderness because art, with its burden of "historical supposition" and humanity, hinders a complete return to the primitive.[52]

Atmosphere

Atmospheric conditions of light and weather figure significantly in the tonality of out-of-door places. Night, rain, fog, sunlight change our perception of places. "The development of the mythical feeling of space," Cassirer asserts, "always starts from the opposition of *day* and *night, light* and *darkness.*"[53] The skies "determine the moods of the people and the landscape," writes Dubos.[54] The sudden light of a meteor causes "the familiar scene of the street," in the twelfth chapter of *The Scarlet Letter,* to take on "a singularity of aspect that seemed to give another moral interpretation to the things of this world than they had ever borne before." Intense heat and the glare of the sun actually help to motivate Meursault's murder of the Arab in *The Stranger;* fog and mud qualify settings in *Bleak House,* storms in *Wuthering Heights.* Uncontrollable natural events, such as storms, earthquakes, and floods, transform civilized, functioning environments into places full of chaos and horror. Snow leaves a city intact but strangely without motion, static.

Writers in the spell of the romantic aesthetic, which associates sublimity with obscurity, favor dim, misty settings, lighted, if at all, by the moon.[55] Classical settings, on the other hand, are customarily bathed in bright sunlight. In the 1853 Preface to his poems, Matthew Arnold observed that the ancient Greek poet endeavored to place "old mythic story . . . in broad sunlight, a model of immortal beauty." Thereafter "Greek light" became a critical commonplace in literary criticism, and it lingers on in the twentieth century among writers who seek to establish a relationship with classical antiquity. In explaining the title *Light in August,* William Faulkner claimed that there was a "peculiar quality to light" in the South, in the month of August, "as though it came not from just today but from back in the old classic times . . . from Greece, from Olympus."[56] Thomas Wolfe also sought to fix his characters in a "moment of timeless suspension" that is flooded with light "old and tragic . . . something like old time and destiny."[57] Faulkner and Wolfe bear out an observation made by Thoreau in *A Week on the Concord and Merrimack Rivers* that "the rays of Greek poetry struggle down to us, and mingle with the sunbeams of the recent day."

Place and Time

Time, being a more subjective and abstract perception of the mind, welcomes the imagistic help that place can offer. The passage of time may be more concretely known through the physical changes in places. In Virginia Woolf's *To the Lighthouse,* "Time Passes" is the title of a section that has nothing directly to do with time but with the effect on a summer cottage of the winds and "certain airs" in a succession of seasons; the cottage is a more eloquent spokesman of the passage of time than the characters who inhabit it. In *Paradise Lost,* Isabel MacCaffrey points out, "past and future become not periods, but places" through the powerful architectural and geographical presence that Milton is able to create in the poem; she cites this as an example of "the modulation of time into spatial effects."[58] The tempo of action may be controlled by the manner in which places are introduced. Time moves slowly when an orderly discovery of a landscape is made to the observing eye, as was customary in eighteenth-century narrative. Time accelerates when places are discovered in quick succession, as when Jane Eyre approaches Thornfield after a long absence: "At last the woods rose; the rookery clustered dark. . . . Another field crossed—a lane threaded—and there were the courtyard walls, the back offices; the house itself, the rookery still hid."[59] The life of Maggie, in Stephen Crane's novel, winds down quickly as she takes to walking farther and farther "into gloomy districts near the river"; the last hours of Quentin

Compson's life in *The Sound and the Fury* are marked by his aimless wandering in neighborhoods along the Charles River; in *Heart of Darkness* the narrower the Congo River becomes the nearer Marlow is to discovering the long-sought secret of Kurtz's existence in Africa.

A stock-in-trade of romantic and Victorian poetry was revisiting a once-familiar place and experiencing again the feelings associated with it but now with an overlay of changed feelings, as in "Tintern Abbey" and "Locksley Hall." Wordsworth sums up the idea in "The Vale of Esthwaite":

> No spot but claims the tender tear
> By joy or grief to memory dear.

The interplay of place and time gives form to the poet's reflective life; to the novelist it yields up character, incident, and the world they inhere in. Proust's revivification of people and times of the past depends on his recreation of places; his great work, writes Georges Poulet, is "une recherche non seulement du temps, mais de l'espace perdue."[60] It could not have been otherwise. Without mentioning Proust, Bachelard establishes the primacy of space in the operation of memory: "Here space is everything, for time ceases to quicken memory. . . . The finest specimens of fossilized duration concretized as a result of long sojourn, are to be found in and through space. The unconscious abides. Memories are motionless, and the more securely they are fixed in space, the sounder they are" (9). A geographically remote place awakens the memory of remote times. This accounts for the effect of out-of-the-way places in local color fiction. Being so far removed from the rest of America, the coast of Maine and the secret places where Mrs. Todd gathers herbs, in Sarah Orne Jewett's *The Country of the Pointed Firs*, are ideal stimulants to stir the "seldom visited bays of memory."[61] Besides the association of place with memory, Proust and Jewett share a remarkable verbal association of odor and memory: of Mrs. Todd's herb garden, Jewett writes: "There were some strange and pungent odors that roused a dim sense and remembrance of something in the forgotten past" (14).

Ruins are man-made markers of the passage of time, places consecrated by the great events in the history of mankind that once occurred there and, in turn, consecrating time by reason of their tangible witness of the past. Ruins continue the influence of the past on the present as either monition or model. Eighteenth-century aesthetics found beauty in desuetude and a special charm in architecture whose forms had become obscured and whose practical functions had become superannuated. But picturesqueness may conceal horror if the ruin preserves some evil thing out of the past, as the Gothic house does. To the realist of the nineteenth century ruins testify to the folly of the past rather than to its greatness or awesomeness. In the works of Dickens ruins are the detritus of the past, the accumulation of dilapidated buildings and broken things that suffocate the inhabitants of the present.[62] Ruins in contemporary writing presage the coming catastrophe, what the places of the present may be expected to become. Such are the ruins of Dresden in Vonnegut's *Slaughterhouse Five,* of a suburban shopping center in Walker Percy's *Love in the Ruins,* of a New York apartment house in Bernard Malamud's *The Tenants,* of war-torn London in Thomas Pynchon's *Gravity's Rainbow.* As though to fly in the face of imminent doom, an American architect, James Wise, specializes in designing artificially ruined buildings to house business establishments. Since the primeval world of the past and the world-to-come stand outside of historical time, they may be made to represent either a dark or a golden past, a heavenly or infernal condition of the future. They are the proper settings of utopias and dystopias, and, conceived as either Urvelt or Nachvelt, they are the strategic places from which primitivists and science fiction writers launch their criticism of the present real world.

Whereas ruins cannot fail to signify the passage of time, either sentimentally or satirically, natural places are timeless, unchanging, and overpowering to man with their suggestion of infinity. Such is Melville's sea, Gide's desert, or Mann's mountain, which Frye appropriately calls a symbol of "anti-time." Yet ruins, when they are almost lost in antiquity, can also approach the condition of timeless natural places. British fiction has a tradition that finds a transcendent value in the most ancient English ruins: Stonehenge at the close of *Tess of the D'Urbervilles,* Cadbury Rings in Forster's *The Longest Journey,* Bragdon Wood in C. S. Lewis's *That Hideous Strength,* an ancient burial place in W. H. Hudson's *Hampshire Days.* American fiction must labor more to confer age upon a new land; Cooper and Cather do it by pondering the remains of lost Indian civilizations, Hawthorne and Faulkner by dwelling on the manners of defunct cultures. If history is short in America, geologic time may be invoked to fill it out to respectable mythic proportions. Thornton Wilder thus magnifies the setting of *Our Town:* "Grover's Corners lies on old Pleistocene granite of the Appalachian range. I may say it's some of the oldest land in the world . . . two hundred, three hundred million years old." In *Requiem for a Nun* Faulkner uses two pages to trace the geologic history of Yoknapatawpha County, "this knob, this pimple-dome, this buried half-ball hemisphere." In *Hawaii* James A. Michener takes fourteen pages to describe the geologic formation of the Hawaiian islands and in *Centennial* a hundred pages to bring Colorado from three billion six hundred million years ago to thirteen thousand years ago when man first arrived there.

In the literature of quest journeys, timeless places of the past or future intersect the present world and produce a visionary experience for the hero that may be either regenerative or shattering. Dante's privileged view of the realms of the after-life wins him a profound knowledge of the kind of behavior he must practice in the real world. Hardy's Jude is cruelly deceived when the Heavenly Jerusalem he thinks he sees from his humble lookout in Brown House turns out to be worldly Christminster. He spends his life seeking the vision, in vain— unlike Christian in *Pilgrim's Progress,* who is told by Evangeline to seek "yonder shining light" and eventually does and is saved. Conrad's Kurtz is shattered in primitive Africa, while Marlow, though terribly shaken by following Kurtz into "the heart of darkness," is convinced that his journey up the Congo River, "on a prehistoric earth, on an earth that wore the aspect of an unknown planet," was ultimately for the good: "It seemed somehow to throw a kind of light on everything about me—and into my thoughts." Saul Bellow's Henderson is another successful venturer into the primeval world of an Africa "beyond geography," where he finds not a depraved Kurtz but a philosopher-king who helps to cleanse him of the civilized complexities that have wasted his energies and turn him toward a wholesome identification with things and animals. Such journeys into the remote interior of Africa are also journeys back in time. Marlow feels that his trip up the Congo River is "like travelling back to the earliest beginnings of the world," and Henderson has the same feeling: "I felt I was entering the past— the real past, no history or junk like that. The prehuman past."[63] When he returns to America, a new man, Henderson repeats the course of Western history in the stages of his journey: from a village "older than the city of Ur" to an Arab settlement on the edge of the jungle, to Ethiopia, Khartoum, Cairo, Athens, Rome, London, and finally Newfoundland.

A mythic Africa is not the only primeval world, of course. The American forest serves the purpose in Faulkner's *The Bear;* Mexico supplied D. H. Lawrence, in *The Plumed Serpent,* with an experience of "the old prehistoric humanity . . . of the days before the glacial period"; and James Dickey's canoeists have no farther to go than a river in Georgia to find a place sufficiently primitive to shake them out of their suburban complacency. Science fiction and fantasy supply the taste for the Urvelt with primitive places that lie mysteriously close to our own—under the polar ice cap, in the middle of a mountain, on an uncharted island where the world of the geologic past, with dinosaur monsters and cavemen, is still to be found.

Behind twentieth-century literature's interest in the Urvelt— particularly behind Conrad and Lawrence—lies Herman Melville, whose works express a life-long fascination with the primeval world, whether in the form of a paradisal island, as in *Typee,* or a forbidding wasteland, as in "The Encantadas." The "primitive forests" and the "eternal ocean," Melville writes in *Pierre,* "are the only unchanged general objects remaining to this day, from those that originally met the gaze of Adam." The timeless world of the sea was more attractive to Melville than the forest at his door, and the sea and its terrors constituted for him the primitive world, through which his heroes make their way in fragile ships. Islands at first offer refuge, but at the last these, too, give out and universal desolation reigns. In "The Encantadas" Melville uses the Galapagos Islands as his most powerful image of the Urvelt.[64] Human beings cannot survive there, but only reptiles, the most forlorn of which are the antediluvian tortoises, who "seemed newly crawled forth from beneath the foundation of the world"; but the islands are an inferno, too, "looking much as the world at large might, after a penal conflagration" and serving as a prison-house for an assortment of desperate and abandoned human beings.[65] Melville's combined primeval and future (post-nuclear-bombed) world intersects the present world in a most terrifying way:

> Nay, such is the vividness of my memory, or the magic of my fancy, that I know not whether I am not the occasional victim of optical delusion concerning the Gallipagos. For, often in the scenes of social merriment, and especially at revels held by candle-light in old-fashioned mansions, so that shadows are thrown into the further recesses of an angular and spacious room, making them put on a look of haunted undergrowth of lonely woods, I have drawn the attention of my comrades by my fixed gaze and sudden change of air, as I have seemed to see, slowly emerging from those imagined solitudes, and heavily crawling along the floor, the ghost of a gigantic tortoise with 'Memento *******' burning in live letters upon his back. (153)

Time-shifts in stream of consciousness writing dissolve the consistency of settings. The African setting of "The Snows of Kilimanjaro," for example, is abruptly abandoned when we follow Harry, in his fevered consciousness, to Montmartre. But, though fractured, places presented in a stream of consciousness have a practical function as time-markers, for the reader may be oriented in the time of a recollected event by the setting in which it occurs. A break in time sequence is signaled by a change of setting, and the return to the place where the recollecting person is located signals the return to the original time period. When we crawl with Benjy under the fence, we know what time in the history of the Compson family we are in; when we accompany Benjy and Luster in their walk along the golf course fence, we know that we are back in the present.

Place and Motion

There is a reciprocal relationship between place and motion as they are represented in literature. Frequent movement between places is always a most popular motif because journeys at least promise life and action, while remaining in a place necessarily diminishes the opportunity for change and increases the need for description. A new place means new adventures, new people for the hero to encounter, new objects to handle, new ideas to contemplate. Free movement opens up a world with a variety of interests, whereas restriction to a single place is more consonant with tragedy and death. A sense of motion may be achieved merely by the quick succession of different settings or by the order in which the details of a single place are described. Edgar's description of a cliffside in *King Lear,* in concentrating on the diminishing size of objects, induces a feeling of vertigo in Gloucester. This is an extreme case; more commonly, the reader may receive a sensation of motion when he reads a description of a place as it is approached from a distance and traversed from periphery to center. The quality of a place in literature is subtly determined by the manner in which a character arrives at it, moves within it, and departs from it. The general impression of a place often depends on its position in a series of places visited by a journeying character, whose moving point of view confers comparison and climax on otherwise static places. It is more exciting to hear about a place from a visitor than from a resident. Homer appreciated that, as well as the fact that a sailor's approach to places by sea is more attractive than by approach by road over land. The sea approach is more symbolic, of course, the road more realistic, and the path even more realistic than the road. Of the distinction between the road and the path, O. F. Bollnow writes: "The path does not shoot for a destination but rests in itself. It invites loitering. Here a man is *in* the landscape, taken up and dissolved into it, a part of it."[66] The romantic poets made the walk across the land an important part of their imagistic repertoire because they felt that a man with his feet literally on the ground is more likely to be in touch with the truths of nature. The earth-oriented walking character gets into prose fiction somewhat later, and is particularly noteworthy in the novels of Hardy.[67]

The narrative of a journeying hero is rich in places that are interesting not only because they are exotic but because their meaning is a mystery until they are explored. They may harbor good or evil for the hero; they may not be what they appear to be, and they are full of surprises, unexpected dangers, and pleasures. Even the return journey is fraught with the perils and temptations of false home places, and the home place itself may have changed so much that it conceals some ultimate catastrophe, as Ithaca does in the *Odyssey*. The original destination of a journey will vary with the age in which a work is written: the ancient epic hero goes to battle places to test his prowess, the Christian hero to a holy place, the romance hero to the land or garden of love, the naturalistic hero to the city to make a new life, the primitivistic hero to the wilderness to find a past way of life.

The circular journey, consisting of a trip out to a number of places and a return to the starting place, suggests a closed universe of limited possibilities. The linear journey, on the other hand, originates in the hope that some foreign place harbors a truth that the familiar home place cannot supply. Sometimes this turns out to be the case, as in the *Aeneid* and *Pilgrim's Progress*. More often, however, the distant destination is no more rewarding than the home place, which deceives by its routine dullness. The traveler, says Emerson in "Self-Reliance," "carries ruins to ruins," and Concord has as much to offer as Rome. Homer holds a perfect balance between the exotic and the home place: Odysseus is excited by the wonders he has beheld all over the known world, but Ithaca still bears the ultimate truth for him. Journeys carry the hero through a series of places representing the perils that his particular culture has identified as being important. On his ten-year homeward trip Odysseus encounters the physical and spiritual tests a Greek leader was expected to withstand; Bunyan's hero faces the embodiment of every spiritual hazard in the life of a Christian believer. Both are victorious over a "landscape of difficulty."

A pair of travelers on different courses—lovers, friends, father and son—increases the range of places and produces a narrative structure of great force in which two series of places and adventures converge in the end on one place: Odysseus and Telemachus in the great hall in Ithaca, Candide and Cunegonde on the shore of Propontis, Bloom and Stephen in the little house on Eccles Street, Tess and Clare at Stonehenge. Sometimes the traveler is not a principal in the story but a transient who is used to introduce the scene and to be, like the reader, an interested witness of the action. Kenneth Burke calls this character the "'poetic traveler' so recurrent in nineteenth-century work."[68] Such expository aides are the reddleman in *The Return of the Native* and the narrator in Poe's "Fall of the House of Usher."

Historically, the novel has favored heroes in motion, movement out to an unknown periphery or movement inward. On the outward journey a character acquires new personality traits as he passes through a succession of challenging places. The inward journey takes a character like Marlow into a hidden place of awful revelation. Isabel Archer has both kinds of journey: from the severe restriction of her room in Albany she travels "out" to Europe and romantic adventure, but from the moment of her discovery of her husband's true nature she travels inward to an imaginary place of confinement. Some novels set up contrasting movements of characters. In *The Scarlet Letter* Hester Prynne proceeds from the scaffold to the periphery of the town and into the woods, or into a state of freedom, while Dimmesdale is gradually drawn from the seclusion of his study toward the scaffold and confession. In *Light in August,* a latter-day Hester, Lena Grove, calmly passes through the frantic center of action in Jefferson and comes out at the other end unscathed, while Joe Christmas moves in tortured circles of flight and concealment. In *Moby-Dick* Ahab travels across the seas straight to his objective—"The path of my fixed purpose is laid with iron rails, whereon my soul is grooved to run," while Ishmael, though he accompanies Ahab on the *Pequod,* actually has no part in the chase of the white whale and sits still, sometimes entranced as in a tantric state and sometimes observant, at the calm center of the world—"while ponderous planets of unwaning woe revolve round me, deep down and deep inland there I still bathe me in eternal mildness of joy."[69]

In works involving both place and motion there is likely to be either harmony or tension between these two aspects of the physical context, balance or imbalance, and the writer often plays one off against the other. This may be observed in individual scenes as well as over an entire work. The reaping scenes in *Anna Karenina* and Lawrence's *The Rainbow,* for instance, convey a concord of place and motion, of motion and the mood of the characters involved. Harmony between place and motion may be observed in the descending and ascending movements of the journey through Dante's *Inferno* and *Purgatory* as well as in the falling and penetrating movements in *Paradise Lost*.[70] In many of Hardy's works, however, there is a tension between place and motion; Tess and Jude become more and more alienated from the beautiful countryside they tortuously traverse and retraverse. In *Light in August* tragic consequences flow from the friction between characters who are rooted to a single spot—Reverend Hightower and Joanna Burden—and characters in perpetual motion—Lena Grove and Joe Christmas. One might posit a whole conception of American literature turning on the conflict of the desire to remain fixed in a paradisal place and the impulse toward motion.[71]

The physical properties of places, interesting though they are in themselves, have an important function in relation to other narrative elements. They serve as markers of various subjects and themes, and they help to flesh out plot and character with concrete details.

PLACE AND PLOT

Each kind of writing makes a selection of the places found to be most appropriate for its purposes—the palace front in classical drama, the manor house or ruined abbey in the Gothic novel, the valley or cave in the romantic lyric, the city street in the naturalistic novel. Heroic stories honor the spots where gods have visited and the fields where warriors have fought and died. Love stories must give some account of the places where lovers first meet, make love, and repine; Book V of the *Aeneid* is an early and prime example. Petrarch is credited with being the first modern poet to make a sentimental association of his beloved lady with specific places: the sweet spot *(dolce loco)* where love's tyranny first seized him (*Rime* lxxxv); the woods and hills and rivers which he finds inhabited by his Love (*Rime* xxxv); the Rhone River washing her feet, and Mount Ventoux, where he thinks of her on his famous climb. Later, romantic poetry carried the association of place with love far beyond what Petrarch dared, and no subsequent writing could fail to organize settings in accord with the development of the relationship between lovers. In *Faust,* Part I, the progress of love from innocence to guilt is artfully presented in pairs of contrasting scenes: Margaret's room and Martha's garden are first the scene of love's discovery and later of love's pain; the mountains are first the spot where Faust indulges in love's romantic rapture (Forest and

Cavern) and later the place where love's horrible obscenities are revealed on Walpurgis Night. The subjective coloration of places is naturally very intense among lovers. The valley of Wahlheim, where young Werther adores Charlotte, seems to be a "terrestrial paradise" compared to the false society of the court in town; but, in despair over the impossibility of having the love of Charlotte, Werther abandons Homer for Ossian, whose melancholy scenery—deep caverns, the moss-covered tombs of warriors, the moonlit sea—better suit his mood. The once-paradisal countryside now appears gloomy and damp; a murder and a flood change the whole aspect of Wahlheim. "He felt a sudden horror at the sight of the spot that he remembered so fondly. . . . Love and attachment, the noblest feelings of human nature, had been turned to violence and murder."[72] A third example of the close articulation of love-scene and love-plot may be drawn from Faulkner's *Light in August*. The affair of Joe Christmas and Joanna Burden, from the author's and partially from Joe's point of view, goes through three distinct "phases." At first Joe must sneak into the house and take her by stealth. In the second phase, Joanna is aroused and abandons herself to violent love-making, often out-of-doors, "without walls"; sometimes she requires him to break into the house and, in Gothic fashion, find her hidden in closet. To Joe, Joanna's licentiousness is alarming—"as though he had fallen into a sewer."[73] In the third phase a remorseful Joanna withdraws from sexual contact. The lovers are "stranded . . . upon a spent and satiate beach." Faulkner summarizes the three phases in a burst of place imagery: "During the first phase it had been as though he were outside a house where snow was on the ground, trying to get into the house; during the second phase he was at the bottom of a pit in the hot wild darkness; now he was in the middle of a plain where there was no house, not even snow, not even wind" (235–36).

No one outdoes Proust in the rich association of places with the love of women. Marcel's love affairs in *Remembrance of Things Past* have their inception in the identification of women with places; indeed, his desire to possess a woman is equivalent to his desire to possess the place with which he identifies her. Of Albertine and the beach where he first saw her Marcel writes in *The Guermantes Way:* "I cannot say whether it was the desire for Balbec or for herself that overcame me at such moments; possibly my desire for her was itself a lazy, cowardly, and incomplete method of possessing Balbec."[74] Ultimately Marcel's desire to possess woman and place becomes a metaphor for his desire to possess the world, to consume it in an act of almost religious devotion. When he surprises Gilberte in the park of Swann's villa at Com-

bray in *Swann's Way,* he describes the setting in which she is standing
as a holy place: the hawthorne hedge "resembled a series of chapels,"
the sun lights the scene "as though it had shone in upon them through a
window," and the scent of flowers "was as rich, and as circumscribed
in its range, as though I had been standing before the Lady-Altar."[75]
The Champs-Élysées, where he sees her next, is "turned into a Field of
the Cloth of Gold." The presence of woman transforms place from
ordinary reality to a condition of intense life and beauty. Swann is of
the same mind as Marcel when he observes that Odette's presence in
the vulgarly decorated apartment of the Verdurins "gave the house
what none other of the houses that he visited seemed to possess; a sort
of tactual sense, a nervous system which ramified into each of its
rooms and sent a constant stimulus to his heart." Later Odette, now
Madame Swann, has the same effect on the boy Marcel when he observes her walking in the Bois de Boulogne, "letting trail behind her the
long train of her lilac skirt, dressed, as the populace imagine queens to
be dressed, in rich attire such as no other woman might wear." The
Allée des Acacias becomes for the adoring boy "the Garden of Woman
. . . like the myrtle-alley in the Aeneid."

But of course it all turns out to be an illusion. In Proust love is a
function of the lover's feelings only, and the significance of places is
created only by association with those feelings. When the feeling of
love passes, the women and the places they transformed sink back into
dull reality. Thus when Marcel visits the Bois de Boulogne years later
and can no longer see Odette walking there, the whole place loses its
wonder and reverts to the common order of things: "Nature began
again to reign over the Bois, from which had vanished all trace of the
idea that it was the Elysian Garden of Woman." The narrator is thus
led to the conclusion that place as well as time exist only as long as one
has belief in them: "houses, roads, avenues are all fugitive, alas, as the
years."

A progression may be detected that leads from the associations of
loved women with highly colored scenes such as the Tansonville villa
park, the beach at Balbec, and the Bois de Boulogne, to the gradual
darkening and diminishing of the place of love. Albertine is first seen
silhouetted against the wonderful seascape at Balbec and is later the
unwilling prisoner in Marcel's Paris apartment. The river Vivonne,
which excited so much wonder in the narrator in *Swann's Way,* is
traced in *The Sweet Cheat Gone* to its source in "une espece de lavoir
carré ou montaient des bulles." Within *Swann's Way* itself the staircase is a place that goes through a process of decline echoing Marcel's
disillusionment with love. The staircase of his childhood in the house at

Combray holds the child's world together: it was "as though all Combray had consisted of but two floors joined by a slender staircase" (60). Each night Marcel's mother ascends the staircase to kiss her son goodnight, but one night this ritual, so essential to the happiness of the boy, is cancelled because the parents are busy with a guest downstairs, Swann. Many years later Swann pays for the misery he unknowingly caused when he pines for his mistress, Odette, as he mounts the "monumental staircase" at Madame Saint-Euverte's fancy reception. He would much rather have "raced up the dark, evil-smelling, breakneck flights" to Odette's dressmaker, a "pestilential, enviable staircase" where "one saw in the evening outside every door an empty, unwashed milk-can set out." Instead, Swann must climb to the top of Madame Saint-Euverte's staircase, lined with statuary and servants in livery, enter the concert-room, and join what now appears to him a monstrously ugly company of people.

Staircases in the poetry of T. S. Eliot are arranged in an order the reverse of Proust's, Eliot's transvaluations moving from the sordid to the sublime and Proust's from the sublime to the sordid. In the early poems Eliot's personae mount the stairs to a degraded love: there is Prufrock, who fondly thinks he has "time to turn back and descend the stair"; the man in "The Portrait of a Lady," who is at least aware of his lowly function—

> I mount the stairs and turn the handle of the door
> And feel as if I had mounted on my hands and knees;

and "the young man carbuncular" in *The Waste Land,* who "gropes his way, finding the stairs unlit," to the room of the weary typist.[76] In "Ash-Wednesday," however, the man on the stairs renounces human love ("the blessed face") as he is "climbing the third stair" and sees below him a woman in a garden. The naturalistically located stairs leading to ugly rooms in which fruitless love is practiced in Eliot's early poetry become, in "Ash-Wednesday," the winding stairs to divine love (that Daniel Arnaut speaks of in Dante's *Purgatory*) and, in "A Song of Simeon," the vision of "mounting the saints' stair." The two kinds of staircases in Eliot also reflect the "recurring exaltation and humiliation" that one is bound to experience on the "ladder of love" leading to God in *The Dark Night of the Soul* of St. John of the Cross. In Proust the ladder of love leads only to humiliation. Swann passes from the Combray staircase, where an innocent child's love of woman and world is created in a glow of wonder and longing, to "the despicable,

enormous staircase" of social hypocrisy, which he knows how to esti-
mate, and finally to the pestilential staircase to his degraded love,
which he cannot throw off: "he thought of the house in which at that
very moment he might have been, if Odette had but permitted, and the
remembered glimpse of an empty milk-can upon a door-mat wrung his
heart."

The structure of events and themes is thus supported and paral-
leled by the arrangement of places in a narrative. Plot is a map of a
story's physical environment as well as the pattern of its events, or, as
Eudora Welty puts it, "Location is the crossroads of circumstance."[77]
The complexities of warfare are reduced to three settings in the *Iliad:*
the Greek camp, from which Achilles finally issues; the Trojan city,
which produces Hector; and the plain outside the city walls, where the
two champions meet. The *Aeneid* occurs on three stages—Troy, Carth-
age, and Italy (because of its scale the least successful)—and the challenge of each is successively mastered by the hero. Three of E. M.
Forster's novels are built on a triad of places, the most familiar being
the mosque, cave, and temple of *Passage to India.*[78] Home, farm, and
town are the three places in which Paul Morel experiences three kinds
of love in Lawrence's *Sons and Lovers;* New York City, the Long
Island suburbs, and the ashy wasteland between form the three distinct
scenes of frustration and death in *The Great Gatsby.*[79] The prime example of a complicated three-part literary geography is *The Divine Comedy.* Dante is careful to make each detail of character and theme fit
precisely the place in the afterworld where it is encountered; the physical context of the poem, including the downward and upward movement of the travelers, is a vast metaphor supporting the ethical,
philosophical, and religious superstructure of meaning. Dante gave the
religious faith of his time a poetic cosmos in which to live, a localization so vivid that it still impresses the imagination of the West long
after the system of belief it was devised to localize has ceased to
compel assent.

Dante's is a familiar device in quest narrative: the hero's movement through a series of climactically arranged places reinforces the
sense of a completed mission. The plot of the *Odyssey* consists of two
such quests—Telemachus's for his father and Odysseus's for his homeland—and two series of places to go with them: the fantasy places
Odysseus reports in retrospective narrative and the actual, historical
Greek sites Telemachus visits. One series is deftly counterpointed
against the other, until the end of the book when the two merge their
quests and bring the action, now all in the present, to a fitting climax in
the great hall of the king in Ithaca. James Joyce in *Ulysses* follows his

model in mixing allegory with reality except that he combines in one series of places in contemporary Dublin both naturalistic and symbolical qualities. The epic *Gilgamesh* presents two sets of places but in a simpler manner than the *Odyssey:* actual geographical kinds of places figure in the story before the death of Enkidu, but after his death the disconsolate hero seeks his ancestor Utnapishtin in a number of purely symbolical places.

The form of a plot may be determined, among other things, by the movement of the central character through successive places. To summarize the variety of such movements: traveling in a circle, or going out from and back to the point of departure *(Odyssey);* traveling a straight line to a selected point *(Iliad);* visiting a number of points along an endless line (the picaresque novel); going from the periphery to the center *(Heart of Darkness);* going from the center to the periphery and back (the quest narrative, like *Gawain and the Green Knight*); moving up from depths to heights and falling from heights to depths (the hourglass plots of *Thais* and *Sister Carrie*); progressing from confinement to open space *(Jane Eyre),* or going from open space to confinement *(The Stranger),* or from confinement to open space and back to confinement *(The Portrait of a Lady).*

Intensification of plot and theme are aided when all action and imagery are concentrated in a central place. Conrad's *Heart of Darkness* is a striking example of this kind of centripetal force in literature. The title itself suggests the strong focus of a central place toward which Marlow moves the reader step by step—from the broad expanse of the Thames River estuary, across the sea to the coast of Africa, and down the ever-narrowing shores of the Congo River to Kurtz's Inner Station. Henry James defines this form in his preface to *The Wings of the Dove:* "one began . . . with the outer ring, approaching the center thus by narrowing circumvallations," and Martin Turnell observes a similar form in Proust, whose book "is really a pyramid of circles which grow smaller and smaller as one approaches the summit."[80] An often repeated central setting, a place where the destinies of the characters periodically converge, may become so dominant that it takes on the force of an image representing the whole book in the mind of the reader. Of this order are the scaffold in *The Scarlet Letter,* the bridge in *For Whom the Bell Tolls,* the wilderness in *The Bear,* the stairs outside Singer's room in *The Heart Is a Lonely Hunter.*

Impressions of spacious or crowded plots may be achieved by the selection and manipulation of settings. A desert or ocean scene creates a sense of disposable space; a room or a valley, a sense of spatial limitation. An impression of expanding or contracting space may also

be conveyed by the number and variety of settings, as well as by the
number and variety of characters active in those settings. "Space is the
lord of *War and Peace*, not time," observes E. M. Forster in *Aspects of
the Novel*, and it is Tolstoy's large expenditure of attention on many
different kinds of places and people and his frequent shifting from one
place and person to another that creates the spacious effect. Concentration on fewer kinds of places and on people with similar concerns
results in a sense of contracted space in *Crime and Punishment*. The
sudden expansion and contraction of space in a single work can be very
engaging. The epic is a literary form of the broadest dimensions, yet its
most common motif, as W. P. Ker notes, is "the defence of a narrow
space against odds."[81] From the broad Mediterranean world the *Odyssey* suddenly narrows down to the locked hall at Ithaca; after the broad
perspectives of Europe and the Atlantic Ocean, Marlow, as we have
noted, barely squeezes past the dense vegetation of the Congo; conversely, from cramped quarters on land, *Moby-Dick* moves out to the
seven seas and the cosmos. By alternating the point of view between
the Christians and the Saracens and between Roland's army and Char-
lemagne's, the poet of *The Song of Roland* accentuates the action at
the pass, just as Hemingway enlarges and narrows the scope at the
close of *For Whom The Bell Tolls* by tracing the progress of a special
courier from the mountain gorge to the headquarters of General Golz.

Less complex than these patterns is the pair of contrasted places
that are used to support polarities of plot, character, and theme. Such
are the good and evil gardens in Spenser's *Faerie Queene*, the alternating localities in Shakespeare's comedies, Eden and Hell in *Paradise
Lost*, river and shore in *Huckleberry Finn*, forest and town in *The
Scarlet Letter*, public and private scenes in Whitman's "When Lilacs
Last in the Dooryard Bloom'd" and in Eliot's *Four Quartets*.[82] Other
contrasts of place and idea are made by picturing the same place at
different times in history—the Thames River of Elizabethan days and
our own, as in Eliot's *The Waste Land;* at different seasons of the
year—the vacation house in summer and winter, in Virginia Woolf's
To the Lighthouse; at different hours of the day—the market place of a
colonial town in broad daylight and at night, in *The Scarlet Letter*.
Carlos Baker advances the thesis that "the total structure" of *A
Farewell to Arms* turns on "the deep central antithesis between the
image of life and home (the mountain) and the image of war and death
(the plain)." Baker elaborates: "The Home-concept . . . is associated
with the mountains; with dry-cold weather; with peace and quiet; with
love, dignity, health, happiness, and the good life; and with worship or
at least the consciousness of God. The Not-Home concept is as-

sociated with low-lying plains; with rain and fog; with obscenity, indignity, disease suffering, nervousness, war and death; and with irreligion."[83] From this point of view the plot of Hemingway's novel may be seen as the effort of the hero to escape from the plain and take up his abode in the mountains. In *The Magic Mountain* the high-perched sanatorium is a vantage point above the darkling plain where ignorant armies are about to clash. But after World War I the mountains lose their privileged role. Lawrence's unhappy lovers move from the paradisal, feminine English countryside in the first half of *Women in Love* to the tragic dead end of the Alps in the second half. The attempt to scale a mountain in Norman Mailer's World War II novel, *The Naked and the Dead,* ends in a farce.

PLACE AND CHARACTER

On the simplest level of allegorical characterization, the place inhabited by a person or being—castle, cave, forest—is merely a sign representing the type of person he is and his function in the story. The eighteenth century enriched this by associating the character of a person with the kind of dwelling place he produced for himself, Alexander Pope's Twickenham being an example from real life, Darcy's Pemberley from literature. This leaves room, of course, for the creation of false impressions, a form of hypocrisy Jane Austen takes pains to point out in Henry Crawford, whose "landscape improvements" are dictated only by his desire for "social prestige." Henry James, in *The Portrait of a Lady,* holds onto this tradition in his characterization of Osmond, whose elaborately devised home in Florence conceals rather than reveals his true character and serves as a trap to catch Isabel. While the eighteenth century commended the power of an individual to modify environment, particularly his dwelling or estate, the nineteenth century was struck by the power of environment to shape and modify character. Realism came to insist on a causal relationship between place and person For Balzac and Dickens a habitation is not only an expression of the person living in it but a condition influencing his life.

Contrasted dwellings may serve to represent a conflict within a single character or the conflict between characters. Two houses, one "on that bleak hill-top" and the other in a pleasant valley, are the poles of antithetical sets of characters in *Wuthering Heights.*[84] The contrast of characters in terms of their dwelling-places is so frequent in James

as almost to constitute a stereotype, if it were not in the hands of the
master himself; in the item of bachelor apartments alone, we have
Roderick Hudson's artist's studio compared to Rowland Hallet's grand
rooms, Newman's first floor on Boulevard Haussmann and Valentin's
basement in an ancient house, Strether's undistinguished hotel and
Chad's "perched privacy" on fashionable Boulevard Malesherbes.[85] In
To the Lighthouse one reader discovers "a dialectic of window and
lighthouse" that is used to objectify the opposed traits of Mr. and Mrs.
Ramsay.[86] The characterization of Emma Bovary turns on the discrepancy she cannot help noticing between the sordid provincial locales she
must live in and the romantic places of her reading, "the immense
territory of rapture and passions."[87] Her dream city, seen from a mountain top, is splendid "with domes, bridges, ships, forests of lemon
trees, and white marble cathedrals whose pointed steeples were
crowned with storks' nests," while poor Yonville-l'Abbaye, seen from
a distance, "brings to mind a cowherd taking a noonday nap beside the
stream." Tension in Thomas Mann's portrayal of the writer Aschenbach, in *Death in Venice,* is gained from his alternation between the
high country where he does his best creative work and the low country
where he seeks his pleasure. Yielding to "an impulse towards flight
from the spot which was the daily theatre of a rigid, cold, and passionate service" (that is, the place where he does his writing), he is torn
between taking a vacation at a mountain retreat or in Venice, the only
place that "had power to beguile him."[88] He chooses Venice, which is
an Elysium on the beachside at Lido but an inferno on the cityside with
its narrow streets, canals, and "fever-breeding vapours." On the
beach, Aschenbach succumbs to forbidden love and in the city to
cholera, a plague that had started in "the hot, moist swamps of the
delta of the Ganges" and had spread thence, "following the great caravan routes" westward to "several points on the Mediterranean lit-
toral."

There is a moral principle involved in the choice a character makes
between alternative places; the implication is that if Emma and Aschenbach had accepted the right places, the reality of Yonville and the
rigors of mountain country, they would not have turned out so badly.
Realistic though their authors are, they put an allegorical construction
on place as a "landscape of difficulty" of the sort found in *Pilgrim's
Progress.* Does one linger in Beulah Land or strive to reach the
Heavenly City? A link between Bunyan's outright allegorical use of
place and Flaubert's and Mann's realism may be found in *Jane Eyre.*
The insular Jane measures the world by England: life as a missionary
beside St. John Rivers "under Eastern suns, in Asian deserts" would

be a self-sacrificing act of Christian penance; life "in a southern clime, amongst the luxuries of a pleasure villa" as the mistress of Rochester would be "a fool's paradise"; the "correct choice" is life as "a village-schoolmistress, free and honest, in a breezy mountain nook in the healthy heart of England." Henry James's people reflect the same moral strenuousness in choosing places of constraint over places promising freedom.

A character's subjective response to places may serve to convey states of mind and feeling in a concrete way. "The impression produced by a landscape, a street or a house should always, to the novelist, be an event in the history of a soul," writes Edith Wharton.[89] A response to a place becomes material for characterization when it is individualized, that is when it does not conform to the customary response and when it cancels or exaggerates the impact place qualities usually have. Milton could not have wholly subscribed to Satan's brave rationalization of his predicament—

> The mind is its own place and in it self
> Can make a Heaven of Hell, a Hell of Heaven—

but T. S. Eliot, with romantic poetry behind him, though publicly proscribed, could endorse the subjective principle in these lines from "Preludes":

> You had such a vision of the street
> As the street hardly understands.

The ancient idea that microcosm repeats macrocosm becomes in the romantic aesthetic the correspondence of inner and outer worlds. Romantic writers discovered that places could be used as a fruitful source of imagery to objectify the inner life just as an earlier literature—*The Divine Comedy, Faerie Queene, Pilgrim's Progress*—had used symbolic geography to objectify the religious or political faith of a time. Wordsworth claimed in *The Prelude* that what he saw of the outside world

> Appeared like something in myself, a dream,
> A prospect in the mind. (II. 351–52)

Coleridge could have said the same for his "Ancient Mariner." Shelley in *Alastor* and Keats in *Endymion* devise elaborate systems of "visionary" geography to set forth the moods of the poet's life.[90] The sea and the land bear "a strange analogy to something in yourself," wrote Herman Melville, whose entire literary production may be viewed as a lifelong manipulation of a set of places he encountered in four years of sea travel as symbols of his feeling and thought. Francis Thompson's "The Hound of Heaven" is one of many concretizations of personal religious scepticism worked out through the analogy with place and motion: the disbeliever flees God at first in places on earth:

> I fled Him, down the nights and down the days;
> I fled Him, down the arches of the years;
> I fled Him, down the labyrinthine ways
> Of my own mind—

and then in places of a cosmic order:

> Across the margent of the world I fled
> And troubled the gold gateways of the stars.

Young Goodman Brown's walk through the woods in Hawthorne's story is an objectification of the inner doubts he is having about the religious professions of his neighbors. A common feature of a good deal of twentieth century writing is identified by Marshall McLuhan as *"le paysage intérieur* or the psychological landscape" that is presented in a discontinuous way in such works as *Ulysses* and *The Waste Land:* "Landscape is the means of presenting, without copula of logical enunciation, experiences which are united in existence but not in conceptual thought."[91]

The inevitable form of characterization by means of place is the journey of the representative hero in search of himself and the world. Confrontation with places is an age-old means of revealing character, whether they are the allegorical places of romance, the geographical places of realism, or the places filtered through the consciousness of the twentieth-century hero in *Ulysses*. Uprooting the hero and turning him loose to discover the world in a series of varied places is the essential narrative form of the heroic monomyth. The places in his journey become the concrete markers of the universal human experiences he encounters in each, and, arranged in an order of increasing difficulty, they dramatize either mastery in epic narrative or failure in naturalistic fiction. The victory of character over circumstance in Jane Eyre, for example, occurs in four stages in four different—and allegorically named—places, each presenting the heroine with a menacing predicament and personage to overcome: Mrs. Reed at Gateshead, Reverend Brocklehurst at Lowood, Rochester at Thornfield, and Reverend St. John Rivers at Marsh End. The case of Lily Bart in Edith Wharton's *The House of Mirth* is presented in a descending series. She is caught in a "clearly traced process of narrowing," observes R. W. B. Lewis in an introduction to the novel, "as she moves from the spacious grounds at Rhinebeck to the more restricted domain at Roslyn to the oppressive suite in the hotel to a single room in a boarding-house to the narrow bed in which she dies."[92]

The dislocation of the hero is a modern adaptation of the ancient journey of the hero in the world. How the hero will fare in unfamiliar places—the provincial in Paris, the American in Europe—is a perennially interesting question, perhaps more intriguing in our time when disorientation is such a common experience. To describe this motif in the work of James, Henry Dupee invents a useful term, "the transplantation plot, the device of modern novelists for unsettling the mind of a character—'transvaluing' his values—by removing him to an exotic place."[93] The ancient hero used more prowess than judgment to extricate himself from dangerous places, but Strether, we find, repeats some of Odysseus' trials—escape from the enchantress and return to Penelope (Mrs. Newsome, alas!)—and the result of his travels is similar, what James calls a "process of vision" in the preface to *The Ambassadors*. Of another one of James's pilgrims, Longmore in "Madame de Mauves," it has been said, "the narrative is a journey to understanding. . . . His physical movement—back and forth between Paris and Saint-Germain—parallels his intellectual movement."[94]

Having categorized in general terms some of the properties of place and the use of the place in plot and characterization, I propose now to narrow the focus sharply to the role of place as it functions in the formation of imagery and, even more minutely, to the metaphor that draws an analogy between the human body and places.

3

A RHETORIC OF PLACE II
The Metaphor of
Place and Body

SETTING AND METAPHOR comprise the two formal uses of place in literature. Setting is established by fixed descriptions or by indirect references in the narrative or in the speeches of characters. Dozens of descriptive details in speeches and songs, for example, go to build up the rich island locale of *The Tempest*. While setting is readily recognized and appreciated, place metaphors are more subtle and often escape notice even though commonly used. The setting for the appearance of the ghost in Act I of *Hamlet* is effectively provided by a few references to the late hour and the cold air ("a nipping and an eager air"), yet place imagery not related to the setting abounds in the characters' speeches. In the long speech of the ghost in Scene 5, besides references to the royal bed and to the orchard where he was killed, there are two metaphors comparing the body to places: poison, he says, was poured "in the porches of mine ears," and poison coursed through "the natural gates and alleys of the body." Normally, minute metaphor and major localization are used together. Place may occur as a fleeting landscape in one of Homer's epic similes or as the whole scene-at-large of the *Iliad*; it may be only a passing respectful allusion to "the secret top of Oreb" at the start of *Paradise Lost* or a vivid realization of Hell in the remainder of Book I. The two functions, setting and metaphor, are often combined in a single place: the heath in *The Return of the Native* is not only the setting of the action but a symbol of the author's evaluation of that action in terms of theme. Of course, other classes of imagery may have multiple functions, too: animal imagery underlies character grouping in Jonson's *Volpone*, a succession of different animals marks stages in the progress of the hero in *Henderson the Rain King*, and the hat worn by Charles Bovary is emblematic of the structure of the whole novel in which he appears.[1] But no class of imagery is so ubiquitous and versatile as place imagery.

Of all the sources of metaphor available to the writer, place is probably the richest. On the simplest colloquial level we characterize emotional states with expressions such as "I'm on a cloud" and "He's in a rut," and we readily turn place names like Watergate and Kremlin into symbols for complex political activities. Place offers to the writer a vast store of potential metaphors to describe the human mind, body, and behavior. Body metaphor is a natural and primitive form. More sophisticated is the transcendental impulse that has enriched literature with imagery drawing analogies between places and ideas in the mind, "a geography of the soul" that began to thrive, no less than the geography of the great explorers, in the Renaissance.[2] The mind, writes Sir John Davies in *Nosce Teipsum,* is a vast body "wherein are men, beasts, trees, towns, seas, & lands." In order to get at the "growth of a poet's mind," Wordsworth incorporates both outer and inner places in *The Prelude,* the country landscape he knew in his boyhood as well as landscape that serves to objectify some "prospect of the mind." This correspondence he prepares for in *The Recluse:*

> Not Chaos, not
> The darkest pit of lowest Erebus,
> Nor aught of blinder vacancy, scooped out
> By help of dreams—can breed such fear and awe
> As fall upon us often when we look
> Into our Minds, into the Mind of Man—
> My haunt, and the main region of my song. (788–94)

This awe of the interior landscape is shared by many poets—by Emily Dickinson in this stanza:

> One need not be a Chamber—to be Haunted—
> One need not be a House—
> The Brain has Corridors—surpassing
> Material Place—;

by Robert Frost in "Desert Places":

> They cannot scare me with their empty places
> Between stars—on stars where no human race is.
> I have it in me so much nearer home
> To scare myself with my own desert places;

and by Gerard Manley Hopkins in "No Worst, There is None":

> O the mind, mind has mountains; cliffs of fall
> Frightful, sheer, no-man-fathomed. Hold them cheap
> May who ne'er hung there.

In the concluding chapter of *Walden,* Thoreau has a brilliant paragraph of mind-place metaphor in which he implores the reader to "be a Columbus to whole new continents and worlds within you, opening new channels, not of trade, but of thought." Thoreau found the idea in a seventeenth-century poem by William Habington:

> Direct your eye inward, and you'll find
> A thousand regions in your mind
> Yet undiscovered. Travel them, and be
> Expert in home-cosmography.

Books, or products of the mind, are often compared to places. Proust saw his work as a "grande Cathédrale," and it is as a "vast minster" that Longfellow, in six beautiful sonnets, conceives the *Divine Comedy.* Wordsworth thought of the *Prelude* "as a sort of portico to the Recluse, a part of the same building."[3] The first plate in Blake's *Jerusalem* pictures a reader at a doorway leading into a dark room. The analogy of books and ships is common. In a prefatory poem, "In Cabin'd Ships At Sea," Whitman calls his book of poems "a lone bark cleaving the ether." Melville classifies whales in terms of book sizes, each species "according to his Folio, Octavo, or Duodecimo magnitude," and he often hints that his book must have the "bulk" of the whale it celebrates and the same driving unity as the whale-hunting *Pequod:*

> . . . though it was put together of all contrasting things—oak, and maple, and pine wood; iron, and pitch, and hemp—yet all these ran into each other in the one concrete hull, which shot on its way, both balanced and directed by the long central keel; even so, all the individualities of the crew, this man's valor, that man's fear; guilt and guiltiness, all varieties were welded into oneness, and were all directed to that fatal goal which Ahab their one lord and keel did point to. (701)

Melville also compares his "Cetological System," and presumably the book in which it is developed, to an unfinished building, "the great Cathedral of Cologne . . . with the crane still standing upon the top of the uncompleted tower." He goes on to say that "small erections may be finished by their first architects; grand ones, true ones, ever leave the copestone to posterity. God keep me from ever completing anything. This whole book is but a draught—nay, but the draught of a draught" (195–96). A book may be like a body. "The shape of *Ulysses,*" observes Marshall McLuhan, "is that of the city presented as the organic landscape of the human body."[4] Swift's *A Tale of a Tub,* writes Cary Nelson, "is a total gastro-intestinal system, a digestive tract in which the intestines empty into the mouth."[5]

Comparisons of places to human behavior and manners seem not to be as natural as body and mind metaphors and are often found in writers who have a tendency toward preciousness. Even such a minute gesture as a smile on the face of a host, the artist Gloriani in Henry James's *The Ambassadors,* can evoke in Strether's mind a large landscape: "the famous sculptor seemed to signal almost condolingly, yet oh how vacantly! as across some great flat sheet of water. He threw out the bridge of a charming hollow civility on which Strether wouldn't have trusted his own full weight a moment" (182). More modest is Isabel Archer's discovery that her husband expects her to be "attached to him like a small garden-plot to a deer-park." In *Of the Farm* John Updike is capable of writing of a conversation in which "suffocating tunnels of tension broke onto plateaus of almost idyllic reminiscence that imperceptibly narrowed again."[6]

BODY-EARTH METAPHOR

Since the body is the measure of all things for man, language and literature abound with comparisons of the human body to places, landforms, and buildings. The most common form of body metaphor is "geomorphic anatomy," or the analogy of parts of the body with earth and its various forms. Thus, the entire human anatomy is laid under tribute to describe a mountain, which is said to have a foot, belly, breast, rib, back, shoulder, brow, and bald head; or a river, which may have a head, mouth, arm, and elbow. The comparison works the other way when features of the body are made to correspond to the objects and places of earth. "All flesh is grass" according to Isaiah, eyes are deep pools, legs are trunks of trees.

A most extreme example of the body-world analogy is Phineas

Fletcher's *The Purple Island* (1633), a long poem in which the first five cantos make a systematic comparison of every detail of the human anatomy to places and buildings in an island world called the Isle of Man. The kind of comparison Shakespeare momentarily lights on when the ghost of Hamlet's father reveals that Claudius killed him by pouring poison "in the porches of my ear" is in Fletcher drawn out to twelve seven-line stanzas, beginning:

> The Portall hard and drie, all hung around
> With silken, thinne, carnation tapestrie. . . .

Shakespeare, too, was fond of such conceits, as for example this exchange between Dromio of Syracuse and Antipholus of Syracuse at the end of Act III in *Comedy of Errors* when they are talking of a kitchen wench by the name of Nell:

D: She is spherical, like a globe; I could find out countries in her.
A: In what part of her body stands Ireland?
D: Marry, sir, in her buttocks. I found it out by the bogs.
A: Where Scotland?
D: I found it by the barrenness; hard in the palm of the hand.
A: Where France?
D: In her forehead, armed and reverted, making war against her heir.
A: Where England?
D: I looked for the chalky cliffs, but I could find no whiteness in them; but I guess it stood in her chin, by the salt rheum that ran between France and it.
A: Where Spain?
D: Faith, I saw it not; but I felt it hot in her breath.
A: Where America, the Indies?
D: O, sir, upon her nose, all o'er embellished with rubies, carbuncles, sapphires, declining their rich aspect to the hot breath of Spain, who sent whole armadoes of carracks to be ballast at her nose.
A: Where stood Belgia, the Netherlands?
D: O, Sir, I did not look so low.

Another humorous, erotic working of the body-world conceit is *Erotopolis: The Present State of Betty-Land* (1684).

The popularity of such labored comparisons in Renaissance literature rested on the belief in the correspondence of microcosm to macrocosm. Sir Philip Sidney states the principle briefly when he writes that God "in our bodies hath framed a Counterfet of the whole world."[7] Sir Walter Raleigh has the same analogy in his *History of the World,* saying of man that "the bones of his body we may compare to the hard rocks and stones. . . . His blood . . . may be resembled to those waters which are carried by brooks and rivers over all the earth; his breath to the air."[8] Behind Renaissance commonplace on this subject was the effort of pre-Socratic philosophers to discover a uniform substance throughout creation. Plato reflects this interest when he writes in *Philebus* that the universe sustains man's body because it has the same constituents. Longinus commends Plato for his comparison of the body with landscapes, buildings, and gardens in *Timaeus.* The Greek philosophers must have been responding to the primitive need of man to believe that there is harmony between himself and his surroundings, that the body and its environment are continuous. To the primitive perception nature must appear to be an animate creature because it is subject to the same laws of creation, dissolution, and regeneration that govern the life of man.

In identifying himself with earth, man both aggrandizes his finite body and humanizes the world, or brings vast amorphousness into relation with a limited, well-known form. The world becomes intelligible to man's consciousness, observes Ernest Cassirer, "only when it is thus analogically 'copied' in terms of the human body"; the body of man "becomes, as it were, a model according to which he constructs the world as a whole."[9] Ancient religious sanction was given to this kind of identification in myths portraying earth as the offspring of gods and portraying man as the offspring of the union of a god with earth. Cosmogonic myths—the Sumerian-Akkadian story of Tiamat, the Scandinavian story of Ymir—account for the creation of the world in the dismemberment of the body of a god. Thus, men may be said to inhabit the body of a god, an awesome thought for primitives if not to men of more sophisticated times. Christian doctrine may conceive of the world as being the body of Christ, but the idea has never inspired much effective belief. Rather, in the West the notion of a world-body has been used for imaginative purposes of a playful or satirical sort. Lucian in his *True History* seems serious enough in his description of a society of men living in the belly of a whale, but Rabelais turns the idea to humorous account when he tells the story of the twenty-five kingdoms in the mouth of the giant Pantagruel: "they have there the countries Cidentine and Tradentine, that is, behither or beyond the teeth, but it is far better living on this side, and the air is purer." The history of the kingdoms has been written by one of the inhabitants and is

appropriately entitled "The History of the Gorgians." Rabelais's juxtaposition of large and minuscule sizes is playful, with Pantagruel act-
ing as a kindly host of mankind.

The vast disproportion of size between the human body and the
world it inhabits can also be used to mount a satirical attack on the
inconsequence of mankind. This is a notion Mark Twain explored in
"Three Thousand Years among the Microbes": the body of Blitzowski,
"an old bald-headed tramp," is a world inhabited by a populous civilization of microbes.[10] Science fiction is able to restore terror to the
body-world analogy, as in Isaac Asimov's *Fantastic Voyage,* an account of the perilous journey of a miniaturized surgical team in the
bloodstream of a stricken heart patient. In *Ulysses* Joyce speaks of
"the universe of human serum."

If the idea that the world is the body of a god is no longer taken
seriously, the identification of the human body with the earth still
persists in one form or another. Although modern thought cannot believe with Chaucer, in "A Treatise on the Astrolabe," that every one of
the twelve zodiacal signs "hath respect to a certeyn parcel of the body
of a man, and hath it in governaunce," the possibility of subtle cosmic
influences on human behavior is still not out of the question from a
strictly scientific point of view. The ecological theory that the life of
man is inextricably bound up with all other systems on earth restores to
scientific respectability an idea long ago enunciated by Plato in
Philebus that "our little body is fed by the mass of the body without."
Alan Watts sums up the principle in the title of an essay, "The World Is
Your Body." Ecology but confirms the practice of poets for whom the
identification of man with earth remains a favorite metaphor.

Literature of the romantic era is especially rich in the Renaissance
metaphor relating microcosm to macrocosm. "What is man but a mass
of thawing clay?" asks Thoreau, observing a bank in early spring. "The
ball of the human finger is but a drop congealed. The fingers and toes
flow to their extent from the thawing mass of the body. Who knows
what the human body would expand and flow out to under a more
genial heaven?"[11] This is similar to a favorite image of melting flesh in
Whitman: "I effuse my flesh in eddies, and drift it in lacy jags." In
"Song of Myself" Whitman canvasses the earth for analogies with his
body, which is a "translucent mould," has "shaded ledges," incorporates "gneiss, coal, long-threaded moss, fruits, grains, esculent roots,"
and is "stucco'd with quadrupeds and birds all over." The poet goes on
to take the measure of his body with reference to earth forms:

> my elbows rest in sea-gaps
> I skirt sierras, my palms cover continents.

His period of gestation is coterminous with geologic time as well as place:

> I waited unseen and always, and slept through the lethargic mist,
> And took my time, and took no hurt from the fetid carbon.
> Long was I hugg'd close—long and long.

A macrocosmic man like Whitman's is to be found in Melville's *Mardi*, except that Melville cannot limit himself to a single metaphor: sometimes his man is co-extensive with earth—"when these Atlantics and Pacifics thus undulate round me, I lie stretched out in their midst: a land-locked Mediterranean"; then he is "an eagle at the world's end, tossed skyward, on the horns of the tempest"; then a ship—"like a frigate, I am full with a thousand souls . . . as on, on, on, I scud before the wind."[12]

Body-earth metaphor persists in literature today, Raleigh's river of blood occurs again in Dylan Thomas's "Light Breaks Where No Sun Shines":

> From poles of skull and toe the windy blood
> Slides like a sea.

Whitman's world-man appears in Doris Lessing's *Briefing for a Descent into Hell*, whose hero believes that he has spent centuries on a raft being borne round and round the world: "my mind is ringed with Time like the deposits on shells or the fall of years on tree trunks"; the Azores lie "just outside the turn of my elbow." Acknowledging Fletcher's precedent, Joyce calls his *Ulysses* an "epic of the human body" in that each place in the novel is parallel to a different organ of the body: the Bloom house is related to the kidney, a bath to genitalia, a hospital to the womb, and so on.[13] The bodies of Joyce's characters, in turn, are presented in earth terms. Molly Bloom's posterior is a "melonous hemisphere," and the very thought patterns of her famous soliloquy, according to Stuart Gilbert, correspond to the various motions of the earth's rotation.[14] The positions of Molly and Bloom as they lie in bed are given in surveyor's notations: "Listener, S.E. by E.; Narrator, N.W. by W; on the 53rd parallel of latitude, N. and 6th meridian of longitude, W.; at an angle of 45° to the terrestrial equator."[15] The relation of body to earth as set forth in the tattooing of Melville's Polynesians turns up in a twentieth-century character in John Cheever's *Falconer:* "Most of his back was a broad mountainous landscape with a rising sun. . . . Serpents sprang from his groin and wound down both his legs, with his toes for fangs. All the rest of him was dense foliage."[16]

The Female Body and Place

The female body is more commonly associated with earth than the male, probably because woman has functions of reproduction and alimentation similar to earth's and her menstrual cycle corresponds to the movements of earth's satellite, the moon. Because child-bearing and child-raising require repose rather than motion, woman is more intimately tied to fixed places than man. Agoraphobia has a much higher incidence among women than among men.

Harboring the child within her body, woman is herself a place, an enduring place, from the child's point of view. D. H. Lawrence writes of a moment of crisis in the life of Paul Morel in *Sons and Lovers:* "There was one place in the world that stood solid and did not melt into unreality: the place where his mother was."[17] Ma Joad, in Steinbeck's *The Grapes of Warth,* is described as "the strong place that could not be taken." In the tenth lecture of *A General Introduction to Psychoanalysis* Freud points out that female sex organs are associated in dreams with landscapes, male organs with things. Elaborating on Freud, Erich Neumann develops in great detail the correspondence in primitive thought of the body of woman with a wide range of natural places—caves, mountains, woods.[18] As "the fundamental symbolic equation of the feminine," he offers the formula "Woman = body = vessel = world," an archetypal chain which depends on the infant's experience of the mother's body as his first environment. Wordsworth had this process in mind when he wrote in *The Prelude:*

> blest the Babe,
> Nursed in his Mother's arms, who sinks to sleep
> Rocked on his Mother's breast. . . .
> For him, in one dear Presence, there exists
> A virtue which irradiates and exalts
> Objects through widest intercourse of sense . . .
> Along his infant veins are interfused
> The gravitation and the filial bond
> Of nature that connect him with the world. (II.234–244)

The identification of mother with earth underlies what Paul Shepard calls "the sexual anthropomorphism of the world."[19] As well as mother, the earth is also conceived in the role of lover, an idea that may have originated in the practice of agriculture, or the discovery that there is in cultivating the soil a reproductive process comparable with human reproduction. Both Freud and Jung believed that the influence went the other way, that man's sexual experience suggested the possibility of agriculture.[20] From the close association of sexual functions and agriculture, moral conclusions are sometimes drawn: to the feminist mankind's domination of nature through agriculture is parallel to the male's domination of woman through sex; to the champion of agrarianism sound sexual relations must be based on sound agricultural economy since "marriage and the care of the earth are each other's disciplines."[21] Husbandry pertains to both land and wife. The pastoral form in literature honors the combination of animal husbandry with erotic bliss.

Whatever the origin, the analogy of the human reproductive process and the planting and fruition of seed in the soil is the source of the ritual impregnation of earth in a sacred marriage *(hiero gamos)* practiced by most primitives and a whole branch of imagery, which Jung calls "phallic plough symbolism."[22] A crude example is Agrippa's summary of Caesar's affair with Cleopatra in *Antony and Cleopatra:* "He ploughed her and she cropped." One of the most common images is the comparison of a woman to a field, a field of "white desire," for instance, in William Carlos Williams's "Queen-Ann's-Lace." There is such an abundance of this kind of imagery that it is helpful to make a distinction between images in which sexual union with earth is figured on a cosmic scale and images in which a limited, well-defined analogy of body and place is involved. A universalizing tendency of the imagination is at work in figures of cosmic intercourse with earth, sea, or sky; whereas the microcosmic inclination of the imagination finds in particular places analogies with the detailed anatomy of the female body: thus, mountains are breasts; valleys and fountains, the vagina; a grove of trees, pubic hair. A compact example of the eroticized landscape is Venus's invitation to Adonis to be her lover in Shakespeare's *Venus and Adonis:*

> I'll be a park, and thou shalt be my deer;
> Feed where thou wilt, on mountain or in dale:
>> Graze on my lips; and if those hills be dry,
>> Stray lower, where the pleasant fountains lie.

In Baudelaire's "La Géante" it is the poet clambering over the feminine landscape:

Parcourir à loisir ses magnifiques formes;
Ramper sur le versant de ses genoux énormes . . .
Dormir nonchalament à l'ombre de ses seins,
Comme un harmeau paisible au pied d'une montagne.

On a larger scale, cities, countries, and continents are imaged in terms of woman. Giving feminine names to continents is standard, and so changing Americus to America was to be expected, but the association of America with a sexually desirable woman is particularly noteworthy. The psychiatrist William G. Niederland, following Fraiberg, advances the thesis that there is a relationship between geographical exploration and the libidinal desire for the hidden places of the female anatomy.[23] "The woman penetrated is a labyrinth," says Norman O. Brown. "You emerge into another world inside the woman."[24] The idea that exploring a strange country is like intercourse with a strange woman comes across very clearly in the description of K.'s making love to Freida in Kafka's *The Castle:*

> K. was haunted by the feeling that he was losing himself or wandering into a strange country, farther than ever man had wandered before, a country so strange that not even the air had anything in common with his native air, where one might die of strangeness, and yet whose enchantment was such that one could only go on and lose oneself further.[25]

To Columbus the western hemisphere appeared to be "like the half of a very round pear, having a raised projection for the stalk . . . or like a woman's nipple on a round ball."[26] Later explorers and land agents described the continent as a virgin waiting to be ravished by enterprising Europeans. In his Elegy XIX John Donne makes amusing use of this metaphor in a poem comparing America to a woman being addressed by her lover:

> O my America! my new-found-land,
> My kingdom, safeliest when with one man manned,
> My mine of precious stones, my empery,
> How blest am I in this discovering thee!
> To enter in these bonds is to be set free;
> There where my hand is set, my seal shall be.

In *The American Scene* Henry James was able to express the idea in the genteel language of his time when he observed that the American land "seemed to plead . . . to be liked, to be loved, to be stayed with, lived with, handled with some kindness, shown even some courtesy of admiration. What was that but the feminine attitude?—not the actual, current, impeachable, but the old ideal and classic; the air of meeting you everywhere, standing in wait everywhere, yet always without conscious defiance, only in the mild submission to your doing what you would with it."[27] Moved by the unusual topography of Cape Cod, Thoreau represents the state of Massachusetts as the body of a woman:

> Cape Cod is the bared and bended arm of Massachusetts: the shoulder is at Buzzard's Bay; the elbow, or crazy-bone, at Cape Mallebarre; the wrist at Truro; and the sandy fist at Provincetown,—behind which the State stands on her guard, with her back to the Green Mountains, and her feet planted on the floor of the ocean, like an athlete protecting her Bay,—boxing with northeast storms, and, ever and anon, heaving up her Atlantic adversary from the lap of earth,—ready to thrust foward her other fist, which keeps guard the while upon her breast at Cape Ann. (14)

The image of America as a female body was the staple of a set of American poets, in the 1920s and 1930s, who made a return to the native land a part of their program as writers; America is a reclining nude woman in MacLeish's "Frescoes for Mr. Rockefeller's City"; the union of man as city and woman as country is used by William Carlos Williams in *Paterson;* the "hobo-trekkers" of Hart Crane's *The Bridge* know the States as

> a body under the wide rain. . . .
> They lurk across her, knowing her yonder breast.

American writers who became disillusioned with America used the image of the degraded woman to express their disillusionment. Daisy and Jordan in *The Great Gatsby* betray the American dream, and their betrayal is performed on the very site where Dutch sailors first beheld the "fresh, green breast of the new world." Caddie in *The Sound and the Fury* betrays the dream of the South, ending up with a Nazi general: "ageless and beautiful, cold serene and damned," this was the same woman who used "to smell like trees."

THE EMBRACE OF EARTH AS WOMAN

The Renaissance correspondence of macrocosm and microcosm resulted in a common metaphor of the marriage of mind and matter. It
can be found as late as Wordsworth's prospectus to "The Recluse"
when he speaks of the "intellect of Man" being "wedded to this goodly
universe." To represent the more passionate identification of man with
nature, romantic writers resorted to images of sexual embrace with
earth. Goethe early explored the possibilities in the Forest and Cavern
scene in *Faust*. Upon overhearing the invocation to the Earth Spirit
that Faust delivers as he admires the wilderness, Mephistopheles cyn-
ically attributes Faust's love of nature to his sexual love for
Marguerite:

> A supernatural delight!
> To lie on mountains in the dew and night,
> Embracing earth and sky in raptured reeling,
> To swell into a god—in one's own feeling—
> To probe into earth's marrow with vague divination . . .
> Then overflow into all things with love so hot,
> Gone is all earthly inhibition,
> And then the noble intuition—*(with a gesture)*
> Of—need I say of what emission?[28]

There is classical precedent for the suspicion of lechery in pastoral
sentiments (Battus in Idyll IV of Theocritus), but in this parody of
Faust's feeling for nature Goethe seems to be recognizing the sentimental excess of this topos in Romantic writing. Even Wordsworth
was tempted by the sexual suggestions of natural places. In "Nutting,"
a young boy in search of hazel nuts forces his way "through beds of
matted fern and tangled thickets" into a "dear nook . . . a virgin scene"
and there subjects "both branch and bough" to a "merciless ravage."
But in Book XIV of *The Prelude* Wordsworth was to temper this "early
intercourse/ In presence of sublime and lovely Form" with a "love
more intellectual" than sexual. Francis Thompson has a similar problem in choosing between sexual union with nature or sexual union with
God in the tradition of religious mysticism; in lines 60 to 110 of "The
Hound of Heaven" the poet attempts to find relief for his "smart" by
"commingling heat" with the setting sun and seeking the breasts of the
sky to slake his "thirsty mouth." Wordsworth would not have found
this to be a "holy passion," and neither does Thompson, for whom only

God can be a proper lover: "Naked I wait Thy love's uplifted stroke!"
There is no reticence of this sort among writers fully committed to
romanticism. Byron misses no opportunity "to mingle with the Universe" and its elements in "The Island":

> Her woods, her wilds, her waters . . .
> . . . they woo and clasp us to their spheres,
> Dissolve this clog and clod of clay before
> Its hour, and merge our soul in the great shore.
> Strip off this fond and false identity! (II.16)

D. H. Lawrence is close to this in "Renascence," the first draft of
which reads:

> Oh but the water loves me and folds me,
> Plays with me, sways me, lifts me and sinks me
> As though it were living blood
> Blood of a heaving woman who holds me
> Owning my supple body a rare glad thing supremely good.

But no one outdoes Whitman's daring celebrations of sexual union
with the night in Sections 21 and 22 of "Song of Myself":

> Press close bare-bosom'd night—press close magnetic nourishing night!
> Still nodding night—mad naked summer night;

the sea:

> Cushion me soft, rock me in billowy drowse,
> Dash me with amorous wet, I can repay you;

and the land:

> Far-swooping elbow'd earth—rich apple-blossom'd earth!
> Smile, for your lover comes.

The poet is especially bound to earth by sexual links. The true American poet, according to Whitman in "By Blue Ontario's Shore," can
serve his land only by

> Attracting its body and soul to himself, hanging upon its neck
>   with incomparable love,
> Plunging his seminal muscle into his merits and demerits.

The poet laureate of Maryland, in John Barth's *The Sot-Weed Factor*, is given the same advice by his friend Burlingame: "I love the world, sir, and so make love to it! I have sown my seed in men and women, in a dozen sorts of beasts, in the barky boles of trees and the honeyed wombs of flowers; I have dallied on the black breast of the earth, and clipped her fast; I have wooed the waves of the sea, impregnated the four winds, and flung my passion skyward to the stars! . . . 'Tis the only way for a poet to look at the world."[29]

Sexual intercourse with landforms continues to be an attractive metaphor among writers who continue the pastoral tradition. Scenes of plowing, mowing, and planting invite strong sexual overtones in the writings of regionalists and naturalists. The dithyrambic manner of Whitman may be imitated by Lawrence in his poem "Renascence," but it is in the regionalist manner that he opens *The Rainbow* when he describes the relation of the Brangwen men to the land they farm:

> They knew the intercourse between heaven and earth, sunshine drawn into the breast and bowels, the rain sucked up in the daytime, nakedness that comes under the wind in autumn, showing the birds' nests no longer worth hiding. Their life and interrelations were such; feelings the pulse and body of the soil, that opened to their furrow for the grain, and became smooth and supple after their ploughing, and clung to their feet with a weight that pulled like desire, lying hard and unresponsive when the crops were to be shorn away.[30]

Naturalists tend to see the process as more mechanical. Here is Frank Norris describing mass farming operations in *The Octopus:*

> Magnus Derrick's thirty-three grain drills, each with its eight hoes, went clamouring past, like an advance of military, seeding the ten thousand acres of the great ranch; fecundating the living soil; implanting deep in the dark womb of the Earth the germ of life, the sustenance of a whole world, the food of an entire People.[31]

Steinbeck adopts the same imagery but a different tone as he sees the land taken out of the loving hands of his Oklahoma yeomen and mistreated by mechanized farming techniques:

> Behind the harrows, the long seeders—twelve curved iron penes erected in the foundry, orgasms set by gears, raping methodically, raping without passion. . . . No man touched the seed, or lusted for the growth. . . . the land bore under iron, and under iron gradually died; for it was not loved or hated."[32]

In Steinbeck's *To A God Unknown* a new settler in the West sees his newfound land as his wife:

> He flung himself face downward on the grass and pressed his cheek against the wet stems. His fingers gripped the wet grass and tore it out, and gripped again. His thighs beat heavily on the earth.
>
>   The fury left him and he was cold and bewildered and frightened at himself. He sat up and wiped the mud from his lips and beard. . . . For a moment the land had been his wife.[33]

John Updike takes mowing a field as an occasion to use the same sort of metaphor in *Of The Farm:*

> The tractor body was flecked with foam and I, rocked back and forth on the iron seat shaped like a woman's hips, alone in nature, as hidden under the glaring sky as at midnight, excited by destruction, weightless, discovered in myself a swelling which I idly permitted to stand, thinking of Peggy. My wife is a field. (59)

In a more daring exercise of this sort, the narrator compares his second wife's "landscape" with his first wife's and finds the whole world in her:

> My wife is wide, wide-hipped and long-waisted, and, surveyed from above, gives an impression of terrain, of a wealth whose ownership imposes upon my own body a sweet strain of extension; entered, she yields a variety of landscapes, seeming now a snowy rolling perspective of bursting cotton bolls seen through the Negro arabesques of a fancywork wrought-iron balcony; now a taut vista of mesas dreaming in the midst of sere and painterly ochre; now a

gray French castle complexly fitted to a steep green hill whose
terraces imitate turrets; now something like Antarctica; and then a
receding valleyland of blacks and purples where an unrippled river
flows unseen between shadowy banks of grapes that are never
eaten. Over all, like a sky, withdrawn and cool, hangs—hovers,
stands, *is*—is the sense of her consciousness, of her composure, of
a non-committal witnessing that preserves me from claustrophobia
through any descent however deep. I never felt this in Joan, this
sky. I felt in danger of smothering in her. She seemed, like me, an
adventurer helpless in dark realms upon which light, congested,
could burst only with a convulsion. The tortuous trip could be
undertaken only after much preparation, and then there was a
mystic crawling by no means certain of issue. Whereas with Peggy
I skim, I glide, I am free, and this freedom, once tasted, lightly,
illicitly, became as indispensable as oxygen to me, the fuel of a pull
more serious than that of gravity. (46–47)

In another work of his, *Bech,* Updike seems to disavow such elaborate
conceits when his author-hero admits, "We fall in love . . . with women
who remind us of our first landscape. A silly idea." Man's first landscape is the mother, of course, and in *Of the Farm* the narrator's
mother and his second wife compete for his affections, the mother
offering her farm to him and the wife her body with all its evocations of
ideal landscapes. (Bachelard speaks of the second mistress of man
being projected upon nature: "The wife-mistress landscape takes its
place beside the mother landscape.")[34] In the end Bech leaves the farm
and returns to the city with his wife. Another Updike hero, Harry
Angstrom in *Rabbit, Run,* finds in sexual intercourse a relief from the
crowdedness and clutteredness of space in urban living.

Romanticism used sexual metaphor to accentuate the union of the
poet with nature. Twentieth-century literature, reacting to the increasing removal of people from natural surroundings, finds in sexuality a
substitute for the actual experience of nature. If Updike's hero cannot
live on a farm, he can at least know the "landscape" of his wife through
sexual intercourse. When sexual relationships between people falter,
as they have in the twentieth century, another resource is available in
cosmic sexuality, or the association of sexual feeling with cosmic
places instead of people. The "chief tragedy" of our time, Lawrence
believed, is that "we have lost the cosmos, by coming out of responsive
connection with it." In order "to re-establish the living organic connection with the cosmos, the sun and earth," Lawrence in his fiction offers
imagery of sexual union on a grand scale, not the "petty little love" of
the minuter aspects of nature made so popular by Romantic poets.[35]

The heroine of Lawrence's *St. Mawr,* Lou, rejects men since she finds more satisfaction from the spirit that dwells in the wild landscape of the ranch she has bought in the American Southwest:

> It's here, in this landscape. It's something more real to me than men are, and it soothes me, and holds me up. . . . It craves for me. And to it, my sex is deep and sacred, deeper than I am, with a deep nature aware deep down of my sex.[36]

Her mother, however, remains sceptical: when she learns that her daughter paid only $1200 for Las Chivas ranch, she remarks, "Then I call it cheap, considering all there is to it: even the name." Like Goethe and Updike, Lawrence cannot quite avoid having reservations about the idea of sexual union with the landscape. In calling attention to Lawrence's occasional scepticism, Richard Poirier makes an important distinction: "Lawrence values the redemptive power of imagination even when its particular exertions are preposterous."[37] In a short story entitled "Sun" Lawrence presents a more sensual woman, one who is sexually fulfilled by bathing "naked in the sun" and makes a daily ritual of "mating" with the sun, which is personified as a lover: "sometimes he came ruddy, like a big, shy creature. And sometimes slow and crimson red, with a look of anger, slowly pushing and shouldering." In the spell of such a transcendent experience, the woman, like Lou in *St. Mawr,* wonders, "Why admit men!" But she turns to men finally and yearns for a strong-looking peasant: "He would have been a procreative sun-bath to her, and she wanted it." Her experience is similar to that of the maidens in Greek myths who have intercourse with the sky and sea gods and are then turned over to human lovers. Ursula in *The Rainbow* is another sun and moon worshipper: "She wanted the moon to fill in to her, she wanted more, more communion with the moon, consummation" (300). Her mortal lover, Skrebensky, "like a loadstone weighed on her." Later, in her affair with Winifred Inger, cosmic and human love coincide: in the presence of her beloved teacher, "the girl sat as within the rays of some enriching sun, whose intoxicating heat poured straight into her veins." Though Gudrun's sinister, life-negating mood is the opposite of her sister's, it is expressed in the same kind of imagery in *Women in Love:* she seeks "her consummation" among the "immortal peaks of snow and rock."[38] While Ursula hates "the unnaturalness" of the Alpine landscape, Gudrun thought "it was so beautiful, it was a delirium, she wanted to gather the glowing, eternal peaks to her breast, and die" (450).

As well as landforms and the heavenly spheres, infinite space, sky, and air are common elements in metaphors of cosmic intercourse. In Camus's "The Adulterous Woman," a wife leaves the bed of her husband and feels sexually fulfilled when she exposes herself to the night and the sky in a remote North African town. In Yeats's "Leda and the Swan," the woman is described as being "mastered by the brute blood of the air," an appropriate figure for Zeus the sky-god. William Carlos Williams imagines "the wind that presses tight" upon a woman in "Kore in Hell," "revealing the impatient mountains and valleys of her sweet desire," while Faulkner reflects a mood more in keeping with the modern wasteland when he reports Dewey Dell's brooding on her pregnancy in *As I Lay Dying:* "the dead air shapes the dead earth. . . . It lies dead upon me, touching me naked through my clothes." The heroine of Anais Nin's *Ladders to Fire* feels that "The warmth of the day was like a man's hand on her breast, the smell of the street like a man's breath on her neck. Wide open to the street like a field washed by a river."[39]

Imagining herself to be a receptacle of love, the female surrenders to the embrace of the world. The passionate male makes an assault upon love objects. "Sweating, I kissed and embraced the cold scaly trunk of a pine tree," declares the hero of William Styron's *The Confessions of Nat Turner;* "I thirsted to plunge myself into the earth, into a tree, a deer, a bear, a bird, a boy, a stump, a stone, to shoot milky warm spurts of myself into the cold and lonely blue heart of the sky."[40] In a similar manner, Birkin, in Lawrence's *Women in Love,* after being beaten by Hermione, flees to "the open country, to the hills . . . to a wild valleyside" and there induces an orgasm by rolling around naked in the lush, erotically "responsive vegetation." Like Lou in *St. Mawr* he feels that he has no need for a human partner: "He knew now where he belonged. This was his place, his marriage place" (104). But there are instances of male characters being fulfilled by the elements of earth in a passive way like women. Michel, in Gide's *The Immoralist,* gives his body to the sun in a daily ritual like that performed by the woman in Lawrence's "Sun":

> I turned my steps towards some mossy, grass-grown rocks, in a place far from any habitation, far from any road, where I knew no one could see me. When I got there, I undressed slowly. The air was almost sharp, but the sun was burning. I exposed my whole body to its flame. I sat down, lay down, turned myself about. I felt the ground hard beneath me; the waving grass brushed me. Though I was sheltered from the wind, I shivered and thrilled at every breath. Soon a delicious burning enveloped me; my whole being surged up into my skin.[41]

Michel's wife, on the other hand, favors the countryside of Normandy with its "narrow coombes and gently rounded hills." Their story is the desperate struggle of the barren landscape of the desert against the fertile farming country. Cosmicity is also an issue between another unhappy pair in Paul Bowles's *The Sheltering Sky:* the husband must have "the proximity of infinite things" whereas the wife is drawn to a series of lovers in tiny rooms.

In Camus's *A Happy Death* the principal character, Mersault, experiences sexual union with earth, sky, and sea on different occasions in Algeria, but it is hardly the same Algeria that Camus uses for a setting of *The Stranger.* In this earlier version the country is beautiful and fruitful: the carob trees "drench all Algeria with the smell of love," a fragrance "like a mistress you walk with in the street after a long stifling afternoon."[42] Here Mersault has a "wedding to the earth . . . the evening flowed into him like a tide." The terms are very much like those used to describe the experience of the hero (now called Meursault) on the beach in *The Stranger,* but the results are the opposite. It is the sun that is "pouring" into poor Meursault, and the sun is not like a lover but an enemy: "the glare of the morning sun hit me in the eyes like a clenched fist." The sun drives Meursault to madness and murder, whereas the evening air leads Mersault to a feeling of conquest and a willingness to accept "this love-soaked earth." Before this, Mersault has had a not quite satisfactory experience with a mountain, and after this a final embrace by the sea. The three sexual experiences with earth complete his transition to death, a happy death in that he is absorbed by the earth: "And stone among the stones, he returned in the joy of his heart to the truth of the motionless worlds" (151). This is thoroughly romantic, like Wordsworth's account of Lucy's naturalistic immortality:

> No motion has she now, no force;
>   She neither hears nor sees;
> Rolled round in earth's diurnal course,
>   With rocks, and stones, and trees.

Camus rigorously expunges such romantic notions from the later attempt to record his experiences in North Africa; Meursault has no happy union with the cosmos. Bathing in the sea may be an occasional solace for him, but at the end of his ordeal, or at the beginning of his new awareness of man's real condition, he expresses the bitter separation of man from the world in a metaphor that ironically employs a conventional figure of embrace: "I laid my heart open to the benign indifference of the universe."[43]

Camus's radically different versions of the same material mark the shift of literature away from the romantic identification with earth and woman toward expressions of enmity against the cosmos and woman. In so far as the diminishment of man's heroic role in modern times is often expressed in terms of sexual failure, it is not surprising to encounter feelings hostile to woman and the fecundity of earth she has long symbolized. Such feelings constitute the kind of superficial relief that spite can bring, but they also reflect a deep male awareness of the double function of earth as both the source of life and the condition of death, an ambivalence also reflected in sexual intercourse as the origin of new life as well as a "spending" of the male in a kind of death. In a moment of rage against womankind, King Lear asserts the two-fold nature of woman and earth:

> But to the girdle do the Gods inherit,
> Beneath is all the fiends';
> There's hell, there's darkness, there's the sulphurous pit.

The earth as well as his daughters mistreats Lear: "Here I stand your slave," he shouts to the elements in the storm scene. In Lear's imagery the body of woman is made to correspond to the Christian cosmology: the upper parts are like heaven where the gods dwell, the lower parts are like the earth's dark, hidden center where a fallen god is held prisoner in disgrace. Dante's happier view of woman in *The Divine Comedy* has Beatrice occupying a garden at the top of Mount Purgatory, the last stopping place on the way to the celestial spheres making up heaven. Still, Beatrice must be renounced by her lover before he can proceed, just as Christian in *Pilgrim's Progress* must leave the land of Beulah before reaching the heavenly city. Woman and the earth she represents may thus be either good or bad, a "paradys terrestre," writes Chaucer in the Merchant's Tale, but "paraunter she may be youre purgatorie!"

THE GARDEN AND WOMAN

Nowhere is the ambivalence of earth-woman imagery so sharply drawn as in the tradition of the good and evil gardens. Eden was good until woman consorted with the earth-spirit in the form of the serpent and until man allowed his desire for woman and the fruit of earth to get the better of his obligation to a transcendent spirit. The earth lapsed into a fallen condition. Edmund Spenser sharpened the opposing gardens in his description of the Garden of Adonis and the Bower of Bliss in *The Faerie Queene*. One is presided over by Venus, the spirit of true love and regeneration, and its predominant feature is "a stately Mount," under which is "a strong rocky Cave" where Adonis, her lover, dwells "in eternal bliss" (III.6. 43–48). But in the Bower of Bliss, Acrasia, the evil enchantress is ensconced in a landscape of "many covert groves, and thickets close" which resemble the "subtile web" she wears as she lies in wait for unsuspecting lovers (II.12.76–77). The dangerous sexuality of woman is associated with earthiness in the form of vegetation, while her intercessionary powers, like Beatrice's, are associated with high places connecting earth and heaven.

Cosmic intercourse, paradoxically, is an effort to transcend sex, a means of satisfying a metaphysical longing for union of the body with the most spacious features of man's environment. As we have seen, the opposite tendency of the imagination associates the body with particular, well-defined places, such as the garden, cave, island, valley, or forest bower. Limitation and enclosure are more comforting than the mystery and possible danger of limitless spaciousness, and such places easily become associated with ease, beauty, and the pleasure of love. The *locus amoenus* of rhetorical tradition was this kind of place, the *dignus amore locus* of Petrarch. They serve as synecdoches of earth, concentrating all of earth's goodness into an easily comprehended area—"In narrow room Nature's whole wealth," as Milton expresses the idea in Book IV of *Paradise Lost*. Enclosed places are protected by divine and man-made barriers from their surroundings, which are therefore conceived as different and even hostile.

Enclosure automatically bestows special value on places and things, and the island, valley, and garden are readily conceived as earthly paradises. But there is a price to pay for their worth: because of their concentrated richness and exclusiveness, paradisal places require constant protection and create feelings of guilt and fear of loss instead of the free, expansive feelings inspired by the spaciousness and openness of cosmic places. Even death lurks in the garden *(et in Arcadia ego)*, and, as Proust avers, the only true paradise is the one we have lost.

All of the attributes of enclosed places are easily transferred to woman, especially the garden, which Sir Kenneth Clark denominates as "one of humanity's most constant, widespread and consoling myths."[44] Although woman is but one of the delights of the Biblical garden, in time the body of woman becomes more and more the engrossing motif of garden imagery. This metaphorical identification is nowhere more decisively advanced than in the Song of Songs, where the poet-lover, searching for a way to define the preciousness of his beloved, speaks of her as "a garden enclosed . . . a spring shut up, a fountain sealed." In subsequent Christian interpretation the bride in the Song of Songs came to be known as the Virgin Mary, whose person then was identified with the garden. Always intriguing to Christian poets was the paradox that the body of Mary, though chaste and shut away from the world, still miraculously bore fruit. A line attributed to John Donne states it succinctly: "O Frutefull garden, and yet never tilde."[45] A medieval lyric by Adam of Saint Victor goes:

> She is that sealed fount, ne'er dying,
> That walled garden, fructifying
> By the good seed in it sown.

In "Epithetes of our Blessed Lady" a Renaissance poet relates the garden to Mary and Eden to Mary's chastity:

> Moste pleasant garden plot, true *Paradise* of praise,
> Erected in the roome of *Paradise* of iore . . .
> All closely wall'd about, inviolate it stayes,
> No serpent can get in, nor shal for evermore. . . .

The association of the garden with a religious figure like Mary points up the easy adaptability of place images to a number of literal and transcendent meanings. In the Christian adaptation the woman in the garden represents the highest spiritual perfection possible on earth before the ascent to heaven, as in Dante; in the homiletic tradition the garden became a "garden of virtues"; in millennialism the garden was the seat of the perfect life of man; in the courtly love tradition the walled garden was both the scene and the symbol of the feudal ideal of court life as well as the physical analogue of the body of the woman who stood at the center of this ideal. Chaucer suggests the grosser side of the garden-body analogy when in the Merchant's Tale he has May provide her young lover with a duplicate of the key her husband uses to open the "smale wyket" of his garden. Gaining entrance into the garden is crucial. In a modern version of the garden-woman parallelism, Hawthorne's "Rappaccini's Daughter," a young man, intent upon meeting the lady of the garden, is shown a "private entrance" through the wall by an old woman servant, whom he bribes with gold:

> His withered guide led him along several obscure passages, and finally undid a door, through which, as it was opened, there came the sight and sound of rustling leaves, with the broken sunshine glimmering among them. Giovanni stepped forth, and, forcing himself through the entanglement of a shrub that wreathed its tendrils over the hidden entrance, stood beneath his own window in the open area of Dr. Rappaccini's garden.

In the figurative language of the garden place, penetration of the vagina is disguised here as entry into the garden by opening the garden gate, with the help of a procuress, and forcing a way through curled vegetation.[46] In describing two homosexual affairs in *Maurice,* E. M. Forster uses the garden on the grounds of a once-noble house now in a state of decay. We see the garden at night; on his way to an assignation with Alec, a lower-class person, Maurice "entered the estate at its lower end, through a gap in the hedge" whereas in the preceding affair with the upper-class Clive he had arrived at the main entrance of the estate in a brougham.

While daring enough as a sexual metaphor in medieval and Renaissance literature, the garden proved too tame to represent the wild passion and vague motivation that romantic writers often favored. Places with sexual meanings in their writing are likely to be less well-defined and wilder than the garden: the riverside, valley, cave, and underground chasm. Coleridge very aptly designates this preference in his description of Xanadu, where there is indeed a traditional garden paradise:

> And here were gardens bright with sinuous rills
> Where blossomed many an incense-bearing tree;
> And here were forests ancient as the hills,
> Enfolding sunny spots of greenery;

but directly beneath this is a "deep romantic chasm," the source of unrest and sexual passion:

> A savage place! as holy and enchanted
> As e'er beneath a waning moon was haunted
> By woman wailing for her demon-lover!

And from this chasm, with ceaseless turmoil seething,
As if this earth in fast quick pants were breathing,
A mighty fountain momently was forced.[47]

In romantic imagery water falling from great heights or welling up from great depths replaces the garden fountain contained by a marble basin and walls. Faust compares his passion to a cataract bursting from rock to rock as it moves into an abyss (I. 3350–51). Keats's Endymion meets a number of women in riverside scenes that combine both the traditional pastoral restfulness and the new romantic turbulence. Early in Book II of *Endymion* the hero meets a nymph by "a sparkling fountain side/ That near a cavern's mouth forever pour'd" (84–85). Promise of sexual fulfillment seems assured by the fact that the fountain soars high into the air and then "downward, suddenly began to dip" as it disappears into the cavern. But the "poor Naiad" in attendance there turns out to be but a child whose function is to gladden the hero on his way, and the disappointed Endymion complains: "for me / There is no depth to strike in" (160–161). Later, however, in a "sounding grotto, vaulted vast," he reaches a climax with the mature Cynthia, of whom he says:

Now I have tasted her sweet soul to the core
All other depths are shallow. (904–905)

Endymion's quest carries him through "the dark earth and through the wondrous sea" and into the sky; it is "an initiation into the mysteries of earth,"[48] and, in view of the analogy of woman with earth, sea, and sky, it is also an initiation into the mysteries of sex.

Two varieties of love are represented by two kinds of place in the poetry of the romantics: passive, innocent, conventional love is to be found in a pastoral setting—Margaret's "Hüttchen auf dem kleinem Alpenfeld" in *Faust;* passionate, painful, dangerous love is associated with the turbulent river in the depths of earth. One kind of love is domestic, revolving around house and field, the other is mysterious and springs from the elements of earth itself, from the archetypal water in stream and ocean. Because their passionate moods collided with public and private standards of taste, romantic writers were easily led to substitute places for the body in their reports of sexual encounters. It is hardly an exaggeration to say that in eschewing grossness and straining for transcendence, poets of the nineteenth century transferred the erotic impulse from the person of the beloved to the places associated with the beloved. Endymion's attention is centered less on women than on the places where he meets them. The same substitution occurs when the lover is enthralled by secretly observing the room of his lady friend, a motif to be examined later.

THE FOREST AND SEXUALITY

The forest lying beyond the garden is another place of great sexual significance, reflecting literature's continuation, in at least one aspect, of ancient and primitive tree-cults. Even though it is an image opposed to the enclosed garden, since it threatens to engulf it, the forest is also equated with woman by virtue of its vegetation and periodic renewal of vegetation. Like the garden it is a fertile place, though its vegetation, being wilder than the well-cared-for and well-contained plants of the garden, signifies an unruly sexuality that threatens tragedy for those who become involved with it. The garden is the body of a woman in a passive condition, waiting to be enjoyed, while the dense vegetation of the forest may portend the active entrapment of the male in the unseen, mysterious reproductive process that leads to revelation or to death. In so far as woman is identified with the forest, sexual intercourse may be a male's way into nature and the world.

English literature, though lacking actual forest models, abounds with passionate encounters in the "greenwood." It is in "a planted woodland" of only two acres—yet full of "darkness and shade, and natural beauty"—that Miss Crawford in *Mansfield Park* attempts to dissuade Edmund from being a clergyman. It is in a remnant of the ancient English forest that Lady Chatterley has her affair with a game-keeper. A man at home in the woods, his "green-stained stone cottage" has a surface that looks "like the flesh underneath a mushroom, its stone warmed in a burst of sun.[49] Little by little the lady of the sterile English manor house ventures "beyond porch and portal" and dis-covers the world of sexuality in the woods. At first she sees the woods as "giving off a potency of silence," but after several visits she is moved by "forest energy," a notion that Lawrence advanced in an earlier version of the novel:

> She realised there were two main sorts of energy, the frictional, seething, resistant, explosive, blind sort, like that of steam-engines and motor-cars and electricity, and of people such as Clifford and Bill Tewson and modern insistent women, and these queer, vacu-

ous miners; then there was the other, forest energy, that was still
and softly powerful, with tender, frail bud-tips and gentle finger-
ends full of awareness.[50]

Her sexual explorations with Mellors lead finally to anal intercourse,
the "phallic hunt" coming at last to "the very heart of the jungle . . . the
core of the physical jungle, the last and deepest recess of organic
shame" (280–81).[51] It is consistent with the point being made here that
when it is a question of the male's anal sexuality, Lawrence does not
use forest imagery, as in the case of Birkin and Gerald wrestling in
Women in Love.

The woods in *Lady Chatterley's Lover* are a remnant of "wild, old
England," and they are doomed to disappear just as the love of Lady
Chatterley and Mellors is doomed. In E. M. Forster's *Maurice* there
are no woods left, "no forest or fell to escape to today," and homosexual love is carried on in the figurative "greenwood" that Maurice and
Alec roam. In their treatment of woods Lawrence and Forster contribute to the long-standing notion that the end of the forest in England in
some way corresponds to the end of a healthy sexuality in England. On
his return to England after an absence of seven years, Byron's Don
Juan observes that "the Druids' groves are gone," having been replaced by housing developments, "Groves, so call'd as being void of
trees" (XI.21,25). Buildings dominate London, and although Mansion
House is "a stiff yet grand erection" (XI.25), there is no true sexuality
in England: the parks have "neither fruit not flower/ Enough to gratify a
bee's slight munchings" (XI.65), and fashion alone "serves our thinking
people for a passion" (XI.33). Forest remnants represent ancient times
when human feeling were more wholesome.

Instead of encouraging the exercise of sexual instincts, the forest
may inspire restraint and sublimation. Thus Oedipus, in seeking refuge
in the grove at Colonus, is returning to the body of woman in a ritual
manner that expiates the actual possession of his mother's body earlier
in the palace at Thebes.[52] Hunters are associated with the chaste Diane
and are even fastidious in their use of the woods, like the boy in
Wordsworth's "Nutting" who is afflicted with "a sense of pain" because in stripping the hazel tree of its fruit he may have offended the
feminine "spirit in the woods." The hunter's sexuality may be
transferred to his animal prey; animal and forest may "coalesce," as
Faulkner puts it, or in Northrop Frye's words, "the quasi-sexual object
of pursuit becomes the surrounding forest itself."[53] Thus it is not unusual for the hunter to eschew woman and take the woods for his bride.
This is the case with Cooper's Leatherstocking, who loves the forest

because it is pure, "untouched by hands of man," and who rejects opportunities for marriage in *The Deerslayer* on the grounds that his sweetheart is the forest itself, "hanging from the boughs of the trees, in a soft rain—in the dew on the open grass—the clouds that float about in the blue heavens—the birds that sing in the woods—the sweet springs where I slake my thirst."[54] Thoreau confided the same sentiment to his Journal: "How rarely a man's love for nature becomes a ruling principle with him, like a youth's affection for a maiden, but more enduring! All nature's my bride."[55] Walden pond in the early morning is seen "throwing off its nightly clothing of mist" like a maiden arising from sleep. The game-keeper in *Lady Chatterley's Lover* is reluctant to begin an affair because he knows that "the seclusion of the wood" will be broken by his taking on a woman. The wife Paul Bunyan takes, in Frost's poem, is "sawed out of a white-pine log," and the mythical woodsman

> Wouldn't be spoken to about a wife
> In any way the world knew how to speak.

Paul and Leatherstocking are romantic idealists who, unable to tolerate the violation of either woods or woman, remain chaste sons of the forest. Of Leatherstocking, Annette Kolodny writes: "Sexuality looms, for him, as a power far too destructive and uncontrollable, carrying with it, always, the threat of violation. Better to remain the son, he seems to be saying, rather than run the risk of violating the Mother."[56] She shows how Cooper takes pains to describe the house of the settlers' leaders, Judge Temple, as a phallic intrusion upon the wilderness, a male assault on a feminine place often described as the "matted and wild luxuriance of a virgin American forest." If agriculture is an aspect of the male sexual domination of woman, it is no wonder that the American woodsman remains chaste and turns away from the settlements from which men set out to ravage the earth.

Hemingway's Nick Adams is another refugee from civilization and sex when, in "Big Two-Hearted River," he flees to the Michigan woods on a fishing trip. He is most sensitive about opening up himself to sexual feeling, refusing to allow himself "too much" of a "thrill" in his fishing for trout and avoiding wilderness places that are too feminine:

> It would not be possible to walk through a swamp like that. The branches grew so low. You would have to keep almost level with the ground to move at all. . . . In the swamp the banks were bare, the big cedars came together overhead, the sun did not come

through, except in patches; in the fast deep water, in the half light,
the fishing would be tragic.[57]

Death as well as entanglement with earth-bound feminine vegetation is
involved here, for it was in such a swamp on a river that the young
Hemingway hero was wounded. Faulkner's most dedicated woodsman, Ike McCaslin, gives up his wife rather than accept the farm that
was carved out of the wilderness—"the woods would be his mistress
and his wife." In "Delta Autumn" he scorns his cousin for being a "doe-
hunter," a man so depraved that he kills a doe on a hunting trip and
abandons the black mother of his child. Two young Texans in Norman
Mailer's *Why Are We in Vietnam?* venture alone into the frozen Alas-
kan wilderness "to get all the mixed glut and sludge out of their systems." The sexual temptation is strong—homosexual exploration of
each other and cosmic intercourse with "the magnetic North Pole
orifice"—but a day spent in the wilds without company and weapons,
witnessing animal life and a display of Aurora Borealis, brings them to
a realization of the divinity of the animal and a condition of chastity.

To dramatize conflicting uses of the wilderness American literature has developed the pair of opposed woodsmen, one who practices
and condones the exploitation of the land and its resources, and one
who sets himself against the course of American history and lives in the
forest without harming or changing it. Thus Leatherstocking is paired
with Hurry Harry in *The Deerslayer,* Ishmael with Ahab in *Moby-Dick,*
Arthur Bridges with his brother Curt in *The Track of the Cat,* Ike with
Cass in *The Bear,* D. J. and Tex with their magnum-wielding fathers in
Why Are We in Vietnam? The hero's way with women is often
transferred to his relationship to the land: sexually brutal men are
careless with nature, sexually gentle men use land without damaging it.

The personification of the forest as female is a sublimation of the
male's feeling for women, an attempt to idealize sexuality in such a
way that the object of love is replaced by its symbol. The male ideal in
this version is "To live in paradise alone," as Andrew Marvell expresses it in "The Garden":

> Such was that happy garden-state,
> While man there walked without a mate.

The forest may be female, but female characters are almost always
shown by male writers to be repelled by the woods and everything
pertaining to them. Cooper's heroines invariably lose themselves in the

woods; all the women of the Luckett family in Conrad Richter's trilogy of American settlers, *The Awakening Land,* are terrified by the Ohio forest, and some give up their lives to it. To Cassy Dawson in Caroline Gordon's *Green Centuries* trees in the fields are acceptable while trees in the deep woods are not because they shut out the sun. Of course, the forest-fearing woman is not based on either historical or psychological fact, though the literary stereotype has no doubt influenced the attitudes of generations of women.[58]

BUILDINGS AND THE BODY

In addition to the correspondence of the body and landforms there is the correspondence of the body and buildings, a metaphor probably springing from the analogy of earth and buildings. In antiquity different building levels were commonly compared to earth's surface, subsurface, and sky: to the Greeks the sky was a ceiling that had to be held up by a god; in the Old Testament angels descend from heaven on a stairway, the earth has a foundation of carpentry and masonry, and the earth is a tabernacle made by God, who "stretcheth out the heavens as a curtain, and spreadeth them out as a tent to dwell in" (Isaiah, 40.22). If earth and buildings are related as well as earth and body, then it follows that body and buildings are in turn associated. In *Timaeus* Plato moves freely from one kind of association to another: while the neck of the body is an isthmus separating the head from the breast, the diaphragm is a "partition" or fence separating the nobler part of the soul from the baser, and the heart is "established in the guardroom" (69d, 69e, 70a–b). Thoreau has no trouble at first comparing Cape Cod to the arm and shoulder of a woman, and then, as he approached Provincetown, to a house: "We had for days walked up the long and bleak piazza which runs along her Atlantic side, then over the sanded floor of her halls, and now we were being introduced into her boudoir" (*Cape Cod,* 188).

Earth, the body, and a building are beautifully brought together by Edmund Spenser in *The Faerie Queene* when he compares the body and mind of Alma to her castle. The analogies are elaborately worked out, the rooms of the castle corresponding as nearly as possible to the organs of the body, both external and visceral, and to the functions of the mind. Even the voiding of waste is accounted for in a rare humorous passage:

And all the rest, that noyous was, and nought,
By secret wayes, that none might it espy,
Was close conuaid, and to the back-gate brought,
That cleped was *Port Esquiline,* whereby
It was auoided quite, and throwne out privily. (II.9. 32)

The relation of the building to earth is suggested in the following:

Not built of bricke, ne yet of stone and lime,
But of thing like to that Aegyptian slime,
Whereof king Nine whilome built Babell towre;
But O great pitty, that no lenger time
So goodly workemanship should not endure:
Soone it must turne to earth; no earthly thing is sure. (II.9.21)

The body of man and the buildings he makes all have the same substance, the impermanent clay of earth. Spenser's House of Alma probably inspired Fletcher's *The Purple Island,* in which the prefatory
poem by Francis Quarles begins: "Mans Bodie's like a house." The
body-building conceit abounded in Renaissance literature, and it still
turns up, as this from a real estate columnist: "I am a building. . . . I
have skin which consists of brick. . . . Inside I have nerves that are
made of copper wires. . . . My pipes are much the same as the blood
vessels in your own bodies"; and this from a poem by Anne Sexton:

Some women marry houses.
It's another kind of skin; it has a heart,
a mouth, a liver and bowel movements.

Earth, body, and buildings set bounds to protect man from the
terror of disorientation threatened by undifferentiated space. The earth
is man's largest dwelling-place, marked off from unlimited outer space
by sky, sea, and land, and distinguished from indefinite time by the
cycle of seasons. The body is the smallest shelter of individual identity,
and the house is an intermediate refuge, enclosing the body and the
things that nourish it. Artemidoras said that the house is the image of
self, and Freud claims that "the only typical, that is to say, regularly
occurring representation of the human form as a whole is that of the
house."[59] In *Nature* Emerson has it, "Every spirit builds itself a house,
and beyond its house a world, and beyond its world a heaven." The
house may be purely imaginative and still be comforting, as it is with

Eudora Welty when she writes in *Delta Wedding:* "when you felt,
touched, heard, looked at things in the world, and found their fra-
grances, they themselves made a sort of house within you, which filled
with life to hold them."[60] A less happy compulsion to contain the things
one loves in a figurative as well as literal house is a persistent theme in
Proust's *Remembrance of Things Past:* "We construct our house of life
to suit another person, and when at length it is ready to receive her that
person does not come: presently she is dead to us, and we live on, a
prisoner within the walls which were intended only for her."[61]

The female body is especially associated with buildings. Woman is
earth, woman is the garden or the epitome of earth; as earth is a
building, so woman is a building. The garden, when it is walled, is an
image combining both earth and building. As such it appears nowhere
more decisively than in the Song of Songs, in which the lover compares
his beloved to "a garden enclosed." Her brothers have a different
interest—to see that their sister does not turn away suitors and yet
does not receive all men promiscuously—and they compare her to a
building: "If she be a wall, we will build upon her a palace of silver; and
if she be a door, we will inclose her with boards of cedar." To which
the maiden dutifully replies, "I am a wall, and my breasts like towers."
This passage is crucial in the history of Christianity as the origin of the
metaphor which equates Mary with the church building.[62] The wall
which originally protected the maiden's chastity eventually becomes
the church building enclosing sacred space. By the thirteenth century
the body of Mary and the facade of the church were made to coincide
in a type of picture called Mater Ecclesia. Moreover, just as in the
Hindu Tantras the interior of a temple is thought to be a womb, so in
Christian imagery the womb of Mary was equated with the rooms of a
building, a way of representing the miraculous conjunction of the
infinite divine with the limited reality. "Love, rekindled in the Virgin's
womb," writes Georges Poulet, "is the immense sphere of the divinity
mysteriously reappearing in the narrow sphere of the human body."[63]
Thirteenth-century masses make copious references to Mary's womb
as the "vessel of honor," "chamber of seemliness," "gate of the world,"
"hostel of the highest King." The paradox of infinite extension lodged
in finite space is cause for wonder in a Spanish mass: "God whom the
world cannot contain, in thy womb He enclosed Himself, becoming
man." Twentieth-century versions of the mass seem to eschew the
vivid metaphors of medieval times, retaining only the rather abstract
phrase "worthy dwelling." In his devotion to Mary as the ultimate
figure in medieval Christianity, Henry Adams observes that her architecture, the Gothic, is feminine, while the Romanesque is male: "No

architecture that ever grew on earth, except the Gothic, gave this effect
of flinging its passion against the sky." For him the Chartres cathedral
was the Court of the Queen of Heaven, and if one refuses to believe
that "the Virgin herself made the plan . . . at least one can still sometimes feel a woman's taste, and in the apse of Chartres one feels nothing else."[64]

Although Pauline tradition equates the church with the body of
Christ, it is the femininity of the church that Paul emphasizes when he
compares the devotion Christ has for the church with the devotion a
man should have for his wife: "Husbands, love your wives, as Christ
also loved the church" (Ephesians 5.25). Further, as Christ treats the
church well because it is his body, so man must love his body and his
wife's body. The identification of Christ and Mary with the church
appears to be an adaptation of earlier cosmogonies in which the whole
earth was conceived as being the body of a god.

The image of woman in the walled garden combines two place
metaphors. Just as Mary's body is a wall enclosing Jesus, a church
housing Christian believers, so the body enclosing a lady's chastity is
like the wall protecting the delightful things in a garden. Breaking
through the wall into the garden is symbolical of the lover's assault
upon his lady; breaking into the church and defiling it is the work of the
enemies of Christ. The profanation of the chaste body of woman is
tantamount to an attack on the church. Thus Satan is pictured by
Milton as leaping over the wall of the Garden of Eden and forcing his
way "into God's fold:/ So since into his Church lewd Hirelings climb,"
an image combining sexual activity with clerical politics (IV. 192–93).
William Blake must have had Milton in mind when he wrote two poems
(numbers 5 and 6) in the Note-Book of 1793. In the first of these the
poet sees a chapel in the midst of "the garden of love," and in the
second a serpent forces his way through the "pearly door" of "a chapel
all of gold" and spits out his poison on the bread and wine of the altar:

> I saw a serpent rise between
> The white pillars of the door
> And he forc'd & forc'd & forc'd
> Till he broke the pearly door.

Here the conquest of the garden-woman by the courtly lover is subor-
dinated to the building-woman being raped by Satan. A Blake sketch
accompanying the poem in the Vala Manuscript shows the female geni-
tals in the form of church portals.[65]

In a familiar romantic motif, a lady's bedroom appears to her lover as both a holy place and a cause of erotic thrill. A famous example is Goethe's *Faust* almost spending his passion ("Und fühle mich in Liebestraum zerflieszen") as he contemplates Marguerite's room, which he likens to a shrine. Saint-Preux, observing Julie's room in *Nouvelle Héloise,* has a similar reaction: "Here I am in your chamber, here I am in the sanctuary of all that my heart adores. . . . O Julie! it is filled with thee, and the flame of my desires pours out on thy every vestige." Chateaubriand's René returns to the home of his youth to see the room "where my sister had received my first confessions into the bosom of her love." Pierre Glendinning in Melville's *Pierre* has a glimpse of his fiancée's "most secret inner shrine," which seems to be "sanctified by some departed saint"—compare Chaucer's Troilus, who calls Criseyde's palace a "shryne of which the seynt is out," and Faust, to whom Marguerite's room is a "Heiligtum"; Pierre is "rooted" as he catches sight of "the snow-white bed reflected in the toilet-glass." A suggestion of breaking into the church is retained in Keats's "The Eve of Saint Agnes," in which an old woman leads the lover to Madeline's room:

> He follow'd through a lowly arched way,
> Brushing the cobwebs with his lofty plume. . . .
> Through many a dusky gallery, they gain
> The maiden's chamber, silken, hush'd, and chaste.

Once there Porphyro hides himself in a closet that is stored with sweets:

> a closet, of such privacy
> That he might see her beauty unespied. . . .

As noted before, a garden is transformed into chapels when Proust's Marcel sees Gilberte on the grounds of Swann's villa in Combray.

The description of sexual intercourse in terms of building imagery continues into the twentieth century. A most striking example is D. H. Lawrence's *The Rainbow* in which Will Brangwen experiences a much more intensive sexual consummation with Lincoln Cathedral than with his wife:

> Here the stone leapt up from the plain of earth, leapt up in a

manifold, clustered desire each time, up, away from the horizontal
earth, through twilight and dusk and the whole range of desire,
through the swerving, the declination, ah, to the ecstasy, the
touch, to the meeting and the consummation, the meeting, the
clasp, the close embrace, the neutrality, the perfect, swooning
consummation, the timeless ecstasy. There his soul remained, at
the apex of the arch, clinched in the timeless ecstasy, consum-
mated. (190)

Unlike Lawrence, most twentieth-century writers dwell on the sordidness of sexuality rather than its ecstasy, although they find it effective to retain the system of imagery that identifies the female body with
holy places. In a novel ironically entitled *Sanctuary,* Faulkner uses the
name Temple Drake for a heroine who is first raped in a corn crib and
then abused for several weeks in a Memphis whore house. The corn
crib is part of a ruined plantation, the oldest one in Yoknapatawpha
County; the whore house was once an upper-class dwelling in the city.
The delapidated buildings of a fallen civilization are the settings for the
Southern woman's undoing. Blake's defiled chapel reappears in Norman Mailer's *The American Dream* when the hero has both vaginal and
anal intercourse with his murdered wife's maidservant, a feat described as "bringing spoils and secrets up . . . from the red mills" of the
Devil to the "chapel" of the Lord.[66] The same pair of sacred and profane love-places is suggested in a conversation between Tristan and
Isolde in *Finnegans Wake.* Joyce uses the legend that Isolde came from
a town near Dublin, Chapelizod (Chapelle d'Iseult), a name on which
he is fond of punning. "Sad one of Ziod," Tristan says to Isolde, "I
must also quickingly to tryst myself softly into this littleeasechapel. I
would rather than Ireland."[67] Some time later, presumably, he asks her,
"Why do you so lifesighs, my precious?" and she replies, "I am not
sighing, I assure, but only I am soso sorry about all in my saarasplace."
The vagina is being figured here not only as a chapel located for the
convenience of people in a large parish but also as a privy (chapel of
ease) and a place of sorrow *(saarasplace).* Possibly the anus is suggested by *saar* for the Saar region (Satanic mills) and *sore* (sore ass
place). After a number of sordid affairs and murders, Mailer's hero
finally leaves the wicked city, where women have been sacrificed to the
male and phallic towers, and journeys to the desert, where he has a
vision of "jewelled cities shining in the glow of a tropical dusk." Unlike
Christian, however, he does not enter the Heavenly City but strikes
out for the Mexican jungle, a feminine place free of the contamination
of the city towers.

The association of the body with secular buildings begins to assume particular importance in the novel of the eighteenth century.[68] The garden and church of earlier times do not disappear, of course, but become appendages of the noble house, which in its totality as an estate comes to represent family distinction, social organization, and individual character. Even before the eighteenth century the "house poem" had become a thriving sub-genre, and eventually house and grounds became an important source of material in long prose narratives. "For Jane Austen, in *Mansfield Park*," writes Alistair Duckworth, "the estate as an ordered physical structure is a metonym for other inherited structures—society as a whole, a code of morality, a body of manners, a system of language."[69] Sexuality comes into the picture by way of the role of the estate as a counter in the games of courtship and adultery. In Goethe's *Elective Affinities*, for example, a noble couple and their two guests search for a solution to their sexual imbroglio by passionately concerning themselves with the improvement of an estate according to the principles laid out in an English book on landscaping; the sophisticated exchange of lovers proceeds hand in hand with the construction of an informal summer house overlooking the old family castle.

The female heroine is more sensitive to houses than the male because women have had to be more concerned with shelter in a permanent place. Even an exceptionally undomestic type like Cathy in *Wuthering Heights* is attracted to the comfortable house at Thrushcross while Heathcliff takes to roving. It is no accident that emphasis on place begins to assume real importance in fiction when the plight of female characters is the subject. The settlement of a young lady in a suitable house through marriage is the theme—and houses the principal setting—of a considerable body of fiction dealing with the immensely popular subject of courtship. The heroine's adventures consist of a progress from one house to another, each with a potential husband who possesses, or will inherit, a noble house, dower house, manse, or estate cottage—some dwelling consistent with the heroine's conception of her worth as a prize. Her encounters are almost as much with houses as with people. Of a James heroine it is perfectly plausible to say, "Isabel's whole career is presented in terms of a succession of houses."[70] Isabel herself expresses the relation of houses to the affairs of the heart when she writes to a suitor, "I am not, I am really and truly not, able to regard you in the light of a companion for life; or to think of your home—your various homes—as the settled seat of my existence" (*The Portrait of a Lady*, I.166). For James, at least, the male is also adept in the language of houses; as he stands before a lady's house in

Wings of the Dove, Merton Densher has this reaction: "It was the language of the house itself that spoke to him, writing out for him, with surpassing breadth and freedom, the associations and conceptions, the ideals and possibilities of the mistress" (73).

Two different versions of the house-heroine motif predominate: the Gothic or melodramatic, in which a very passive heroine is subjected to terror by the machinations of a monstrous villain in a series of houses and is miraculously saved by a nobleman in disguise; and the sentimental version, in which the heroine lives in a very real world of polite intrigue and makes the best use of her wit and intelligence to secure for herself an honorable husband and dwelling place. While the tone and characterization differ considerably in these two forms, the settings remain about the same: the castle or great house with a nearby forest, the remote cottage, the deep glen or mountain top—these are the perilous places where the virginity and freedom of the heroine are endangered in a succession of imprisonments and flights. Like the garden of earlier literature, the house is both the symbol of the woman's body, which male villainly plots to violate by penetrating, as well as the place where the horrible event may occur. The heroine's fear of being raped is expressed by her fear of an intruder breaking into a building; the flight through corridors and stairways to more concealed rooms is a suspenseful analogy with the male's destruction of one defense after another until the ultimate seat of chastity is reached. The heroine agonizes in a nightmare of ambivalent feelings: she desperately wants to escape from precincts made abominable by unholy passions, but she is also attracted by curiosity and by desires she dare not admit to herself. Another paradox in her predicament is that the house which should be her protection and refuge becomes instead the trap in which she must fight off totally unexpected sexual attacks, the lust of a father, old man, or clergyman, the as-yet-unbridled passion of a prospective husband.

It is from the lingering hold of the past, from the accumulation of ancient wrongs perpetrated in the old rooms and passageways, that the heroine seeks to escape in the Gothic novel. The sentimental courtship novel, on the other hand, is pointed more to the practical perils and pitfalls of contemporary society that women are likely to encounter in their drive for freedom. *Jane Eyre* strikes a balance between the Gothic and the sentimental. The old horrors are still there but as a feminist heroine Jane is far from passive in contending with them and is not afraid to take to the open road in search of house and husband. Even upon reaching Thornfield Hall, which would seem to be a worthy final destination, she continues to express a desire to roam the world:

I climbed the three staircases, raised the trapdoor of the attic, and
. . . looked out afar over sequestered field and hill, and along dim
sky-line—. . . then I longed for a power of vision which might
overpass that limit; which might reach the busy world, towns,
regions full of life I had heard of but never seen. . . . (95).

Admired by Virginia Woolf, the sentiment of this passage is more in
character with male rovers, like Oliver Twist, who similarly peers out
on the world, than with Gothic heroines or even with Jane Austen's
ladies, who feel they must wait for their chances to improve their lives
and do not often venture abroad to make opportunities for themselves.[71] From the inhospitable home of her aunt and the prison-like
boarding school Jane makes her way to a manor house with a potential
husband. But Thornfield Hall, like its master, is tainted with sexual
evils and must be destroyed by fire—its "blackened ruin" is compared
to a lover "stone dead." The awesome Gothic building yields to the
simpler Ferndean, a small manor house that has been converted to a
hunting lodge, where Jane will presumably find happiness as the wife of
a man cut down, like his estate, to manageable size. Ferndean occupies
an "ineligible and insalubrious site" in the gloomy woods, but it harbors no past wrong and its natural setting comports more with nature
than with society; Jane is confident that she can "rehumanize" Rochester there, and on their first day together she leads him "out of the wet
and wild wood into some cheerful fields." Ferndean is not nearly as
grand as Pemberley, which finally falls to Elizabeth Bennet's patient
efforts in *Pride and Prejudice,* but middle-class ambition is sometimes
willing to compromise a little. The parsonage at Mansfield Park
satisfies Fanny Price: it "soon grew as dear to her heart, and as thoroughly perfect in her eyes, as everything else within the view and
patronage of Mansfield Park had long been." Sexual interest is missing
from this apt formulation of the Austen ideal; what counts is the "view"
or aesthetic value and the "patronage," or the social and economic
perquisites of a great estate in eighteenth-century England.

As the chances of individual advancement diminished and the
spiritual tone grew darker in the course of the nineteenth century,
heroines of courtship novels are not even granted a parsonage or a
Ferndean. They are more likely to remain trapped in houses that are
still pictured with Gothic imagery, though the melodrama once associated with those places yields to the more normal behavior required
by realism. Dorothea Brooke, in *Middlemarch,* having anticipated her
marriage with Casaubon as a wonderful voyage on the open sea, soon
learns that "the large vistas and wide fresh air which she had dreamed

of finding in her husband's mind were replaced by anterooms and winding passages which seemed to lead nowhither."[72] They spend their honeymoon in Rome, where he pursues his antiquarian researches at the Vatican, "lost among small closets and winding stairs," while Dorothea has her first doubts about her marriage as she sits "in an inner room or boudoir of a handsome apartment in the Via Sistina." Rome has become "the oppressive masquerade of ages" for her, and she yearns for "the light of years to come in her own home and over the English fields and elms and hedge-bordered highroads." The death of Casaubon delivers Dorothea from confinement with a man who "forgot the absence of windows and . . . had become indifferent to the sunlight," both so essential to her. She is now able to part the curtains of the house he has left her and look out "towards the bit of road that lay in view, with fields beyond outside the entrance-gates. . . . Far off in the bending sky was the pearly light; and she felt the largeness of the world and the manifold workings of men to labor and endurance" (578). But this is not the world she can have now: as she and Will Ladislaw finally discover their love for one another, they look out of the same window upon a storm, "at the drear outer world." To marry Will, Dorothea must give up the house Casaubon left to her and live in London. "How you can always live in a street?" her shocked sister asks. The sacrifice is a little softened when we learn in the epilogue ("Finale") that old Mr. Brooke leaves his country house, the Grange, to Dorothea's son, and the son seems to continue his mother's spirit of independence: he declines to represent Middlemarch in Parliament, "thinking that his opinions had less chance of being stifled if he remained out of doors."

Dorothea Brooke's direct descendant, Isabel Archer in Henry James's *The Portrait of a Lady,* also experiences courtship and marriage in terms of diminishing vistas and restrictive buildings. After being rescued from life in a dull house in Albany, New York, Isabel tastes freedom at Gardencourt, an English country house much like Fanny Price's Mansfield Park, Jane Eyre's "cheerful fields," and Dorothea's lighted countryside. But circumstances force Isabel to spend her life in the Roman palazzo that the villainy of her husband has transformed into a Gothic prison. Dorothea and Isabel are but two of a long line of heroines who experience the tragic passage from opening vistas to restrictive places. James's Catherine Sloper, George Eliot's Maggie Tulliver, Stephen Crane's Maggie, Madame Bovary are dissatisfied with the places society has assigned to them in both the literal and figurative sense, places and situations that restrict their freedom to develop themselves equally with men. Although they make heroic efforts to seek other places where they may be free, their efforts to escape are rarely successful and they find themselves pushed back into the constraining room or house, often by the very men who gave promise of helping them.

In the place imagery of these tragic women there is a remarkable reiteration of the opposition of confining places to open vistas. To the examples cited from Brontë, Eliot, and James may be added Flaubert's Emma Bovary, whose dream it was that beyond the "boring countryside . . . there stretched as far as eye could see the immense territory of rapture and passions." Here another repeated association occurs: limitation of space and confinement go hand in hand with sexual unfulfillment. Sexual relations with lovers and husbands diminish as space and movement become more confined. Restricted movement is regularly associated with sexual deprivation in the fiction of Henry James, for whom movement is essentially travel. In "Four Meetings" when the narrator identifies pictures in Caroline's photo album as sites he has visited in Europe, Caroline blushes over the young man's knowledge of places she too would like to visit: "She looked as pretty as if, instead of showing her photographs, I had been making love to her." The same kind of exchange is to be found between the narrator and Miss Jane in "Europe": Miss Jane is said to have "flirted" with him through talk of going to Europe. James's heroines are as incapable of seizing spatial freedom as they are of taking sexual gratification. A later generation of women would at least experiment with mobility and so progress beyond the traditional binding of woman to the homeplace.

The case of woman may be, however, the case of all humankind. The old, time-honored, unquestioned associations with place are subject to change as the face of the world itself is being changed. And the pain of adjustment is most apparent as it involves the sexual life of the individual—or at least this is the report that literature offers. Literature thus preserves the fundamental and primitive association of body and world, body and place, portraying the disorientation of the individual in a changing world and the possibilities of reorientation.

4

THE WRITER AND PLACE
The Case of
Herman Melville

THE PLACES HERMAN MELVILLE VISITED in his youth gave him his start as a writer, and shaped the view of the world that he sought to convey throughout his career. However, sensitivity to place is a variable in the creative life of writers. Strong feelings about specific places are absolutely essential for some like Melville, while others never seem to require the inspiration or material that places may offer. Middlesex countryside was the occasion for many a poem by John Keats, but the vales of Kent failed to move Conrad, who averred that he was "not a topographical writer."[1] The novels of Thomas Hardy could not have been produced without the author's attachment to a particular region in England; Gertrude Stein, on the other hand, hardly needed the stimulus of place, and her writing depends not at all upon localization. "For her," writes William Troy, "reality resides in the timeless consciousness rather than in space," and William Gass agrees that Stein lacked the "enlarged sense of locale" that characterizes so many other Americans.[2]

The place where a writer is brought up may have a decisive influence on his career. St. Ives, Cornwall, was the Eden of Virginia Woolf's youth, writes a biographer, and "provided a treasury of reminiscent gold from which Virginia drew again and again."[3] André Gide attributes his artistic sensibility to his attempt in his writing to "reconcile the discordant elements" of the two distinctly different French provinces where he spent his childhood holidays.[4] Eugene Ionesco traces many of the "preoccupations and obsessions" in his plays to the loss of a paradisal childhood place.[5] A child's experience of the city, confirmed by a young man's newspaper writings, started the careers of great realists like Dickens, Dostoevsky, and Dreiser.

The place where writing is done, as distinguished from the place one is writing about, may be of importance to an author and to the work he produces. This was true of Pope at Twickenham, Melville at

Pittsfield, Hemingway at the L Bar T Ranch in Wyoming. The estate
Pope created for himself, writes his biographer, "nourished in his consciousness the dramatic personality" that speaks in satires and epis-
tles."[6] Failure to have a satisfactory place in which to write may create
tension and torment in the writing itself. Nietzsche was convinced that
his life was "spent in the wrong places, places that should have been
precisely forbidden to me."[7] D. H. Lawrence uses the term "savage
pilgrimage" in a letter to describe his lifetime search for a place where
he could fulfill himself as person and writer. "After he had left his home
village," says one of his biographers, he "never found a permanent
home and was condemned to be an exile for ever."[8] Of this quest Mark
Schorer says: "To discover a place where the vital connections could
be maintained intact was the motive of Lawrence's life as it increas-
ingly becomes the motive of his heroes and heroines."[9] Novels such as
St. Mawr, The Plumed Serpent, and *Kangaroo* are attempts to assimi-
late the life and spirit of alien places. Henry James, on the other hand,
sees a distinct danger in exotic surroundings, and in the preface to *The
Portrait of a Lady* he passes on to us

> the rather grim admonition that romantic and historic sites, such as
> the land of Italy abounds in, offer the artist a questionable aid to
> concentration when they are not the subject of it. They are too rich
> in their own life and too charged with their own meanings merely
> to help him out with a lame phrase; they draw him away from his
> small question to their greater ones. . . . The real truth is, I think,
> that they express . . . more than, in the given case, one has use for;
> so that one finds one's self working less congruously, after all, so
> far as the surrounding picture is concerned, than in the presence of
> the moderate and the neutral, to which we may lend something of
> the light of our vision.

A writer's productivity may depend upon his continued relationship to a place. Hardy may have stopped writing fiction because he
exhausted the possibilities of his beloved Dorsetshire and Wiltshire,
though Faulkner never seems to have grown weary of his "postage
stamp" of a county in Mississippi. Changes in a place may alienate the
writer who has been accustomed to draw material from it. After several
distinguished novels with an English scene, E. M. Forster gave up
fiction because, as he explained, "the English countryside, its reality,
and creative retreat into it, were more plausible than they are today."[10]
It was an England transformed by industrialism and war that sent
Lawrence abroad. The alienation of the writer from his homeland has
grown to be so common in the twentieth century that literary historians

have a special term, expatriates, for writers who live and work away from home, and a number of books, including an entire number of the magazine *Mosaic,* have been devoted to the subject.[11] In the writing of expatriates—Hemingway, Camus, Joyce, Nabokov, Lawrence—we find frequent use of special themes: finding an alternative homeland, recalling the native homeland, and returning to the original homeland.[12]

Certain kinds of places, drawn from personal experience or literary stores, may have a special attraction for some writers over their entire career. Houses figure prominently in Austen and James, domes in Shelley, the dell in E. M. Forster, islands in John Fowles, bathrooms in Salinger. Matthew Arnold regularly employs a symbolic landscape in which three distinct regions—"The Forest Glade, the Burning or Darkling Plain, and the Wide-Glimmering Sea"—stand for general conditions in the life of an individual and in the history of mankind.[13] John Steinbeck had a passion for unusual shelters and hiding places. Near the end of their tribulations the Joads are living in a boxcar, a couple in *Cannery Row* make a pleasant home in an abandoned factory boiler, Mack and the boys live in some large rusty pipes (but only in "damp" weather), Pirate lives with his five dogs in "a deserted chicken-house in the yard of a deserted house on Tortilla Flat." Steinbeck's fleeing heroes hide in culverts *(Of Mice and Men, In Dubious Battle)* and caves of vines *(The Grapes of Wrath, Pastures of Heaven).*[14] Makeshift housing was quite common in the Great Depression, but of course Steinbeck had plenty of precedent among American writers before him. Huck Finn lived in a "sugar-hogshead" when he grew tired of the Widow Douglas's house. In considering "how slight a shelter is absolutely necessary," Thoreau, in *Walden,* suggests that a "man who was hard pushed" might do worse than a railroad toolbox measuring 6×3 feet if he were to bore "a few auger holes in it, to admit the air at least."

Some writers may become so obsessed with certain places that they can be read as a kind of language of the psyche. In Hemingway the good place is where the hero experiences love and death, and the bad place is where the hero is wounded. Neither place is ever forgotten by Hemingway's many personae: "terrain is what remains in the dreaming part of your mind," says Colonel Cantwell in *Across the River and into the Trees.* The good place is the forest edge where the pine trees meet the meadow, and it is there that Nick Adams first makes love ("Fathers and Sons"), restores his spirit after the shocks of war ("Big Two-Hearted River"), and, as Robert Jordan in *For Whom the Bell Tolls,* prepares to meet his death as a soldier:

He touched the palm of his hand against the pine needles where he lay and he touched the bark of the pine trunk that he lay -

behind. . . . He was waiting until the officer reached the sunlit
place where the first trees of the pine forest joined the green slope
of the meadow.[15]

In the Hemingway scheme of values the worst possible condition, for
both animal and man, is to be wounded, and the Hemingway hero is
wounded in World War I on the bank of the River Piave in Fossalta,
Italy. The place where the river bends and the water is "slow and a
muddy blue" haunts Lieutenant Henry in *Farewell to Arms*, Nick
Adams in "Big Two-Hearted River" and in "A Way You'll Never Be,"
and Colonel Cantwell, who finally lays the ghost of the bad place by
defecating on the exact spot where he had been wounded in World
War I. The bad place, the wide and slow river, is elsewhere countered
by the swift-running trout stream, where the hero recuperates in "Big
Two-Hearted River" and *The Sun Also Rises*. (The lost consolation of
the trout stream is to be noted among contemporary American writers.
"Where were the trout streams of my youth?" asks a character in John
Cheever's "The Housebreaker of Shady Hill." Polluted trout streams
symbolize the fall of Edenic America in Richard Brautigan's *Trout
Fishing in America*, though in Brautigan's *In Watermelon Sugar* the restored trout stream is the center of religious rites in a post-apocalyptic
world.)

High land and low land make another pair of opposed places in
Hemingway. In a world that left few desirable places for his restless
characters, the low places were to be avoided—the swamp in "Big
Two-Hearted River" where fishing would be "a tragic adventure,"
where the branches of trees were so low "you would have to keep
almost level with the ground to move at all"—and the high places were
to be sought out—the upland trout streams in Michigan and France for
sport, "the slope of the hill above the road and the bridge" for Jordan to
die on, the snow-covered peak of Kilimanjaro ("great, high, and unbelievably white in the sun") to go to after death. The description in *The
Sun Also Rises* of the view of the Spanish countryside from the high
road crossing the Pyrenees presents one of the most beautiful landscapes in all of Hemingway's works.

Nietzsche, writes Bachelard, is an "ascensional poet" and his
"cosmos is one of heights."[16] Albert Camus was also drawn to heights,
not to enjoy and die on heroically as Hemingway, but as a point from
which to observe the world and the human condition. Such are the
balcony in *The Stranger*, the terrace in *The Plague*, the House above
the World in *A Happy Death* from which can be seen the Bay of Algiers
and the whole space of the world. Only after experiencing the perspective from above can an individual enter freely into the life below. The

despair of Jean-Baptiste Clamence in *The Fall* is that he is "condemned," like Aschenbach in *Death in Venice,* to a flat country, Holland, which he sees as hell compared to his life in France, an Eden,
where he was able to practice his "vocation for summits. It cleansed
me of all bitterness toward my neighbor." It would be ideal to have "a
natural balcony fifteen hundred feet above a sea . . . well above the
human ants."

Perhaps because of the strong influence of Hemingway on him,
Norman Mailer has had a career-long interest in the opposition of high
and low places. His first novel, *The Naked and the Dead,* ends with the
attempt of a platoon of ordinary soldiers to scale Mount Anaka, a
mission that is at first military but then becomes an ideal quest to which
the men are driven by Sergeant Croft, who, like Ahab whom he is made
to resemble, is himself driven by the abstract challenge of nature.
Though the ascent fails, the effort at least raises the men above the
jungle floor, above "the stench of fertility," into the space of the bare
hills where the dangerous terrain drives from their minds the obsession
with sex and creature comfort that has preoccupied them up to that
time. It is their one encounter, in a very long book, with heroic action.
The soldier Roth, who, goaded by Croft, falls from the cliff to his
death, appears much later in *An American Dream* in the person of
Rojack, and this time he makes it around the parapet of a skyscraper in
spite of his father-in-law's attempts to topple him over the side into the
New York street below. An even happier victory over heights occurs
in *Why Are We in Vietnam?* when two young men, having climbed the
"ice ass pinnacle of the Brooks Range" in Alaska, reach a lovely mountain meadow where they have a privileged view of wild animals and
pledge themselves in deepest friendship. (So Ishmael sees the mother
and infant whales in the depths of the sea and makes a tayo pact with
Queequeg.) The astronauts, too, in *Of a Fire on the Moon,* overcome
the fear of falling, but only through a suppression of the ego: since
"one's fear of height must be at least a partial function of the importance of one's ego," then it follows that "a mind without ego . . . is kin
to a body without gravity."[17] The conflict between fear of heights and
life on the plain is resolved by Mailer at the close of *An American
Dream* when Rojack, in the desert at Las Vegas and released from the
terrible experiences among the towers of New York City, regrets that
he was not strong enough to pull down the spires of the city, as though
heights should not be there for man to *want* to climb. This recognition
is like Croft's after the failure to climb Mount Anaka near the end of
The Naked and the Dead: "Deep inside himself Croft was relieved that
he had not been able to climb the mountain. . . . Croft was rested by the
unadmitted knowledge that he had found a limit to his hunger" (701).

His true love dead and her soul on the moon, Rojack heads for the Mexican jungle: the drive of the "idealist"—the name given to Croft by his men—for some abstract transcendence, symbolized by a victory over the heights, is finally allayed and man returns to the plain of ordinary life.

Instead of being opposed, two different places may compete for a writer's attention. Ibsen explored his interest in heights in architect Solness's passion for towers in *The Master Builder* and his interest in horizontality in the roadbuilder Borgheim in *Little Eyolf*.[18] Thomas Mann and Gide were divided in their loyalties between the places of their parents' origin, Mann's mother having come from Italy and his father from northern Europe, Gide's mother from Normandy and his father from Bas-Languedoc. The prairie and the high rock, or mesa, pulled Willa Cather in two directions. Drawn to the Nebraska "table-land" of her youth, Cather yet maintained, even in her prairie novels, a feeling of awe for the home of the Indian cliff-dwellers. The high rock dominates her later novels *The Professor's House, Death Comes for the Archbishop,* and *Shadows on the Rock.*

A writer may find it useful to imagine his work itself in the form of a place. It has been noted in an earlier chapter that Wordsworth thought of *The Prelude* "as a sort of portico to the Recluse," that Proust saw his *Remembrance of Things Past* as a great cathedral, and that Melville liked to think of his massive *Moby-Dick* in terms of a ship, whale, and building. John Keats argued that a long poem has the advantage of giving poetry lovers "a little region to wander in," and he may be referring to his own long poem when in *Endymion* he writes at length about

> the space
> Made for the soul to wander in and trace
> Its own existence. . . .[19]

Virginia Woolf describes a novel as "a structure leaving a shape on the mind's eye, built now in squares, now pagoda shaped, now throwing out wings and arcades, now solidly compact and domed like the Cathedral of Saint Sofia at Constantinople."[20] On a trip to Denver in his later years, Whitman found "the law of my own poems" in the landscapes of the West, "this grim yet joyous elemental abandon—this plenitude of material, entire absence of art, untrammeled play of primitive Nature—the chasm, the gorge, the crystal mountain stream, repeated scores, hundreds of miles—the broad handling and absolute uncrampedness."[21]

Travel is often the spur to composition, and even accidental visits to places may release creative energy. A trip to Africa for his health supplied the spark for Gide's career, beginning with *Les Nourritures Terrestres;* the trips Graham Greene made to Africa "molded him into a writer."[22] From drafting his travel notes Flaubert "learned the techniques displayed, *en raccourci,* in the novels," and from his many travel sketches Henry James drew material for his fictions.[23] The act of travel in itself is sufficient for Michel Butor because a trip for him is "a privileged place for reading" and reading leads to writing. "I travel in order to write," he concludes.[24] Return trips to childhood scenes can be most rewarding. Poems inspired by revisiting places become almost a stereotype for romantic poets. *Huckleberry Finn* grew out of a trip Mark Twain made as a professional writer to the Mississippi River he had known as a youth. A return trip to Nebraska, where she had been brought up, gave Willa Cather the materials for her best early novels; a return to Pennsylvania Dutch country "contributed directly" to "a poetry of meditation" in the later years of Wallace Stevens.[25]

HERMAN MELVILLE: "All the way from Paradise to Tartarus"

Four years at sea fixed upon the youthful mind of Herman Melville a set of places that lasted for a lifetime of writing. He was an early witness of the transformation of the South Pacific islands from their original paradisal state to places degraded by contact with western civilization. Deterioration, decline, the lost paradise were materials he wove into the familiar romantic narrative of the young man's worldwide quest for the ever-disappearing truth and beauty that might be found in the form of exotic places and woman. Just as Byron's, Melville's heroes are turned out of the civilized homeland and forced to explore the frontiers of both geography and speculative thought: the sea, the island harboring good things and bad, the strange culture of exotic people leading the observer to sceptical ideas. It was, as R. W. B. Lewis puts it, a "vexed odyssey" for Melville,[26] not the usual journey from bad to good places as in Dante and Bunyan, nor the fortunate restoration of the tainted place as in Homer. The quest engaged Melville's attention for at least ten years in a series of books, from *Typee* (1846) to "The Encantadas" (1856), that marked the stages in Melville's increasing disillusionment with the world. While the questing hero remains essentially the same in the successive encounters Melville plots for him, the world he explores suffers a declension from paradise to hell—one, in fact, becomes the other.

Melville begins with the image of paradise as an island refuge from the rigors of the sea, a land-place of rest, ease, and beauty; its chief topographical feature is the valley, and its most striking association is with innocence and woman. His very first novel, *Typee*, opens with thinly veiled analogy between an island valley and the female body.[27] The narrator and his companion, Toby, escape from the horrors of life aboard a whaler, steal ashore, and set out for a valley inhabited by reputedly friendly natives, the Happars. After clambering over volcanic rocks in the mountains, on their first night ashore they suffer a kind of symbolic death on a cliffside where a cataract plunges into an abyss, the entrance of hell itself: the water "fell with wild uproar into a deep black pool scooped out of the gloomy-looking rocks that lay piled around, and thence in one collected body dashed down a narrow sloping channel which seemed to penetrate into the very bowels of the earth."[28] In this "infernal place" Toby lies all night "with his knees drawn up to his head," while the narrator is swept by "incessant streams of water." Next day the process of rebirth begins with the discovery of a new land that they see from another cliffside: "a scene which even now I can recall with all the vividness of the first impression. Had a glimpse of the gardens of paradise been revealed to me I could scarcely have been more ravished with the sight. . . . I looked straight down into the bosom of a valley . . . the crowning beauty of the prospect was its universal verdure" (49). To reach this hidden paradise they must spend five days of perilous travel in a river gorge, crawling and sliding "along the oozy surface of the rocks or slipping into the deep pools" and "worming" their way "through the subterranean passages." Then, from tree to tree they drop down to the floor of a valley, where they are greeted by two naked children, a Polynesian Adam and Eve. The place is inhabited by Typees, a people who turn out to be quite friendly in spite of their reputation; Melville's cannibals, like Montaigne's, are more virtuous than supposedly civilized people. In the Valley of the Typees the two wanderers are welcomed back to life after dying and being reborn on their journey over the landscape. The narrator is given a name, Tommo, and is treated like an infant to restore his health; he settles down to a paradisal existence with a native family and a maiden companion, Fayaway. But two serious blemishes gradually turn up: Tommo's leg, diseased through exposure on the mountain trip, cannot be healed with native medicine, and Tommo has good reason to believe that cannibalism is practiced by his hosts. No more than Byron can Melville overlook the two fatal consequences of a civilized white man living in paradise, guilt and death: guilt for having defected from civilization (the whaling ship and the captain) and the danger of being consumed by a life of unmitigated ease. Tommo decides that he must leave Eden and return to ships and the sea; turning his back on the lovely valley and woman, he forces his way to the shore and joins another whaling crew.

In *Typee* is found the first instance of a recurring narrative motif in Melville: the escape of the hero, after a miraculous death and rebirth, to a land-locked valley paradise where he enjoys perfect rest and fleshly gratification; and the eventual rejection of this kind of life for a return to a grim outpost of civilization in the form of a ship at sea. Melville's vision of the earthly paradise is purest in this first book, for after the Valley of the Typees each succeeding paradise is a fainter copy of the first until paradise becomes its opposite, inferno. The outpost of civilization also becomes progressively grimmer until in *Billy Budd* it takes the life of the innocent hero.

Omoo presents Melville's second look at paradise, but the island of Tahiti is in a sad state of deterioration as compared to the pristine condition of Nukuheva in *Typee*. Its population is diseased and dwindling, its land, though still fertile, shows signs of decay. Only one place, Tamai, is truly paradisal, but its peace seems threatened by the imminent arrival of missionaries. (Ironically, it is Western civilization, with its paradise-loving Christians, that has ruined the actual South Sea island paradises.) This time we are allowed only one fleeting look at Eve, this time a planter's wife, who is seen flashing by on horseback, as though in a vision, "along one of the bridle-paths which wind among the shady groves." In keeping with the whole tone of dissolution is the court of Queen Pomaree at Partoowye, where the last of Tahitian royal family lives among a shabby retinue of demoralized natives and opportunistic Europeans. Tommo had been perfectly absorbed into the Typee Valley, whereas the seed of corruption in Tahiti is the imperfect and forced assimilation of Western civilization which is symbolized by the disarray of the royal lodge at Partoowye:

> The whole scene was a strange one; but what most excited our surprise, was the incongruous assemblage of the most costly objects from all quarters of the globe. Cheek by jowl, they lay beside the rudest native articles, without the slightest attempt at order. Superb writing-desks of rosewood, inlaid with silver and mother-of-pearl; decanters and goblets of cut glass; embossed volumes of plates; gilded candelabras; sets of globes and mathematical instruments; the finest porcelain . . . were strewn about among the greasy calabashes half filled with poee, rolls of old tappa and matting, paddles and fish-spears, and the ordinary furniture of a Tahitian dwelling.[29]

The search for paradise and Eve is continued in *Mardi* on a worldwide scale, for Mardi is an archipelago representing the entire world and the narrator, Taji, who, like his predecessors has escaped from the tyranny of a whaling ship, searches among its many islands for Yillah, a girl with whom he had enjoyed an idyllic existence for a short time on "a little green tuft of an isle" before she was mysteriously stolen from him.

The importance of the quest for paradise and woman is emphasized by Melville in a visit Taji makes to the island of Juam, where custom requires that the reigning king immure himself for life in the valley of Williamilla, another glen, "vivid with verdure," bearing a relation to the female anatomy ("the secret places between the salient spurs of the mountains") and reached, like the Valley of the Typees, by passing through "a subterranean tunnel."[30] Though it is "the fairest of the valleys of Mardi" and offers all imaginable paradisal amenities, the present king, Donjalolo, is miserable because he can never see the world outside or breathe "the free ocean air." The luxuries with which he is surrounded make him feminine—"so feminine that he was sometimes called . . . the Girl"—and ineffectual as a ruler since no one outside the valley obeys him. As Taji and his company of world travelers approach the king's twin palaces, where he lives in perpetual shade, they see topographical features suggesting sterility: a "trunkless tree," a waterfall whose volume of water "ere reaching the ground was dispersed in a wide misty shower," and a great river whose "youthful enthusiasm was soon repressed, its waters being caught in a large stone basin." Though he has thirty wives, the king "had never an heir." The episode closes with a royal feast in which the excessive eating and drinking are described in terms suggesting group masturbation. From "a pompous, lordly-looking demijohn," a "special calabash," is poured Marzilla wine, "distilled of yore from purple berries growing in the purple valley of Ardair." Wielding the "polished thighbone" of an ancestor for sceptre, Donjalolo urges Taji to drink the "potent contents" of the calabash:

> "In this wine a king's heart is dissolved. Drink long; in this wine lurk the seeds of the life everlasting. Drink deep; drink long; thou drinkest wisdom and valor at every draft. Drink forever, O Taji, for thou drinkest that which will enable thee to stand up and speak out before mighty Oro himself."
>
> Amazing! the flexibility of the royal elbow and the rigidity of the royal spine! More especially as we had been impressed with a notion of their debility. But sometimes these seemingly enervated young blades approve themselves steadier of limb than veteran revelers of very long standing. (226)

Of course no consummation with women results, and after the feast the king sleeps "in company with his guests, for together they had all got high, and together they must all lie low . . . each king to his bones." Normal heterosexuality is suppressed in the paradisal valley; there "ardent impulses . . . recoil upon themselves" and come to naught. Never seeing the sun as he moves regularly from one of his two palaces to the other, Donjalolo leads a futile existence: "mountain-locked, arbor-nested, royalty-girdled, arm-clasped, self-hugged, indivisible" (210).

In *Redburn,* the novel immediately following *Mardi,* Melville sets aside the world of phantasy and turns his attention to the very real contemporary England. For the first time the emphasis shifts from tainted paradises to infernal regions, and these Melville finds in the cities modern industrialism has made. In a narrow street of Liverpool, ironically called "Launcelott's-Hey," Melville's innocent traveler happens upon a destitute family taking shelter in the cellar of "a crumbling old warehouse . . . some fifteen feet below the walk"; there he hears "the low, hopeless, endless wail of some one forever lost."[31] After failing to get help from indifferent authorities, Redburn returns the next day to the same spot only to find that "in place of the women and children, a heap of quick-lime was glistening." He finds the same destitution in "the cellars, sinks, and hovels of the wretched lanes and courts near the river." The city arouses in him a vision of "old women . . . picking dirty fragments of cotton in the empty lot," an image amazingly like Eliot's in "Preludes":

> The worlds revolve like ancient women
> Gathering fuel in vacant lots.

Redburn offers up a prayer "that some angel might descend, and turn the waters of the docks into an elixir, that would heal all their woes, and make them, man and woman, healthy and whole as their ancestors, Adam and Eve, in the garden." According to a guide book inherited from his father, Liverpool had once been grand enough to merit the praise of poets, a place

> Where Mersey's stream, long winding o'er the plain,
> Pours his tribute to the circling main. (140)

Now, as Redburn stands on the site of the " 'pool' from which the town borrows part of its name," he is struck "with a comical sadness at the vanity of all human exaltation," for the present Liverpool seems nothing but "a brick-kiln": "I now eyed the spot with a feeling somewhat akin to the Eastern traveler standing on the brink of the Dead Sea. For here the doom of Gomorrah seemed reversed, and a lake had been converted into substantial stone and mortar" (152).

If "smoky old Liverpool" is an industrial wasteland, London is the false garden of iniquity. On a brief visit to the city Redburn sees only Aladdin's Palace, a fancy private club where gambling and prostitution seem to be the main attractions. The elaborate furnishings suggest the Bower of Bliss: the frescoed ceiling was "arched like a bower, and thickly clustering with mimic grapes"; the floor was covered with "Persian carpeting, mimicking parterres of tulips, and roses, and jonquils, like a bower in Babylon"; and the oriental ottomans were covered with material "whose cunning warp and woof were wrought into plaited serpents, undulating beneath beds of leaves, from which, here and there, they flashed out sudden splendors of green scales and gold." To the inexperienced Redburn, "The whole place seemed infected. . . . This must be some house whose foundations take hold on the pit" (219–225). It is Redburn's mysterious upper-class friend, Harry Bolton, who introduces the inexperienced Redburn to this vaguely evil place and almost abandons him there, as Toby abandoned Tommo in the Valley of the Typees. But this time the two young men make their escape and return to their ship unscathed.

Only in the English countryside does Redburn find a remnant of Eden, "a green splendor in the landscape that ravished me." In walking one day out of Liverpool he happens upon a "charming little dale, undulating down to a hollow, arched over with foliage." A sign on a gate-post reads: "MAN-TRAPS AND SPRING-GUNS," to which Redburn-Melville, recollecting *Typee* perhaps, responds: "They were not surely *cannibals,* that dwelt down in that beautiful little dale, and lived by catching men!" No, but they were three beautiful English girls in a cottage, "three charmers, three Peris, three Houris," and the loveliest of the three was called Matilda, "by far the most beautiful rosebud I had yet seen in England." An old lady sees to it that the likes of Redburn, a common sailor, has no further contact with the lovely maidens. It was not until *Moby-Dick* was out of the way that Melville returned to the paradisal countryside, the female charmers, and the man-traps.

In *Pierre* the deterioration of paradise into a condition resembling the inferno of the city is sharply drawn. Half of the story is laid in a pastoral setting in the Berkshires, where Melville resided at the time, and half in New York, where he had recently toiled through *Mardi* and part of *Moby-Dick*. The countryside that is still innocent in comparison

with the city in *Redburn* is now discovered to harbor as much evil as
the admittedly wicked city. Melville's friend and neighbor, Nathaniel
Hawthorne, was making the very same point at the same time (1852) in
The Blithedale Romance. Both books are anti-pastoral arguments dis-
puting the romantic celebration of the life lived close to nature as well
as the popular belief that American ruralism offered the world a new
Eden. Ten years earlier, in a short story entitled "Eleonora," Poe had
described the life of a young man in a paradisal valley that changes for
the worse when his loved one dies; his removal to "a strange city" and
betrothal to another woman break the curse of his former love.

Pierre does not have to travel to paradise as Melville's sailor
heroes do, because he is born to it, being the scion of a noble family
appropriately named Glendinning. But the peril to his male soul is
precisely the rural environment, which is described in heavily loaded
feminine terms. The danger is established in the very first paragraph,
which speaks of "the trance-like aspect of the green and golden world"
and its "wonderful and indescribable repose." Pierre is bound to this
place by the two women he loves, his mother and his sweetheart,
Lucy. His mother nurtures him in "heroicness" and near-incestuous
affection; she represents for him the ancestral tie with the family seat,
Saddle Meadows, while Lucy represents the tie of man with earth in a
more general way:

> All this Earth is Love's affianced; vainly the demon Principle
> howls to stay the banns. Why round her middle wears this world so
> rich a zone of torrid verdure, if she be not dressing for the final
> rites? And why provides she orange blossoms and lilies of the
> valley, if she would not that all men and maids should love and
> marry? . . . . So on all sides Love allures; can contain himself what
> youth who views the wonders of the beauteous woman-world?
> Where a beautiful woman is, there is all Asia and her Bazaars.[32]

This may be a "ludicrous conceit," as it has been termed, but only in
the extravagance of its style, for it attests to the point of view Melville
develops in his works, that man is trapped by earth through the agency
of woman. Lucy is "the bait . . . set in Paradise" and Pierre is at first the
willing Adam; but, like the garden in Hawthorne's "Rappaccini's
Daughter," this Eden of the New World is strangely inverted: Pierre's
father is a sinner in having had an illegitimate daughter, Isabel, and it is
she who insinuates herself into Saddle Meadows to exact retribution
from Pierre, who has been enjoying paradise while she has been a
homeless waif. Respect for his father "had long stood a shrine in the
fresh-foliaged heart of Pierre," who now must believe that Eden too is

false. Again reversing the Bible story, Pierre is dismissed from Eden by his mother for having renounced the pure Lucy in favor of the mysterious Isabel. He flees to the city with his dark Lilith and Delly Ulver, a farm girl who is carrying an illegitimate child.

In the city Pierre is able to get a better perspective on the deceptiveness of the country paradise he has had to quit. Just as the white whale in the novel preceding *Pierre* represented the ambiguity of creation, both its beauty and terrible hideousness, so the mountain dominating Saddle Meadows has two opposing aspects. From the piazza of the Glendinning house, as from Melville's own farmhouse, the mountain "presented a long and beautiful, but not entirely inaccessible-looking purple precipice, some two thousand feet in the air, and on each hand sideways sloping down to lofty terraces of pastures" (477). (We recall that Moby Dick first appears in a sea that is like "a noon meadow," his wake a "moving valley," and "on each bright side, the whale shed off enticings.") An old farmer, who had been struck by this pleasant pastoral aspect of the mountain, named it Delectable Mountain; but another aspect of the same mountain inspired a "most moody, disappointed bard" to rename it Mount of the Titans when he noticed, upon a closer look, that the foliage of trees "cunningly masked . . . a terrific towering palisade of dark mossy massiness . . . a hideous repellingness." Melville goes on to describe the mountain with infernal imagery of the sort he had so recently heaped on the white whale; he speaks of "dark-dripping rocks, and mysterious mouths of wolfish caves," of "rocky masses, grotesque in shape . . . which seemed to express that slumbering intelligence visible in some recumbent beasts." In a word, from one point of view Eden can be seen as hell, a place of "stark desolation; ruin, merciless and ceaseless; chills and gloom."

To Pierre and his friends, when they were school-age playmates, one of the half-buried rocks under the mountain had seemed to be a fallen giant, the Titan Enceladus "writhing from out the imprisoning earth." With their shovels the boys once tried to unearth the rock but gave up in despair after "they had bared a good part of his mighty chest." Melville's description of the impotent offspring of the mighty mountain is clearly phallic. To reach the rock you do not follow "the sad pasture's skirt" but go to a field where fragments from "the mystic height" of the mountain have fallen. There you see the "whole striving trunk" of this particular rock, Enceladus, "the turbaned head of igneous rock rising from out the soil." As a boy Pierre had failed to free the half-buried rock, but later as a young man, in a trance, he has a vision of the fallen Titans "now sprung to their feet" and assaulting heaven:

"Foremost among them all, he saw a moss-turbaned, armless giant, who despairing of any other mode of wreaking his immitigable hate, turned his vast trunk into a battering-ram, and hurled his own arched-out ribs again and yet again against the invulnerable steep." Here are remnants of imagery used a short time before to describe the rage of both Ahab and the whale. The sexuality of the rock image is further confirmed by the suggestion that Pierre had an orgasm during his trance: "Recovered somewhat from the after-spell of this wild vision folded in his trance, Pierre composed his front as best he might, and straightway left his fatal closet. Concentrating all the remaining stuff in him, he resolved . . . to wrestle with . . . this new death-fiend of the trance, and this Inferno of his Titanic vision" (483–4).

Melville adapts the myth of Enceladus by changing the classical Mount Aetna to Mount Greylock in the Berkshires and using it to point up Pierre's tragic predicament: "heaven-aspiring, but still not earth-emancipated," Pierre indulges in a "reckless sky-assaulting mood" that is fruitless. In adding the myth of the mountain to the paradisal countryside, Melville fashions a system of land imagery that seems to reach for the same ends he had so recently achieved in the sea story *Moby-Dick*. Pierre is a land-based Ahab whose struggle is to free himself from the restricting paradise of Eden and woman in order to assault heaven, which in Pierre's case is writing a masterpiece, "something transcendently great." He succeeds in freeing himself from Eden and his mother in the first half of the book, but the city, to which he flees with Isabel, turns out to be an inferno. Isabel seems to offer an opportunity for a new start in life, though it is fraught with mystery and the feeling of death. Lucy joins the pair, bringing in again the discredited Eden, now somewhat refined of its evil. Pierre needs both women just as he needs both the influences of land and sea to complete his great book:

> . . . ere that vile book be finished, I must get on some other element
> than earth. I have sat on earth's saddle till I am weary; I must now
> vault over to the other saddle awhile. Oh, seems to me, there
> should be two ceaseless steeds for a bold man to ride,—the Land
> and the Sea; and like circusmen we should never dismount, but
> only be steadied and rested by leaping from one to the other, while
> still, side by side, they both race round the sun. (485)

Even so, Pierre has not the heart for a sea adventure like Ahab's. A short sail on the bay reveals that Isabel is preternaturally drawn to the sea; she had crossed the ocean in her mother's womb, and now she yearns to return to the sea and to death, to "the great blue sluice-way into the ocean . . . where the two blues meet, and are nothing." Shortly after his rejection of the sea journey Pierre learns that his publishers account his book "a blasphemous rhapsody" and his cousin and Lucy's brother have branded him "a villainous and perjured liar." Pierre's love for two women and his assault on heaven end in the city prison, where, like Enceladus, he is buried by rock:

> That sundown, Pierre stood solitary in a low dungeon of the city prison. The cumbersome stone ceiling almost rested on his brow; so that the long tiers of massive cell-galleries above seemed partly piled on him. His immortal, immovable, bleached cheek was dry; but the stone cheeks of the walls were trickling. The pent twilight of the contracted yard, coming through the barred arrow-slit, fell in dim bars upon the granite floor. (502)

Ahab is overwhelmed by sea, Pierre by earth; the failure of both is expressed in phallic symbolism: Ahab cannot take the "battering ram" that is the white whale, Pierre lies prone before the two women he would love.

The failure to transcend earth is the terror of American transcendentalists, accounting for Thoreau's horror upon climbing to the top of Mount Katahdin and discovering only the chaos of uncreated matter. In *Pierre* both infernal city and paradisal countryside block the aspiring hero from his transcendental ends; both land and sea constrain his spirit and lead it to the absolute negation of the buried rock. Commenting on the extensive imagery of stones in *Pierre,* H. Bruce Franklin concludes: "In trying to follow, to imitate, and to become Christ, he succeeds only in becoming Enceladus, a stone borne down by the earth into a granite hell."[33] Christ is the one God who escapes earth after the rock is pushed away from the mouth of his tomb; Enceladus, Prometheus, Satan are eternally bound to earth—like man.

The declension of paradise continues in a pair of related stories which give a contemporary, realistic touch to the relation of sex to paradise and hell. The diptych, entitled "The Paradise of Bachelors and the Tartarus of Maids" is an elaborate allegorical treatment of places Melville had visited, a paper mill in the Berkshires and the Inns of Court in London. In "Tartarus" the process of manufacturing stationery is systematically, and rather too obviously, compared to the process of childbirth. The allegorical intention is struck at the very beginning of the story with the setting of the mill being presented in terms of the common analogy of topography with the female anatomy.

Woedolor Mountain overlooks a ravine called Black Notch, which drops to a

> hopper-shaped hollow, far sunk among many Plutonian, shaggy-wooded mountains. By the country people this hollow is called the Devil's Dungeon. Sounds of torrents fall on all sides upon the ear. These rapid waters unite at last in one turbid brick-colored stream, boiling through a flume among enormous boulders. They call this strange-colored torrent Blood River. Gaining a dark precipice it wheels suddenly to the west, and makes one maniac spring of sixty feet into the arms of a stunted wood of gray-haired pines, between which it thence eddies on its further way down to the invisible low lands.

It is a bitter cold day when the narrator, a seedsman, visits the mill. The mountain "fairly smoked with frost," and frost "made the whole country look like one petrifaction."

The paradisal topography of the Valley of the Typees is now transformed by Melville into hell, and the lovely Berkshire countryside is the scene where women slave before machines. The horrible situation of the maids is compared to the good life of the bachelors; the "mountain nook" where they labor "is the very counterpart of the Paradise of Bachelors, but snowed upon, and frost-painted to a sepulchre." For the bachelors, though they live in the heart of London, enjoy a place which is like paradise, "the sweet, tranquil Temple garden, with the Thames bordering its green beds." Though not in a valley, Temple Bar is like "some cool, deep glen" in the midst of the "heated plain" of the city. "The Temple is indeed a city by itself. . . . A city with a park to it, and flower-beds, and a river-side—the Thames flowing by it as openly, in one part, as by Eden's primal garden flowed the mild Euphrates."

The settings of the two stories are thus the same, paradisal valleys that have been degraded through the chief activities of the modern world, industry and commerce. Temple Bar, once the home of the heroic Knights Templars, is but a superficial Eden inhabited by effete lawyers: the mill valley is an icy inferno. Melville's paper mill is like one of the "dire mills" disfiguring the English landscape in Chapter 1 of Blake's *Jerusalem:*

> The land of darkness flamed, but no light and no repose:
> The land of snows of trembling and of iron hail incessant:
> The land of earthquakes, and the land of woven labyrinths:
> The land of snares and traps and wheels and pit-falls and dire mills.

The effect of industry on people was also Melville's grave concern, as it was Blake's.[34] The maids are the victims of industrialism, their victimization being compared to the drudgery of child-bearing that is forced upon them by chauvinistic males. The sexual meaning is established by the setting of the mill, as we have seen, and more than confirmed by the phallicism associated with the machinery which the girls serve like "tame ministers." One machine is "a vertical thing like a piston periodically rising and falling," another is "a long, glittering scythe" looking "exactly like a sword," before which "like so many mares haltered to the rack, stood rows of girls." The whole process "for the pulp to pass from end to end and come out paper" requires "only nine minutes." Thus Melville, like Blake, associates sexual degradation with the industrialism of the times: "Before my eyes—there, passing in slow procession along the wheeling cylinders, I seemed to see, glued to the pallid incipience of the pulp, the yet more pallid faces of all the pallid girls." The bachelors, on the other hand, are upper-class beneficiaries of the industrial system and sexless, devoting themselves to substitutes like eating, drinking, smoking, and perhaps reading "the *Decameron* ere retiring for the night." The whole allegory of "The Paradise of Bachelors" turns on the contrast of the weak gentlemen of the present age with the heroic Knights Templars in whose precincts the bachelors occupy themselves with very unmanly pleasures. For instance, at the end of their festivities "an immense convolved horn" is brought out, not to be used "to blow an inspiring blast" to battle but as a receptacle for snuff. Just as Donjalolo and his guests, the bachelors have committed the prime Melvillean sin of succumbing to paradise and allowing their lives to become a continuous round of self-indulgence and auto-eroticism.[35]

Through the juxtaposition of these two stories, Melville seems to be saying that industrialism and the subjection of woman to child-bearing go hand in hand and have made a hell out of paradise, enslaved the modern Eve, and turned Adam into an impotent, sybaritic weakling. Had the realistic mode appealed to Melville, he might have continued to find his materials in the social problems of his time and to locate his fiction in the cities, where the evils of industrialism were being compounded. He made several starts in this direction. In addition to his treatment of Liverpool and London in *Redburn,* Book XVI of *Pierre* describes New York in terms of an inferno: the hack-driver is Charon, the streets are paved with the hearts of the dead, the night people being held at a police precinct are "a base congregation . . . poured out upon earth through the vile vomitory of some unmentionable cellar." Chapter XXIV of *Israel Potter* is a description of London

as a "cindery City of Dis." Like T. S. Eliot in *The Waste Land,* Melville relates the passage of thousands of people across London Bridge
to souls crossing into hell: "At times the mass, receiving some mysterious impulse far in the rear, away among the coiled thoroughfares out of
sight, would start forward with a spasmodic surge. It seemed as if some
squadron of centaurs, on the thither side of Phlegethon, with charge on
charge, was driving tormented humanity, with all its chattels, across."[36]
But the city could not long hold the attention of Melville, who required
exotic places to inspire him, especially the Pacific islands where he
started his journeying when he was a most impressionable youth. A
paragraph from *Israel Potter* illustrates how his imagination was pulled
from the city to the island:

> Whichever way the eye turned, no tree, no speck of any green
> thing was seen—no more than in smithies. All laborers, of what-
> soever sort, were hued like the men in foundries. The black vistas
> of streets were as the galleries in coal mines; the flagging, as flat
> tomb-stones, minus the consecration of moss, and worn heavily
> down, by sorrowful tramping, as the vitreous rocks in the cursed
> Gallipagos, over which the convict tortoises crawl. (208)

The Galapagos Islands, described in a set of ten sketches called "The
Encantadas," are at the other extreme from the Valley of the Typees
and, though Melville visited them before the South Pacific islands, he
saves them for last to bring us to the bottom-most point in his passage
from paradise to hell. If the Valley of the Typees is the world before the
fall, the Galapagos are the world after the fall.

For unrelieved gloom and concentrated images of despair and deprivation, Melville's "The Encantadas" invites comparison with the first
two books of *Paradise Lost* and T. S. Eliot's *The Waste Land.* Other
travellers before Melville had been struck by the infernal nature of the
Galapagos Islands: the captain of H. M. S. *Beagle* called them "a fit
shore for Pandemonium"; and his distinguished passenger, Charles
Darwin, also resorted to literary imagery when he described "the
strange Cyclopean scene," which reminded him of "those parts of Staf-
fordshire, where the great iron-foundries are most numerous"—
another interesting association of hell with industrial places to be
included with Blake's "dark Satanic mills" and Melville's own "Tartarus of Maids."[37] Perhaps Darwin related the topography of the
Galapagos to the description of Hell in *Paradise Lost,* a copy of which
he had with him on the *Beagle.* Melville certainly relied on Miltonic
terms for his work, which has many echoes from *Paradise Lost.*

The Galapagos constituted for Melville an image of both the beginning and the end of the world, the "clinker-bound" foundation of creation as well as a place "looking much as the world at large might, after a penal conflagration."[38] Darwin, too, had observed that "the archipelago is a little world within itself," but, while Darwin found this to be most useful for the pursuit of his scientific inquiries into the independent evolution of finches in a limited area, Melville saw the islands, philosophically, as "evilly enchanted ground" with its principal animal life being hellish reptiles. In the giant tortoise Melville found an animal equal to the whale for imagistic development. He saw them as the chief denizens of hell, doomed forever to "lasting sorrow and penal hopelessness" as they drag their ponderous bulk across "the baked heart of the charmed isles . . . in quest of pools of scanty water." Though utterly desolate, the islands teemed with animal life, a fact also observed by Darwin: "one is astonished at the amount of creative force, if such an expression may be used, displayed on these small, barren, and rocky islands." Melville could see nothing "creative" in the countless snakes, spiders, iguanas, tortoises, and birds on the islands but rather an image to confirm the literary tradition that hell teems with the souls of the damned. "Sketch Third" and "Sketch Fourth" of "The Encantadas" are devoted to a description of Rock Rodondo, a 250-foot height from which the entire archipelago can be seen. "Sketch Fourth" is ironically entitled "A Pisgah View from the Rock" and is headed by two lines from the *Faerie Queene* that allude to the Red Cross Knight's vision of saints enjoying eternity in the New Jerusalem. What Melville sees from Rock Rodondo is neither the Promised Land nor the Celestial City "wherein eternall peace and happinesse doth dwell," nor the paradisal valley Tommo had seen from his cliff in *Typee,* but an "archipelago of aridities, without inhabitant, history, or hope of either in all time to come." The view may be as grand as "the universe from Milton's celestial battlements," but the place is in fact "a boundless watery Kentucky," a state Melville in *The Confidence-Man* calls "The Bloody Ground." The Rock itself is the perch of thousands of aquatic fowl who are arranged not according to some natural zoological order but in an infernal hierarchy like Milton's fallen angels—"in order of their magnitude . . . thrones, princedoms, powers, dominating one above another in senatorial array."

No paradisal valley graces the Enchanted Isles but rather a phallic pillar teeming with rapacious animal life. The few human beings who have attempted to live there are condemned to the horrors of isolation and survival. All the men have been tyrants and murderers, one having earned the name of Dog-King because he tried to keep his captives under control with a "dog-regiment"; another, Oberlus, so acclimated to wickedness that "he struck strangers much as if he were a volcanic creature thrown up by the same convulsion which exploded into sight the isle." Like Caliban, owning Sycorax as his mother and the tortoises as his companions, Oberlus is an earth-bound figure whose function it is to reduce other men to his own condition; when he can entice wandering seamen to stay with him on his island, he sets them "to breaking the caked soil; transporting upon their backs loads of loamy earth, scooped up in moist clefts among the mountains . . . and in all respects converts them into reptiles at his feet—plebeian garter-snakes to their Lord Anaconda." Are the Galapagos Islands Melville's America, where slavery thrives and there is no Prospero to administer justice and defend the innocent? The only woman on the islands is Hunilla, a pitiful figure who barely survives after her husband and brother drown before her eyes. Most horrible of all are "two unnamed events" which befell her when passing whale-boats called: "let them abide between her and her God. In nature, as in law, it may be libelous to speak some truths."

"The Encantadas" is Melville's penultimate inferno, his very last being the impression of Palestine he renders in the long narrative poem *Clarel,* written over two decades and published privately in 1876. The island symbolism growing out of Melville's own experience is replaced in this work by the traditional Christian pilgrimage to the Holy Land, but the result remains the same. The grand irony of *Clarel* is that a place, specifically Jerusalem, that was once the source of great spiritual truth, the origin of the hope of heaven, is now a wasteland, stony and barren, "a burial ground of ashes." Stark wilderness is "the root metaphor of the poem," writes Walter Bezanson in his definitive edition of the poem.[39] The earnest seeker after truth is lost, finally, in Jerusalem, and there never comes to him "a message from beneath the stone." Two echoes of earlier works recall Melville's usual contrast of paradise and hell: one character observes that for barrenness and aridity the Holy Land compares only to the Galapagos; another speaker recalls his stay in an "Eden, isled, impurpled," a reference to Tommo's visit in the Valley of the Typees. *Clarel* has invited comparison with Eliot's *The Waste Land* for its "unspeakably desolate impression of aridity."[40] But Melville's poem is a terribly diffuse and crabbed work, with endless philosophical conversations and no effective narrative to hold it together. Dealing with islands and ships somehow seemed to concentrate Melville's powers of adapting the traditional symbolism of paradise and hell to real places.

The Galapagos were the first Pacific islands Melville visited in his sailing days and the last he used in his writings. Before he could bring himself to use them as his penultimate model of hell, he had to exhaust the world in search of a paradisal place that would incorporate both the male and female principles, both action and rest. This happy combination he was never to find anywhere. He discovered that Eden is a female-dominated place, a valley trapping and incapacitating the male hero—the wounded Tommo, the autoerotic Donjalolo and bachelors, the ineffectual Pierre. The male-dominated place is also horrible, because male rapacity devastates the landscape and subjects woman to sexual tyranny, such as experienced by Hunilla and the maidens working in the paper mill. Men at sea turn ships into tyrannical miniature worlds. As it goes about the business of rendering oil from whales, the *Pequod* in *Moby-Dick* resembles a floating inferno, "freighted with savages, and laden with fire, and burning a corpse, and plunging into that blackness of darkness." The production of oil from the body of an animal makes whaling as evil as the production of paper in "The Tartarus of Maids." Imagery of sexual rapacity are also common to both accounts. The final operation in the "cutting-up" of the whale is performed by the mincer, a sailor dressed in the skin of the whale's penis, who cuts pieces of blubber into the try-pots, which are themselves obliquely compared to the womb. At the mill, "a long, glittering scythe" tears the rags ceaselessly fed to it by the pallid girls. The infernal world of the Galapagos is another place dominated by the tyrannical male, whose phallic power is represented by the Rock Rodondo. The curse of being alive is best symbolized by the giant tortoises that, once having been seen, cannot be expunged from the memory of Melville even when he is far away in the Edenic Berkshires many years later:

> . . . when at such times I sit me down in the mossy head of some deep-wooded gorge, surrounded by prostrate trunks of blasted pines and recall, as in a dream, my other and far-distant rovings in the baked heart of the charmed isles; and remember the sudden glimpses of dusky shells, and long languid necks protruded from the leafless thickets. . . . (153)

Here Melville bitterly reverses the common romantic theme of the happily recollected landscape, such as Wordsworth expresses in these lines from "Tintern Abbey":

> oft in lonely rooms, and 'mid the din

> Of towns and cities, I have owed to them,
> In hours of weariness, sensations sweet.

Melville denies, too, the romantic confidence that paradise still abides, the confidence, expressed again by Wordsworth, that earth is

> nowhere unembellished by some trace
> Of that first Paradise whence man was driven.
> *(The Prelude* III.111–2)

Both the Valley of the Typees, with which Melville begins, and the rock-bound Galapagos, with which he ends, present no permanent home to the questing hero. Melville's mind was driven by what he termed the"two-strandedness" of everything; his use of place, of paradise and hell, of land and sea, is at one with other aspects of his writing, with characterization, for example, of which John Seelye observes: "Where contrasting characterization in Shakespeare's plays suggests an affirmative balance, in Melville it is often paradoxical, mutually destructive."[41] No place is good for Melville; only motion matters, the incessant motion of the sea and the ship at sea. Abiding in a place leads to loss of identity, which Melville often expresses as a trance-like state when the spirit "becomes diffused through time and space." The fatal trance may occur at sea as well as on land; hovering "over Descartian vortices," Ishmael almost falls from the masthead into the sea. Death is to be sucked down into the unmoving center of the vortex, while moving with the vortex is the law of life for Melville, as it was the law of the universe for Descartes.[42] Ishmael's escape from the vortex in which the *Pequod* disappears is truly miraculous, but his escape leaves him no better off than he was when he started his journey, for he is now once more "another orphan." The ever-moving Ahab is the tragic hero on whom Melville expends his most loving attention, and another is Taji, "the unreturning wanderer," who at the close of *Mardi* plunges into the vast, undifferentiated "endless sea." The philosophy of Old Bardianna in *Mardi* teaches that "to stop, were to sink in space," and Babbalanja, his expositor, adds the thought, "there is no place but the universe; no limit but the limitless; no bottom but the bottomless" (400). The sentiment is repeated definitively in *Moby-Dick* at the point when another inveterate wanderer, Bulkington, stands at the helm of the *Pequod* on the night of her departure: "But as in landlessness alone resides the highest truth, shoreless, indefinite as God—so, better is it to perish in that howling infinite, than be ingloriously dashed upon the lee, even if that were safety!" The rediscovery of Melville in the twentieth century owes much to his having so movingly expressed the loss of Eden and the consequent feeling of "cosmic homelessness," as Camus later named it.

5

PLACE AND NATIONAL LITERATURE
The American and
His Land

THAT PLACES MAY HAVE A SIGNIFICANT INFLUENCE on a writer is incontestable, though the proposition does not hold for all writers. That a geographical region with distinguishing features may have an influence on a number of writers is less incontestable. There is little doubt about sub-regional influences, such as the Lake District on English romantic poets, Concord on American transcendentalists, New York City on the Knickerbockers; but the more extensive the region and the wider its variety of places, the less precise is the line from environmental cause to literary result and the more we must call on other factors—local history and culture, dialect and folkways—to establish the regional quality of a body of literature.

That a great landmass can have an influence on the literature of a populous nation over hundreds of years is even less incontestable. Yet so great is the prompting of national pride that such claims are frequently made by the literary critics of newly established nations. No national literature ever generated more faith in the influence of geography on art than the infant American literature. Especially after the War of 1812 nationalism and romantic idealism combined to produce a theory that the northern American hemisphere in all its size, topographical variety, and unspoiled primitive purity could not fail to shape a unique American character and a set of unique American achievements. "The nervous, rocky West is intruding a new and continental element into the national mind, and we shall yet have an American genius," Emerson declared in a lecture called "The Young American." He saw the land "as a commanding and increasing power on the citizen, the sanative and Americanizing influence, which promises to disclose new virtues for ages to come." Even Thoreau could sometimes fall in with the popular view of the American scene as a symbol of, if

not precisely an influence on, American philosophy, poetry, and religion; in the essay "Walking" he writes: "I trust that we shall be more
imaginative, that our thoughts will be clearer, fresher, and more
ethereal, as our sky,—our understanding more comprehensive and
broader, like our plains,—our intellect generally on a grander scale,
like our thunder and lightning, our rivers and mountains and forests,—
and our hearts shall even correspond in breadth and depth and gran-
deur to our inland seas." Thoreau and Emerson were merely reflecting
what was more extravagantly said in hundreds of patriotic addresses:
that American literary achievements would be greater than Europe's
because American peaks were higher than Olympus and the Hudson
River broader than the Thames.[1] Of course not all Americans went
along with nationalistic pride of place. Longfellow, in his novel
Kavanagh, Holmes in the poem "Astreae," and James Russell Lowell,
in a number of essays, refused to accept geographical determinism in
literary matters. Lowell ironically called for a new system of criticism
in which a "want of sublimity would be inexcusable in a native of the
mountains" and authors would be required to supply on the title-page
of their works "an exact topographical survey of their native districts."[2]

Later in the century theories of geographical determinism came to
the support of nationalist thought, culminating in the thesis advanced
by Frederick Jackson Turner in "The Significance of the Frontier in
American History" that "the vast free space of the continent" was a
decisive factor in the formation of American character, that democracy
was "born of free" land. Even though Turner's frontier thesis has been
seriously challenged by historians, traces of it can be found in the
claims some literary critics still make for the influence of space on
American literature. Protagonists in the early novelists—Brown,
Cooper, Bird—are denominated "the hero in space" by R. W. B. Lewis
in *The American Adam;* Charles Olson begins his book on Melville
with the declaration, "I take SPACE to be the central fact to man born
in America"; Gay Wilson Allen attempts to show that "space-
empathy" in Whitman's theory and practice is the natural inheritance
of any number of twentieth-century American poets—Hart Crane, Archibald MacLeish, Robinson Jeffers, Wallace Stevens.[3] The same idea
is more discreetly developed in Glauco Cambon's proposition that
nineteenth-century American writers "were exhilarated by so much
geographic and cultural space to conquer" that their successors—
Robinson, Crane, Williams, Stevens—have had to deal with space in
one way or another.[4]

Curiously, environmental determinism has lingered longer among

students of literature than among social scientists. Perhaps the influence of Hippolyte Taine accounts for this, though of his three factors
conditioning a people's literature, milieu is the least stressed and it is
illustrated only by some very general notions of the influence of climate.[5] Geographical determinism lives on in the concept of "spirit of
place," a phrase popularized by D. H. Lawrence in a book dealing,
significantly, with American literature, *Studies in Classic American
Literature:*

> Every continent has its own great spirit of place. Every people
> is polarized in some particular locality, which is home, the home-
> land. Different places on the face of the earth have different vital
> effluence, different vibration, different chemical exhalation, differ-
> ent polarity with different stars: call it what you like. But the spirit
> of place is a great reality. The Nile valley produced not only the
> corn, but the terrific religions of Egypt.[6]

In an earlier version of the book we find the claim that "all art partakes
of the Spirit of Place in which it is produced" and that the American
continent "has produced us the familiar American classics."[7] But with
places having such mysterious effects as effluences and vibrations, it is
no wonder that Lawrence could not demonstrate in any detail the
influence of the American continent on the writers he selects for treatment. Spirit of place is an idea that is more mystical than geographical;
it falls just short of the *genius loci* of antiquity, and indeed Lawrence
uses the classical term when he speaks of "the demon of the continent"
and the "pure daimon" of a great locality. In an age of unremitting
scientific realism the writer does not have the remnants of classical
mythology at his disposal, as, for example, Keats might have in some
mountain glen on Mount Latmos. Consequently, the American continent has been hailed as a new source of magical feeling for place. Carl
Jung, at about the same time as Lawrence, claimed that the local
ancestor-spirits of the original inhabitants of North and South America
cannot fail to have an influence on European newcomers to the land.[8]

Racial theory gets drawn into Lawrence's discussion when he
asserts that "The Island of Great Britain had a wonderful terrestrial
magnetism or polarity of its own, which made the British people."
Indeed, Lawrence's emphasis is more on race than place, just as in
Taine's theory of the influence of environment on literature, land and
moment are simply the occasions of race. There was precedent for this

line of thought in romantic notions that national as well as individual character is shaped by landscape. Thus Byron in *Don Juan:*

And as the soil is, so the heart of man.

Afric is all the sun's, and as her earth
Her human clay is kindled. (IV.55–6)

Patriotic Englishmen were persuaded that British landscape helped create a new kind of literature, just as in their turn American critics saw the vastness of a new continent as the chief determinant in American character. In his earliest work, *The Poetry of Architecture* (1837), John Ruskin tried to prove that national differences in cottage architecture are a direct result of variations in landscape. He later gave up the idea that landscape is "a gigantic instrument of soul culture," admitting in *Modern Painters* that there is no necessary relation between landscape and feeling.[9] But the idea has persisted. Typical is Norman Douglas's insistence on the "civilizing agency" of woodlands: "Who will deny that forests . . . exercise a benignant power . . . upon the mind of a people; that music, architecture, and other generous arts have in forests sought, and found, high inspiration; that some of the sublimest efforts of literary genius could not have been conceived in regions as denuded of timber as Italy, Greece, and Spain are now?"[10] Following Douglas and Lawrence, Lawrence Durrell devotes an essay to the proposition that since "human beings are expressions of their landscapes" a political science could be formed from "the intimate knowledge of landscape, if developed scientifically"; a few minutes' identification with a landscape could give one the key to a national character: "if you sit quite still in the landscape-diviner's pose—why, the whole rhythm of ancient Egypt rises up from the damp cold sand."[11] The well-known ecologist René Dubos calls these remarks "a caricature of the environmentalist point of view" and supplies a corrective: "The patterns of behavior and taste that characterize racial, regional, and national groups are influenced by the ways of life as much as by physical surroundings, by cultural history as much as by natural history"[12] Dubos advances the counter-proposition that "landscape is shaped by human activities," that men determine the appearance of landscape through pursuing their needs and tastes (128). It is this principle rather than Durrell's that Henry Miller adopts in his book on Greece, *The Colossus of Maroussi,* even though Durrell was responsible for Miller's visiting Greece in the first place. Miller discovered that man's history "is written into the earth," and therefore "The Greek earth opens before me like the Book of Revelation."

The deterministic relation between a civilization and the physical conditions of its setting should be left to historians and geographers. Literary discussions of this subject, as we have seen, tend to propagate only vague and undemonstrable generalizations. Literary criticism does better to work with the opposite premise that man has an undisputed influence on his environment, which he alters in accord with principles his culture has fostered in him, literature, of course, being one of the creators and purveyors of that culture. This approach has become popular in American studies since 1950 with Henry Nash Smith's *Virgin Land: The American West as Symbol and Myth,* a book that reverses Turner by assuming that the conception of the West as "the garden of the world," not the West itself as a geographical area, has been a decisive factor in American history and literature. In *The Machine in the Garden* Leo Marx shows how the garden we wanted America to be was in reality destroyed by our passion for industrial progress. The relation of people to land is finally a product of the interaction of three factors: the basic physical nature of the environment, the preconceptions with which it is approached by its inhabitants, and the changes man makes in it. Turner addressed himself to the first of these, Smith to the second, and Marx to the last.

The physical nature of the environment is perhaps the least important of the three. The most striking feature of the American landmass was not at first its size, which was not fully known until much later in the history of the transcontinental migration, but its pristine state, its lack of civilized improvements, and its potential for the kind of human occupation that Europeans were predisposed to assume for it. Although Americans subsequently saw their continent as unique, it was at the beginning no different from other unoccupied frontiers offering people a new chance in life and freer social circumstances. But no new relation to land was contemplated. As European settlers saw it, the only choice was to convert the wilderness into a copy of their native lands or extract what they could from the wilderness and leave it.

Upon individual and family hopes was built the conception of America as a fresh start for mankind, the place on earth for "the old millennial hope" to take shape in, and like all utopias it was not fleshed out with very much concrete detail. Seizing and developing the land occupied the hands of the settlers, but their minds were exercised by the renewal of individual, family, and society in America. The land itself was almost casually assumed, for the ideal was more important than the actual place in which it was to be realized. "The United States," writes Wyndham Lewis, "is rather a site for the development of an idea of political and religious freedom than a mystical *terre sacrée* for its sons, upon the French model."[13] The title of a poem by Wallace Stevens, "Description without Place," suggests the manner in which America existed for generations of settlers:

> Description is
> Composed of a sight indifferent to the eye.
>
> It is an expectation, a desire,
> A palm that rises up beyond the sea . . .
> The future is description without place.

It is natural for people to expect great things from new places, to exaggerate both the good and bad qualities of places they have not yet experienced. The deliberate manner in which Europeans came to settle in America inevitably led to their forming many *a priori* ideas about their destination. Having chosen to emigrate, they were bound to rationalize their decision both to themselves and to those who elected to stay behind. A sharp distinction between the two worlds was thus encouraged, with the Old World delimited by realistic details and the New World adumbrated by hearsay and wishful dreams. There were plenty of obvious faults to be seen in the Old World but only speculations of what might be found in the New. Immigrants were thus forced to conceive of America before experiencing it, and consequently preconceptions of its physical qualities far outstripped reality. It was ironical that many immigrants later discovered that they had exchanged a strong feeling for places in the Old World, unsatisfactory though their lives had been there, for an abstract, unlocalized ideal in the New World. The American experience often meant the postponement of tangible realities for the prospective enjoyment of some future condition; the future of the land was most important since its past hardly mattered. The notion settlers had of the American landscape was projective rather than descriptive. There was little chance for the development of permanent relations to the land since Americans who lived for a time in one place soon moved to a frontier farther west with a fresh set of expectations. The old farm wife in Hamlin Garland's "Mrs. Ripley's Trip" had the same experience as a European immigrant returning to the Old World when, after twenty-three years living on the prairie, she revisits her girlhood home in New York State: "to see the old folks, an' the hills where we played, an' eat apples off the old tree down by the well. I've had them trees an' hills in my mind days and days." Looking forward to a new place and looking back at the old place is a universal American experience. Because it was not possible for Americans to develop much natural feeling for their new surroundings in a short time full of changes, they continued to hold onto their preconceptions, which duly found their way into the "official" ideology spread by mass education, political oratory, and advertising. The literature of the new nation also strengthened and perpetuated images that were slow in being corrected by experience.

American literature has given form to feelings about the land in the way it has responded to actual experiences of the land as these became part of American history. The vague expectations of immigrants were attached to three principal images of the New World as a garden, a wilderness, and a place of treasure. The chance for a new life on what seemed to be the virgin soil of a fresh new continent aroused in Europeans the racial memory of mankind's pastoral past in the classical Arcadia and the Biblical Garden of Eden. The risks of surviving in a primitive land, on the one hand, and the promise of freedom in surroundings entirely different from Europe's, on the other, were expressed in the ambiguous image of America as a wilderness. The possibility of quick fortune supported the conception of America as a place of treasure, an Eldorado where great riches could be taken from the land with little trouble. None of these images could stand as true representations of the New World, though none was entirely false either, and each served to feed the desire to migrate to the new continent in the first place and to continue its settlement westward. None looked toward a new and original relation to environment; each drew on customary European practices of occupying and exploiting new lands. Each ideal prompted a different treatment of the land: the garden wanted cultivation, the wilderness taming, the place of treasure quick consumption. Each was basically opposed to the others: the garden encroaches on the wilderness, the wilderness in time reclaims the garden, and Eldorado ever extends its domain over the garden for its produce and over the wilderness for its timber, furs, ore, and oil. Each has contributed imagistic materials for the value systems that have competed for dominance over the American economy, the garden image underlying various forms of agrarianism from Jefferson to the Southern Fugitives, Eldorado inspiring business aims and a sort of folk capitalism, and the wilderness serving as the symbolical setting of romantic primitivism. The relation of the American to his land is a history of the conflict of these concepts.

AMERICA AS ELDORADO

Of the three preconceptions of America, Eldorado is the oldest and the least specific in its imagery because the place where the riches are to be found counts for less than the riches themselves, and these tend to become a rather abstract end. Phantasy more often than realism dictates the description of places where treasure may be found. The one constant is the imagery of gold and silver, a detail that persists even when the valuable commodity is no longer precious metal. Often the presence of gold on the continent was a hoax. Captain John Smith shrewdly observed as much when he reported of his voyage to New England in 1616: "For our Golde, it was rather the Masters device to get a voyage that projected it, then any knowledge hee had at all of any such matter."[14] But the presence of gold was not recognized as an illusion by the earlier Spanish and Italian explorers who first described the American Eldorado. Their association of the new land with mineral wealth arose quite naturally from their assumption that it was part of Asia, the place of fabled riches, that they had discovered, and the abundance of gold ornaments in the possession of the natives of Central and South America seemed to confirm that assumption and encouraged the idea that gold mines must be abundant. Columbus, as Walt Whitman observes in "Passage to India" was responsible for

> Spreading around with every look of thine a golden world,
> Enhuing it with gorgeous hues.

In a book on the New World written by Peter Martyr in 1533 and translated into English by a man appropriately named Richard Eden, a claim is made that an entire district in Hispaniola was veined with gold from a "livinge tree . . . that . . . spreadeth and springeth from the roote by the softe pores and passages of the earth, putteth forth branches even unto the uppermost part of the earth, & ceaseth not until it discover itself unto the open aire: At whiche time it shineth forth certaine beautifull colours instead of flowers, rounde stones of golden earth

instead of fruites, and thinne plates instead of leaves."[15] The transformation of vegetation into precious metal is a pretty fair image of the
hopes of many newcomers to convert the natural phenomena of the
New World into abstract forms of wealth.

The "search for the mine" was a popular motif of pre-colonial
literature and ever after continued to be a "darling subject" of American literature.[16] In his description of Virginia as "Earth's only paradise," Michael Drayton points out to prospective colonists that as well
as having "the fruitful'st soil" it is also the place "To get the pearl and
gold"; a court masque of the time portrayed Virginian princes reclining
in a gold mine.[17] Over one hundred years later the search for the mine
was still going strong. "The people are all mine-mad," observed William Byrd on his travels through Virginia, which he reported in *A
Journey to the Land of Eden* in 1733. "As you ride along the woods,
you see all the large stones knocked to pieces."[18] Although he had an
eye for the beauty of the land and respect for its agricultural uses, Byrd
himself was not a little smitten with the mining fever. He named his
20,000 acres on the border of Virginia and North Carolina the "Land of
Eden," but he was less impressed with its greenery than with its potential for mining copper: "All my hopes were in the riches that might lie
underground, there being many goodly tokens of mines" (396). It was
most fitting that a river in which the stones "promised abundance of
metal" should be named by him the Potosi, after the center of the
fabulous Bolivian silver mines. The search for buried riches on
America's east coast rivals the better-known Western gold rushes of a
later date. In one Maryland county alone (Montgomery) there are sev-
enty abandoned mines. Preoccupation with religious matters did not
diminish the quest for gold in the North. In his "Life of John Eliot"
Cotton Mather found an argument for white supremacy in the fact that
the Indians never developed the deposits of iron and copper on their
land:

> These abject Creatures, live in a Country full of Mines; we have
> already made entrance upon our Iron; and in the very Surface of
> the Ground among us, 'tis thought there lies Copper enough to
> supply all this World; besides other Mines hereafter to be exposed;
> but our shiftless Indians were never Owners of so much as a Knife,
> till we come among them.

Even such a champion of agrarianism as Thomas Jefferson listed mining before farming in his inventory of the assets of the state of Virginia.

Sometimes the images of mining and farming were interchanged; Judge Temple, in Cooper's *The Pioneers,* describes his estate as a "mine of comfort and wealth." The passion for mining often weakened the motive for farming. Byrd noticed that Virginia settlers neglected "to make corn" and starved their families "in hopes to live in great plenty thereafter" from mining successes. Large-scale farming, with its use of heavy machinery and its calculated exhaustion of the soil, is a kind of mining operation. As early as 1915 Liberty Hyde Bailey observed, "Farming has been very much a mining process."[19]

The conversion of landscape into riches has always bothered some sensitive Americans. Washington Irving is careful to point out that in contemplating the lush fields of the Van Tassel farm, Ichabod Crane thinks only "how they might be readily turned into cash." From what he knew of his neighbors, Thoreau could guess that a beautiful pond like Walden might well have been drained "for the mud at its bottom" by the typical American farmer, "whose fiields bear no crops, whose meadows no flowers, whose trees no fruit, but dollars."[20] The ancestors of the hero in Thomas Pynchon's *Gravity's Rainbow* converted Berkshire timberland "into paper—toilet paper, banknote stock, newsprint—a medium or ground for shit, money, and the Word." Excrement is "our predominant way of viewing the world," writes Theodore Roszak:

> Today, when "realistic" people look at nature around them— mountains, forests, lakes, rivers—what is it they see? Not divine epiphanies, but cash values, investments, potential contributions to the GNP, great glowing heaps of money, the crude shit-wealth of the world.[21]

As a generic place Eldorado has no value apart from its capability of being reduced to an abstract form of wealth by some extractive process. Land and its good are separable, and once the treasure has been extracted—whether it be gold, timber, oil, or crops—Eldorado is abandoned since there is no question of remaining in a worthless place. American literature is thus rich in abandoned places, especially sites ravaged by mining operations. As early in 1849 in *Mardi,* Melville describes one of these in South America: "A vast and silent bay, belted by silent villages:—gaunt dogs howling over grassy thresholds at stark corpses of old age and infancy." In *Roughing It* Mark Twain deplores the "disfigurements far and wide over California" and the waste of humanity caused by gold and silver mining. In *Burning Daylight* Jack

London observes the same kind of destruction wrought by the Gold Rush in Alaska. The Western mining town is probably the most original native expression of the mining craze in America. Established overnight and equipped with the crudest amenities of high living, and just as quickly deserted when the gold runs out, the abandoned mining town is the symbolical end-product of American Eldorado. It is the prototype of other money-making places that have outlived their promise—the abandoned farm, factory, store, gas station.

A story by Scott Fitzgerald, appropriately entitled "The Diamond as Big as the Ritz," perfectly characterizes the dream of America as a place of untold hidden treasure which the lucky wanderer finds and selfishly holds for himself and his family against all others. Fitz-Norman Culpeper Washington is the all-American name of Fitzgerald's opportunist who amasses a fortune by selling chips from the fabulous diamond-mountain he has discovered in Montana. His son, Braddock Washington, with this wealth and the services of a band of Southern ex-slaves, a landscape gardener, and an architect, builds a "house of jewels" where he lives a life of exquisite luxury and seclusion with his family. But wealth corrupts the Washingtons; in order to preserve his world from incursion by outsiders Braddock commits murder and forces his children to lead barren lives, without friends and love. For a while he is "Prometheus Enriched," who is able to make earth serve his vainest wish, but he is finally foiled by an Italian aviator who happens on the mountain retreat, escapes from the cage where such intruders are kept, and returns with an air fleet to destroy the palace and slave quarters. Braddock Washington and his family die in the fire he sets to destroy the mountain, which turns into "a black waste from which blue smoke arose slowly, carrying off with it what remained of vegetation and human flesh."

Like so many other American writers, Fitzgerald was fascinated by the Eldorado image but finally rejects it with the implication that the quest for Eldorado leads to the destruction of the land and human values as well. The selection of the name Washington for his treasure-seeker and an Italian aviator as his opponent suggests that the story is a fable of American history second time around. A now unselfish Columbus rediscovers America and delivers it from the spoliation of its prime hero, the entrepreneurial Washington who has a passion for extracting wealth from the land. In a wider context, Braddock Washington is among those monomaniacal heroes of American literature who seek the power of tyrant-kings over some corner of the earth and its people: Dr. Rappaccini, who rules his magic garden, his daughter and her prospective husband; Colonel Sutpen, who attempts to set up a planter dynasty in Yoknapatawpha County with the help of his Haitian slaves and French architect; and Melville's Creole Dog-King in "The Encantadas," a kind of archetypal colonial imperialist whose plan it is "to lead colonists into distant regions and assume political preeminence over them."

In the Eldoradan use of land, both land and the people engaged in its exploitation are wasted or reduced to some infernal condition. To participate in the California Gold Rush is like "going . . . three thousand miles nearer to hell," Thoreau wrote in his Journal, and Melville calls the South American mines "a golden Hell," in *Mardi*. The *Pequod*, exploiting the sea for its whales, is described as a floating inferno, a "red hell," in which the blubber is rendered; of Stubb's digging ambergris out of the carcass of a whale, it is said in Chapter 91: "You would almost have thought he was digging a cellar there in the sea. . . . His boat's crew were all in high excitement, eagerly helping their chief, and looking as anxious as gold-hunters." The gold mine in Bret Harte's *The Story of a Mine* is a lurid scene, "a heavy Rembrandtish mass of black shadow. . . . The furnace fire painted the faces of the men an Indian red"; the mine claim originates in a murder perpetrated by a Satanic figure.

AMERICA AS A GARDEN

While compulsion, sin, and death are associated with Eldorado, the image of the garden elicits innocence and a sentimental as well as practical regard for land. The idealization of America as the garden of the world sprang from a latter-day hope of mankind in the possibility of an earthly paradise where both material and spiritual goals could finally be realized. America seemed to be the long-lost Eden that Christian scholars had sought the location of for centuries. Paradise was sometimes localized in Europe, in the English countryside, for example, but not with the clear force it could have in a fresh new continent that was innocent of the evils of Europe. If John of Gaunt, In *Richard II*, is afraid that political corruption was about to engulf England, "this other Eden, demi-paradise," Michael Drayton was confident that Virginia was "Earth's onely Paradise." America was the last clear localization of millennial hopes in the form of an agrarian society. Its most loved hero was the young countryman Lincoln, not the entrepreneurial Washington, Lincoln being identified with clearing the land rather than drawing a profit from it. Whitman sensed the chord to which Americans would respond when he pictures the coffin of Lincoln being carried "over the breast of the spring, the land . . . amid the grass in the fields . . . passing the yellow-spear'd wheat" in "When Lilacs Last in the Dooryard Bloom'd."

As a distillation of the Biblical and classical pastoral ideals, the New World Eden, because it was of the present as well as a reflection of the golden past, necessarily incorporated a practical principle, the conversion of virgin land into productive fields through hard work. Man being fallen, the garden could no longer be a natural, God-given place, but a farm-garden cultivated by labor; and the occupant of the garden could no longer be like Spenser's "salvage man" living in a natural state of uncivilized innocence, but a European applying technology and order to an individually owned piece of land. Religious principle confirmed the cultivation of the land to support a European standard of living, for Christian conscience made it impossible to accept the new land as an unearned Eden. Crèvecoeur thought it was sinful to live off "the natural fecundity of the earth," while on the other hand "the simple cultivation of the earth purifies" the soul.[22] "What is a farm," asks Emerson in *Nature* , "but a mute gospel?" As well as serving religious and economic ends, the agrarian use of the land sorted well with the revolutionary ideology of the eighteenth century: If Europe was doomed because of its aristocratic, urban, mercantile corruption, America would be the home of a society of self-sufficient yeoman farmers, the backbone of a strong republic. "Those who labor in the earth are the chosen people of God," wrote Jefferson, while "the mobs of great cities" are like sores to the "support of pure government."[23]

Like Eldorado, the farm-garden also marched across the continent with successive waves of settlers, from Massachusets Bay to the Connecticut Valley in the seventeenth century, to the trans-Appalachian grasslands in the eighteenth century, and in the nineteenth to the Midwestern prairies, the Western plains, and California. The procession persists even today in America's last frontier, Alaska, where settlers start seedlings indoors in order to be ready for the short growing season. The garden ideal was an important emotional spur in the process of transforming wilderness into settlement, determining the shape of the landscape, the locations of clearings, dwellings, roads, towns. The land area involved was tremendous, and much of America became "a well-ordered green garden magnified to continental size," "the world's largest-scale utopian experiment in creating a nation on the model of a pastoral garden."[24] The radical transformation of the landscape could not fail to have a profound effect on American character as well as on the political fortunes of the country. The successful carving out of a continental empire against the competition of the Spanish and French was made possible by the fierce agrarianism of American settlers, the passion to own and farm the land. The garden image proved to be a more effective instrument of national politics than the Eldorado image. Unlike classical forms of pastoralism, the American variety was revolutionary: Its encouragement of widely scattered small freeholders strengthened the democratic principle and fostered radical causes.

But, having served its purpose, the idea of America as the Eden of the New World, like its Biblical prototype, also "sank to grief." Quite early, New England settlers abandoned poor farm land and turned to trade, fishing, and industry for their livelihood. Despite his pastoral idealism, Crèvecoeur had to choose Nantucket as his prime example of successful colonization in the North. Not the soil—the island was barren—but the character of the people in developing the whaling industry accounted for "this happy settlement." By 1904, Henry James was able to write *finis* to agrarianism in New England: "everywhere legible was the hard little historic record of agricultural failure and defeat."[25] In the South the abundance of arable land led, ironically, to farming on a larger scale than was consistent with the democratic ideology of the rest of the country. Crèvecoeur has to admit that in the South "kindness and affection are not the portion of those who till the earth," and Freneau points out in "To Sir Toby" that slavery was a result of "the fruits that spring from vast domains." The plantation, which Southerners like Simms conceived as a model garden in the wilderness, was rejected by Northerners. That left only the West where the pastoral ideal could be achieved. In his last letter Crèvecoeur announces that his farmer will attempt farming in the western wilderness, but Crèvecoeur could not have known that the West (our present Midwest) was to become a great industrial as well as agricultural region and that farming was to become highly industrialized itself. By 1850 there were no subsistence farmers on the prairies.[26] Neither of the two principal agrarian efforts in the United States succeed in fulfilling the pastoral dream because each, to attain practical success, had to resort to large-scale operations that were finally unacceptable, slavery in the South, technology and agribusiness in the West.

The garden image faltered because it had not taken account of American geography, the character of American settlers, and the economics of agriculture. These eventually turned farming in America into big business, successful farmers into entrepreneurs, and unsuccessful farmers into farm labor or city dwellers. The myth of the garden belied

the drudgery of one-crop farming on vast tracts of arable and sometimes semi-arid land and did not foresee the collaboration of agriculture
with the city, where the farmer sold his surplus produce for the machinery he had to use for large-scale cultivation. Not being a farmer to
begin with, the typical immigrant from Europe preferred living in
towns to settling on the land. Indeed, urban population in the Old
Northwest grew at a faster rate than rural population. The man who
chose to farm could not be made into a peasant indefinitely fixed on a
single parcel of land; he was as mobile as the townsman. From the very
beginning of colonization in America settlers prospered only by supple-
menting their farming with income derived from trade, land speculation, and public office. Emerson recognized this when he admitted that
while the American farmer may be "the Caesar, the Alexander of the
soil" he does not get rich by farming but "by other resources, or by
trade, or by getting labor for nothing"; that American farmers are "not
stationary like those of old countries, but always alert to better themselves, and will remove from town to town as a new market opens or a
better farm is to be had."[27] Cooper illustrates the type in Jotham Riddel
of *The Pioneers*, the sort of man, "who changes his county every three
years, his farm every six months, and his occupation every season."
As agriculture prospered more and more in the nineteenth century, the
farmer drew farther and farther away from the soil, often not living on
the land. In these circumstances the soil itself could hardly be imagined
as a mystical substance but instead resembed a crucible in which
chemicals are mixed to produce a marketable commodity. The landscape took on the form not of the cozy European countryside many
immigrants pictured to themselves but of immense stretches of levelled
land without house or hedge or copse. The speed with which agriculture in America moved from the clearing in the woods to illimitable
fields made the garden image inappropriate to describe the American
landscape.

The unpleasant truth is that the pastoral garden image was not the
efficient cause of European settlement on the American continent but
rather its rationalization in acceptable symbols of great emotional
power. The cause was economic and political: the acquisition of wealth
by nations, or, more specifically, by monarchs and their supporters, by
investment corporations and individuals; and the securing of freedom
by dissenting religious and social groups. This conclusion flows from
the assumption that myths do not so much motivate behavior as cor-
roborate behavior already set in motion by other more material causes.

The American experience must not be taken as unique, however.
The history of ruralism in England, while not as dramatically com-

pressed in time nor extended in space, corresponds to, and probably influenced, the American experience. England also had its dream of the garden, its sturdy yeomen, its flight from the land to the city, its transformation of farmers into hired labor. Wherever it occurs, the classical notion of the pastoral life is tenable only as long as the cultivation of the soil remains rather simple and primitive; but as soon as it avails itself of unlimited labor or technological help agriculture becomes an economic activity of great mechanical regularity that inspires no particularly strong feeling for the land it uses except as a commodity to be abandoned once its energy potential is exhausted. "Agriculture started man on his way to modern civilization," writes René Dubos, "but the price was the end of the Arcadian way of life" (259). Agricultural success ironically negates the ideal of the agricultural way of life. The increased productivity of each farm worker and the embarrassing accumulation of agricultural surpluses have reduced the number of Americans engaged in farming to about 4 percent of the total population. Thus, fewer and fewer Americans participate in the so-called good life of the farm-garden. Agriculture is now appropriately known as agribusiness, and agribusiness puts industry on the land, not people; it generates profit in dollars, not a culture based on the land. A program that sought to encourage the attachment of Americans to the land, because of its success, has turned Americans away from the land.

But Arcadia always lives on in the imagination after it ceases to exist as a reality. In fact, in America, "the agrarian myth came to be believed more widely and tenaciously as it became more fictional."[28] Political and economic interests had reason to keep it alive rhetorically, and as late as the 1930s support came from intellectuals in the Southern Agrarian, back-to-earth, and Negro "down home" movements. The post-World War II development of American suburbanism, with its emphasis on the separate plot of profusely planted ground, is a recent expression of the garden image. Suburbia combines the city, where the economic lifeblood is, with the countryside, where the pastoral setting is supposed to survive.

In spite of the honorable position of the garden image in our national ideology, American literature has never been captivated by the farmer and his way of life. Writers may have mourned the encroachment of the machine on the landscape, as Leo Marx has so abundantly documented in his *The Machine in the Garden,* but there could not have been much mourning for the passing of an ideal that had never been more than superficially popular. The historian of "myth of the garden" in America, Henry Nash Smith, must admit that "the agricultural West . . . proved quite intractable as literary material" and the story of the yeoman farmer and his garden "could not be brought to fictional expression."[29]

The pastoral tradition has never really been given new life in American literature. Only lesser literary forms seem to thrive on rural materials: nostalgic poetry like Whittier's "Snowbound," which treats American farm life not directly but only as it is transformed by memory and the enchantment of snow; sentimental romances of Southern plantation life in which aristocratic manners form the true center of interest; and the barnyard variety of humor in local color fiction. The Western celebrates not the farmer but the cattleman, his sworn enemy. The nearest our literature comes to the farmer as hero is the figure of the early settler who had as much to do with the wilderness as with the fields and who was a hunter and warrior as well as a ploughman: Daniel Boone, Davy Crockett, Per Hansa in Rolvaag's *Giants in the Earth*, Orion Outlaw in Caroline Gordon's *Green Centuries*. There are no second-generation farm heroes. When heroes do arise from the farm scene, such as Magnus Derrick in *The Octopus* and Tom Joad in *The Grapes of Wrath*, they are class heroes who are scrupulously removed from ordinaray farming operations. This accords with the western tradition of the great hero—Saul, David, the Redcross Knight—who has his origin "in the ploughman's state" but displays his prowess on the field of battle. The man who stays on the land is no hero.

The anti-pastoral note in American literature is a more dominant strain than the pastoral. In "Rip Van Winkle," that simple story which is now recognized as the prototype of a central myth in American culture, the hero regards his farm as "the most pestilent little piece of ground in the whole country" and allows it to deteriorate "until there was little more left than a mere patch of Indian corn and potatoes." Cooper's woodsman in *The Deerslayer*, Leatherstocking, has nothing but contempt for the clearings made by farmers:

As for farms, they have their uses, and there's them that like to pass their lives on 'em; but what comfort can a man look for in a clearin', that he can't find in double quantities in the forest? . . . It seems to me that the people who live in such places must be always thinkin' of their own inds, and of universal decay . . . the decay that follows waste and violence. . . . Moreover, all is contradiction in the settlements, while all is concord in the woods. . . . No, no— give me the strong places of the wilderness, which is the trees. . . ." (247)

Farm labor "does not make men, but drudges," Emerson wrote in his

Journal on May 20, 1843; "a continent cut up into ten-acre farms is not desirable to the imagination. . . . It is time to have the thing looked into, and with a transpiercing criticism settled whether life is worth having on such terms." Thoreau continues this point of view in the bitterness of his reflections on the early settlers who cleared the land around Concord. A paragraph on Flint's Pond in *Walden* is one of the severest attacks ever made against the conversion of the wilderness to farming: Flint is pictured as a man motivated only by "money values"; he carries the landscape to market; his crops are dollars; and his farm is "a great grease-spot" on the land. As to Flint's descendants, Thoreau's neighbors, it is their misfortune "to have inherited farms, houses, barns, cattle, and farming tools." Farm work turns men into machines, and Thoreau's experiment at Walden was to scale down farming to the simplest level of subsistence in order to allow time for more important activities in the wilderness. Hawthorne's experiment with farming was to join the Fourierist group at Brook Farm for a year, the result of which he records in *The Blithedale Romance* through the viewpoint of Miles Coverdale. As a participant in a cooperative community Coverdale discovers that the farm is a "cold Arcadia" and farming a form of toil that reduces all thought to a brutish level: "The clods of earth, which we so constantly belabored and turned over and over, were never etherealized into thought. Our thoughts, on the contrary, were fast becoming cloddish."[30] So much for Crèvecoeur's belief that virtue may be extracted from the soil. The only thing that makes life bearable for Coverdale is his secret "hermitage, in the heart of the white-pine tree" in the woods near the farm: "It symbolized my individuality." Hawthorne himself had a similar hideaway on a pine-crested hill overlooking the meadows of Concord. "He preferred his hill-top," wrote William Dean Howells, who accompanied Hawthorne on a walk to the spot (probably in Sleepy Hollow Cemetery), "and if he could have his way those arable fields should be grown up to pines too."[31] Hawthorne preferred the wildness of Walden Pond to the pastoral stream that flowed past his house: "A good deal of the mud and river slime had accumulated on my soul; but these bright waters washed them all away."[32] The agrarian experiment in *The Blithedale Romance* comes to a tragic end when Zenobia drowns herself in the oozy depths of the same river.

Hawthorne's neighbor at Pittsfield, Herman Melville, had more experience with farming than either Hawthorne or Thoreau since he lived on a 160-acre farm for thirteen years and worked it to the extent of keeping his family in produce and firewood. Yet Melville considered Arrowhead to be "more of an ornamental place than a farm" and cher-

ished, more than anything else, the view it afforded of Mount Greylock, a neighboring peak that figures in his imagination as the epitome
of wildness.[33] The first half of *Pierre* is an anti-pastoral picture based on
the irony that the lovely Berkshire landscape is honeycombed, underneath, with pits and caves. Just as in *The Blithedale Romance*, the
pastoral scene conceals the destructive passions of the people who
inhabit it. All of Melville's Edens are flawed. His seamen heroes are in
flight from the land and cannot tolerate farming. In *Omoo* the narrator
and his companion, Doctor Long Ghost, after hoeing potatoes for a few
hours, conclude that "although, as a garden recreation, it may be pleasant enough for those who like it—still, long persisted in, the business
becomes excessively irksome." They abandon the field and go off to
hunt bullocks "through some nobly wooded land" in the mountains.

It was not until the latter part of the nineteenth century, with the
new power acquired by the novel through realism, that literature could
do justice to the sad state of the pastoral ideal in America. Hamlin
Garland's *Main-Travelled Roads* is typical of the new point of view
which found "infinite tragedy" in the lives of farm people whom the
world falsely calls "peaceful and pastoral." A further irony of their
situation, according to Garland, is that the "farm-scene, with all its
sordidness, dullness, triviality, and its endless drudgeries" is played
out in the midst of great natural beauty. But beautiful landscape does
not support life, and Garland's people are either broken by toil or
forced to flee. One of his favorite themes is the remorseful return of the
son who abandoned the farm to make an easy fortune in the city. In the
first half of the twentieth century anti-pastoralism was a well-
established theme. Two novelists worth dwelling on, because of their
stature and because they began as eloquent rural apologists and ended
in disillusionment, are Willa Cather and John Steinbeck.

In the literary career of Willa Cather there is a turning from a
pastoral to a mystical relationship to the land. The idealization of farming in *O Pioneers!* and *My Antonia* changes to deep disillusionment in
One of Ours and subsequent works. Alexandra's devotion to the rural
life cannot be dimmed even by the horrible murder of two lovers in an
orchard, and Antonia's romantic diminishment in marriage cannot
shake her love of the land. The trees she plants are like her children,
binding her more strongly to the featureless land she had exchanged for
the beloved homeland of her father in the Old World. Claude Wheeler,
on the other hand, the son of a prosperous farmer in *One of Ours*,
cannot find contentment on the land; he is drawn more and more to the
remaining wild, uncultivated places out of disgust for the American
farmer's mistreatment of the land. The hardships of the first-generation

immigrants sanctify their relation to the land, from which succeeding generations turn away out of new needs or misguided materialism. Claude's brother, for example, gives up farming to become a farm machinery salesman. In France, where he goes to war, Claude is happy to find farmland better loved and better cared for than it is in America. It is ironic that Cather, whose feeling for the Western farmland once amounted to fierce patriotism, had to concede that America is no longer the most suitable place to harbor the pastoral ideal, that the particular place one chooses to settle does not matter nearly as much as the love and labor expended on it. It is a further irony that while Crèvecoeur in the eighteenth century forsook the "accursed" Old World to find the ideal farmer in America, Cather, in the twentieth century, becomes disillusioned with America and finds true devotion to the land in the French peasant. Whereas France of the seventeenth century is pictured as decadent in Cather's *Shadows on the Rock,* France of the twentieth century is redeemed by the sacrifices her people made in World War I resulting in a new love for their native places. Almost like the fictional Claude Wheeler, the author Louis Bromfield also was impressed by the devotion of Frenchmen to their soil: "I had found there a continuity which had always been oddly lacking in American life. . . . It seemed to me that real continuity, real love of one's country, real permanence had to do not with mechanical inventions and high wages but with the earth and man's love of the soil upon which he lived." In returning to operate his old family farm in America, Bromfield did what Wheeler probably would have done if he had not died in the War.

As with most people who want only a lifetime of devotion to the land, Cather saw the relationship to the land as a purely individual matter not essentially involving family, community, or nation. Even land ownership is irrelevant. "We come and go, but the land is always here," muses Alexandra at the end of *O Pioneers!* "And the people who love it and understand it are the people who own it—for a little while." There is a Puritan element in Cather's insistence that perseverance on the land is a test of character rather than a commendable way of life or the foundation of a nation's wealth. There is also the other tendency of Puritanism, the mystical, in Cather's suggestion of a transcendent relationship of her more sensitive characters to the land. Alexandra, for example, has a recurrent vision of being carried off by a fertility god, and Antonia and Jim Burden weave a spell of romance over their unstoried acres by choosing to believe that Coronado had come as far north as Nebraska in his search for the Seven Golden Cities.

When the pioneer spirit of the American western settler petered

out and the romanticization of the farmer's relation to the land yielded
to the profit motive, farming could no longer satisfy Cather's moral and
imaginative interests. She rejected arable land and found another,
more universal symbol of man's destiny on earth, the rock. The
epitome of earth itself, the rock could not be an expression of man's
impact on his environment, as the fields were, but rather the harsh,
unchanging reality of existence itself. Moreover, the rock better
satisfied Cather's Puritan predilection to see the New World as a severe test for the spirit of man to withstand. The rock is further
sanctified for Cather by the long history of man's association with
actual rocks, in particular the Indians living on mesas in the Southwest
and the French settling at Quebec. The rock deeply moves all sorts of
people, not only aborigines and pioneers but an intellectual (Professor
Saint Peter in *The Professor's House*), a cleric (Father Latour in *Death
Comes for the Archbishop*), and an artist (Thea Kronberg in *Song of
the Lark*). Their lives are given new direction when they recognize the
mysterious power of the rock. Alienated from the farming community
she grew up in because it threatens her career as an opera singer, Thea
gets support "out of the rocks, out of the dead people" who once
inhabited the cliffsides of Panther Canon.[34] Gradually coming to love
the wild, stark land so different from his native France, the priest is
deeply moved by two experiences of the rock, one at the mesa where
the Indian city of Acoma once flourished, the other at a cave in a
mountainside where he could hear "one of the oldest voices of the
earth . . . the sound of a great underground river . . . far below, perhaps
as deep as the foot of the mountain, a flood moving in utter blackness
under ribs of antediluvian rock."[35] In building his cathedral in Sante Fe
out of stone locally quarried, the archbishop symbolically unites his
adopted land with the religion of the Old World: "the towers rose clear
into the blue air, while the body of the church still lay against the
mountain." Professor Saint Peter's boyhood identification with "earth
and woods and water" is renewed by his reading a former student's
account of the Blue Mesa, another rock once occupied by Indians:

> . . . now he enjoyed this half-awake loafing with his brain as if it
> were a new sense, arriving late like wisdom teeth. He found he
> could lie on his sand-pit by the lake for hours and watch the seven
> motionless pines drink up the sun. In the evening, after dinner, he
> could sit idle and watch the stars, with the same immobility. He
> was cultivating a novel mental dissipation—enjoying a new friend-
> ship. (263)

In developing respect for a sacred place the aging professor finds a good defense against the shallow passion for new things that characterizes his wife and daughter and a welcome preparation for death. His battle to hold onto earth, as represented by the mesa and his old house, is like that of Melville's aging narrator, in "I and My Chimney," for whom the great chimney of his home is another symbol of the earthbound and the ancient.

The priest's and the professor's rock is quite different from the land as Cather earlier conceived it. The land where the rock exists in its most impressive form, the Southwest, is not good farming country. The light dry desert air that rejuvenates Father Latour, "that wind that made one a boy again," is not typical of an agricultural region:

> He had noticed that this peculiar quality in the air of new countries vanished after they were tamed by man and made to bear harvests. Parts of Texas and Kansas that he had first known as open range had since been made into rich farming districts, and the air had quite lost that lightness, that dry aromatic odour. The moisture of the plowed land, the heaviness of labour and growth and grain-bearing, utterly destroyed it; one could breathe that only on the bright edges of the world, on the great grass plains or the sage-brush desert. (276)

Indeed, the land counts for less than the sky: "Elsewhere the sky is the roof of the world; but here the earth was the floor of the sky. The landscape one longed for when one was far away, the thing all about one, the world one actually lived in, was the sky, the sky!" (235). D. H. Lawrence had a similar reaction to the sky in New Mexico finding "a certain magnificence in the high-up day . . . one sprang awake, a new part of the soul woke up suddenly, and the old world gave way to the new."[36]

Unlike white settlers, the native cliff-dwellers did not change the landscape: "They spent their ingenuity in the other direction; in accommodating themselves to the scene in which they found themselves. . . . They ravaged neither the rivers nor the forest, and if they irrigated, they took as little water as would serve their needs" (237). Thus the mesa Indians achieved an ideal community; the bishop's cathedral may possibly form the nucleus for another. The "little city of stone" atop the mesa and the "tawny church" are structures for men in a world where habitations—beautiful ones—are required to support life.

Willa Cather's etherealization of the relation of humanity to the land struck leftist and sociologically oriented critics of her time as escapism. Maxwell Geismar, for example, complained of her "movement *back* in terms of time and place, this movement *away* from the real areas of human feeling."[37] Our own ecologically sensitive time is bound to see Cather's disillusionment with farming in America as an honest recognition of the failure of the agrarian dream to bring about a healthy condition for both the individual living on the land and the land itself. She was not alone in this perception, and confirmation was to come only three years after *One of Ours* in Ellen Glasgow's *Barren Ground* (1925), which suggests that while the land can be made fertile its servant may remain sterile.

Though tempted, like Cather, by the mystical relationship to the land in *To a God Unknown,* John Steinbeck was willing to face changes in the American farming scene and to examine new ways of organizing farm life. In *The Grapes of Wrath* particularly he takes a long hard look at the deterioration of the old pastoral dream and sets beside it the possibility of a new kind of enterprise in which collective action is more important than an individual's relation to the soil. The two immediately preceding works had tested the fragility of the pastoral ideal. In *Of Mice and Men* it is but a tale told to an idiot by his good friend George, who merely keeps alive the dream of the rabbit farm in order to keep Lennie in line; and for a brief time in *In Dubious Battle* a group of striking migrant pickers desperately hold onto precarious contact with the land when they set up a collective community in an orchard, "a pleasant place," where "the apple trees grew in close to a small white ranch house." With *The Grapes of Wrath* there is a full recognition of the end of the farm-garden image in America as thousands of people are uprooted from their small holdings and replaced by large-scale industrialized farming methods. The possibility of "westering" in the old style is but a sentimental dream, for there is no more land available to settle on. At best they can become hired laborers just to pick crops on large farms and then move on. The old ideal of living on the land dies hard among people who cannot understand what has happened to agriculture in America, principally that mechanization and regimentation of farm labor means the increasing separation of people from the land. "Place where folks live is them folks," is the old belief as it is rendered by Muley Graves, who, in refusing to leave the land, reduces himself to an animal existence. Steinbeck himself seems to hesitate between the remaining force of the old garden image and a hard-headed recognition of its inappropriateness in the new economy; he can never quite tear himself or his most engaging characters away from impassioned nostalgia for the land. But the facts of his story speak for themselves: Westering leads not to a new, independent life on the land but to a new social awareness, the formation of a new social class, the rural proletariat, whose strength is discovered not on the soil but on the highway where they learn the necessity of collectivism. Uprooted from the land by a drought at the beginning of the novel, the Okies are separated from the land by a flood at the end. The land is thus not dependable, though no one dares to admit it. But even while the Joads hold on to the old feeling of kinship with the land, they are developing a new sense of relatedness with other people that has nothing to do with farming but rather with the rights of all men to work and receive adequate wages for their work. The class consciousness Casy introduces to their way of thinking prevails in the end rather than Muley Graves's land consciousness.[38]

Far from supporting the tradition of American agrarianism, *The Grapes of Wrath* clearly faces the fact that the old pastoral dream has been permanently shattered by big business farming and the running out of new open lands. It is the culmination of a line of thought that Steinbeck had begun with his second novel, *The Pastures of Heaven*, and confirmed in *The Long Valley*. The first reads almost like a parable of the history of America as a land of promise. A Spanish corporal discovers a particularly fertile valley while he is pursuing renegade Indians. Richly endowed as the valley is, however, only one settler thrives there, Bert Monroe, who, having failed in many enterprises before migrating to the valley, somehow manages to make a success of a farm that was supposed to be haunted. All the other settlers inherit the curse and lead tragic lives. In the final chapter of *The Pastures of Heaven,* a busload of tourists behold the valley spread out below them and ironically speculate about its potential as the site of a family farm, a refuge for the disaffected, a last retreat for the aged, a fun spot for the wealthy. Twenty years later Steinbeck put the finishing touch on his anti-pastoral viewpoint in *East of Eden,* a long novel that relates the failure of the American dream-garden to the Biblical story of Adam's family. Salinas Valley is like the fallen earth: It has the potential to "feed the world" and to be the home of thousands of happy people, but "there's a black violence on this valley. . . . It's as though some old ghost haunted it out of the dead ocean below and troubled the air with unhappiness."[39]

In such a fallen world the agrarian virtues do not seem to result in a viable economy; for masses of people there is nothing to do but acquire techniques of bare survival, and these the Okies are in fair way of learning by the end of *The Grapes of Wrath*. In another mood and in another narrative mode, the picaresque, Steinbeck has considered the

possibility of people avoiding the economic facts of life by refusing to
accept the traditional American land and work mystiques. For this
purpose a strong infusion of Latin-American blood is required. In *Cannery Row* "a little group of men who had in common no families, no
money, and no ambitions beyond food, drink, and contentment" picks
up a marginal living in the interstices of the commercial society of
Monterey. Mack and his friends are not like large predators but small
animals who yet survive—"the coyote, the common brown rat, the
English sparrow, the house fly and the moth." In *Tortilla Flat* the
"well-browned" paisanos are neither farmers nor factory workers but
likable misfits who live on the outskirts of Monterey "where the forest
and the town intermingle." Each one of them an original, they yet
organize themselves into a temporary society, a sort of Arthurian
round-table fellowship rather than the leftist collective the Okies grope
toward. They survive by developing a casual, parasitic relationship to
the commercial and agricultural activities of the Monterey region.
Theirs is a kind of secondary ecology for a species of man who attempts, for at least a portion of his life, to set himself against the
reigning economic institutions; it may be found again in the sub-culture
of the hippies in the 1960s.

Steinbeck's Okies, on the other hand, represent the masses of
Americans who remain in the economic system by making a radical
change in their function: Instead of staying settled on the land, as their
forebears had done, they must become migrant laborers of farm and
shop. Steinbeck takes them up to the point of change, and then their
story is continued by Erskine Caldwell, who follows them to the cities
where they take temporary jobs in war industries, and by Joyce Carol
Oates, whose second generation migrants attempt, unsuccessfully, to
relocate on the land. Caldwell's uprooted farmers in *Tragic Ground* are
not happy about returning to the land even when they have the chance:
"You just can't keep digging a man up by the roots and setting him
down in different parts of the country and expect him to be satisfied for
the rest of his life."[40] The daughter of migrant farm laborers in Oates's
A Garden of Earthly Delights yearns to establish herself on the land
and to make it possible for her son to have "a whole world to live in—
not just a patch of the world," but the boy resists any feeling of this
kind and succumbs to a passion for destruction: "He wanted nothing so
much as to destroy everything . . . he did not really want to build it
up—he didn't want to step into the place his father had made for
himself; instead he wanted to get rid of it all, destroy it all, everything,
the entire world."[41]

Willa Cather was disillusioned with rural life as she saw it on the great plains, Steinbeck as he saw it in the lush valleys of California. Cather identified the cause in the materialism of individuals, Steinbeck in the monopoly forces of big business spreading to agriculture. William Faulkner's voluminous works, from one point of view, are devoted to tracing the failure of agriculture in the South. Like Hawthorne, Faulkner finds the cause of failure in the guilt of the past, the original Southern sin having been clearing the land for cultivation, when the wilderness was "ruthlessly destroyed by axes, by men who simply wanted to make that earth grow something they could sell for a profit, which brought into it a condition based on an evil like human bondage."[42] In *The Hamlet* Faulkner mourns "the final blue and dying echo of the Appalachian Mountains" that had been left by the woodcutters in ashes, "rank sedge and briers" (174). While he himself professes not to "choose sides at all," his sympathetic characters value woods over arable land and there is never a good word said for farming in all of Faulkner, never the devotion to land that moves some characters in Cather and Steinbeck. The first generation of planters—the McCaslins, Compsons, Sutpens—leave a burden of guilt in the way they abuse the Indians from whom they more or less stole the land and the blacks whom they imported to work the land. Their descendants cannot seem to expiate the sins of the planter aristocracy, and the tenant farmers who supplant them lead sordid, blighted lives, fighting and cheating each other and abusing their womenfolk. As the most pitiable victims of a debased economy and family life, Faulkner's country women are symbolic of earth's declining fertility; their attempts to persevere are sad, grotesque. Eula is a bovine nullity, Lena Grove is bemused with her journey over the countryside, Dilsey rules over a kitchen and a grassless dooryard with three mulberry trees and a pair of jaybirds, and Caddy has lost the "smell of trees." Farmland, whether productive as in the nineteenth century or depleted as in the twentieth, is the setting of tragedy for Faulkner. His "dusty landscape offers, like Eliot's cricket, no relief."[43]

The Hamlet is Faulkner's most damaging attack on farm life. The story of Eula Varner is a reversal of "The Legend of Sleepy Hollow," whose plot it adapts. The school teacher, Labove, is well advised to flee the land because the maiden in this case is a mock-heroic symbol of fertility in a land that is no longer fertile. Eula is eventually married, not to the only true man in the area, McCarron, but to Flem Snopes, the sterile store-keeper, who, like Ichabod Crane, sees the woman and the land that comes with her only in terms of the money into which they can be converted. Those who are closest to the land in *The Hamlet* are Ike Snope, an idiot, who pursues the object of his passion, a cow, through a creekside pasture and Mink Snopes, who murders a man in a dispute over a cow and stuffs the body into the cavity of a tree trunk in the forest. The mock-heroic courtship of Eula, the ironic pastoral idyll of Ike and the cow, and the Gothic horror tale of Mink and Houston are grotesque travesties of country manners and husbandry.

Many American writers agree that it would be better if land could somehow be worked and not owned, since ownership leads to all the abuses undermining the pastoral ideal: land speculation, absentee ownership, large-scale mechanized cultivation, and alienation from the soil. The McCaslin farm is not his to repudiate, Ike heatedly asserts in *The Bear,* nor was it his grandfather's to bequeath, nor the Indians' to sell; God intended man "to hold the earth mutual and intact in the communal anonymity of brotherhood" (247).[44] What constitutes ownership of land? Steinbeck's composite Okie answers: "being born on it, working it, dying on it. That makes ownership, not a paper with numbers on it." Willa Cather's Alexandra has the same idea in *O Pioneers!:* "We come and go, but the land is always here. And the people who love it are the people who own it—for a little while."[45] Man is "but a sojourner in nature," says Thoreau in *Walden,* and agriculture can give him only a false sense of permanence on earth. Marjorie Kinnan Rawlings reflects this truth in *The Sojourners* when Ase Linden turns his farm over to a hired man instead of his own family: "Why, any man had only temporary rights in the earth. . . . No man owned the land."[46] Compare this sentiment with the ancient Greek and Roman pride in continuous possession, with the Old World compulsion to own land in Wordsworth's "Michael," in which the tragedy of the old shepherd lies not in his son's dissolute ways but in his land being "sold into a stranger's hand."

Farming may have the same tragic results as mining. Cooper's Jotham Riddel dies in a forest fire because he is so engrossed in digging for ore. In mining gold men "dig their doom," writes Melville in *Mardi,* and "pile their earth so high, they gasp for air, and die." At the close of *The Hamlet,* Faulkner creates a powerful image combining the tragedy of mining and farming in the spectacle of Henry Armstid digging up the garden of a ruined plantation house for Confederate coins that are supposed to be buried there:

> Armstid dug himself back into that earth which had produced him
> . . . spading himself into the waxing twilight with the regularity of a
> mechanical toy and with something monstrous in his unflagging
> effort. . . . He did not glance up at the sun, as a man pausing in
> work does to gauge the time. He came straight back to the trench,

hurrying back to it with that painful and laboring slowness, the
gaunt unshaven face which was now completely that of a madman.
(366–73)

AMERICA AS A WILDERNESS

Anti-pastoral sentiment in American literature arises not only from
disillusionment with the practical failure of the garden image but from
the long-standing commitment of Americans to the third landscape
archetype of the New World, the wilderness. It is important not to
confuse the wilderness image with the garden or pastoral image. The
essential difference is that land forms, plants, and animals remain in a
natural condition in the wilderness, whereas in the pastoral setting they
are altered through the technologies of agriculture and husbandry. The
pastoral in literature is not, as many readers mistakenly assume, a
celebration of wild nature. Trees, rocks, and wild animals are proper
symbols of the wilderness; fruit trees, flowers, and domestic animals,
of the garden. Devotion to wilderness is a deeply conservative attitude
and is opposed to the alteration of the land, no matter how simple, in
the name of civilization or progress. The agricultural use of land is
incompatible with the continuance of wilderness conditions. "Every
one finds by his own experience, as well as in history," writes Thoreau
in the "Sunday" chapter of *A Week on the Concord and Merrimack
Rivers,* "that the era in which men cultivate the apple, and the
amenities of the garden, is essentially different from that of the hunter
and forest life, and neither can displace the other without loss." The
discovery of America refreshed Europe's conception of wild nature,
and some Americans took pride in their wilderness. For a long time in
American history the farmer doubled as a hunter, and fishing and hunting were leading industries until the middle of the nineteenth century.
But as intensive enterprise reduced the number of wild animals and
converted more and more wilderness to arable land, the feeling for
wilderness was eclipsed and appeared to be merely romantic nostalgia,
at one with sentimental regret over the vanishing red man. With the
accelerated encroachment on the remaining American wilderness since
World War II, there has developed a renewed sensitivity over the use
of land, and the wilderness way seems now to be more dominant than
either the garden or Eldoradan choices. Conservation now wins many
battles against farming and mining. The movement to preserve wil-

derness areas is supported by psychological and ecological needs, whereas the practical results of the garden and Eldoradan ideals are now seen to be sometimes destructive of these as well as of social and economic ends. In an over-civilized time, when the revival of primitive experience seems desirable, contact with wilderness, in sport and leisure, finds more favor than the economic exploitation of land.

Always an ambivalent symbol in the history of man everywhere, the wilderness in America early came to represent both the forbidding aspects of the new continent, its perils and hazards standing in the way of survival, as well as the mysterious source of spiritual health and regeneration. The New England Puritans adapted Christian stereotypes of the dark wood and barren "desert" to American geography and wove them into a religious drama: The forests they found between the Atlantic and the Connecticut River were "Devil's Territories . . . the Utmost parts of the Earth," and the settlers were "the Vine which God has here Planted . . . to take deep Root, and fill the Land."[47] It was a "poor Plantation" grimly accepted by the guilt-ridden Puritans as a fitting testing ground, a new Sinai where new Israelites could prove themselves by working out man's covenant with God, without hindrance from the sinners and false believers of the Old World. The "waste and howling wilderness" was sacralized in their eyes by reason of their being appointed to do God's will there—"casting out the Heathen" and establishing a community of true believers for all the world to behold.

The Puritan religious view of the wilderness later became the foundation of two differing literary psychologies. In one, the Gothic, the wilderness was associated with the destructive aspects of the psyche— what Freud later identified as the unconscious mind. Lacking ruined abbeys and castles, Charles Brockden Brown used the American forest and its denizens "to project the darker impulses of the id."[48] A milder adaptation of Puritanism saw the American wilderness as a testing ground in which to build strong moral character. Thus the historian Francis Parkman thought that taming the American wilderness developed masculinity in English colonists and accounted for their eventual superiority over the French.[49] Ordinary settlers saw the wilderness simply as an inconvenient obstacle to be cleared out of the path of material progress and survival. To a few brave men the wilderness appealed as a place affording freedom from constraints and opportunities for the exercise of prowess and violence.

The religious and practical depreciation of wilderness was countered by romanticism and the vogue for picturesque landscape in the late eighteenth and early nineteenth centuries. Then the forest covering the eastern states became the source of aesthetic pleasure and spiritual health. Later in the nineteenth century, when the settlers reached the treeless plains and the western mountains, the ambiguous feeling about wilderness recurred. Shifting responses can be seen in Nathaniel Hawthorne, who managed to make use of both his ancestors' fear of the "unconverted wilderness" and his romantic contemporaries' esteem of the woods. His characters are imperiled in the forest not so much because it is evil but because they project upon it their own bad conscience. So it is with Young Goodman Brown, who thinks he sees his neighbors misbehave in the woods, and with Reuben Bourne, who lives in terror of the woods because he once yielded to cowardice there. It is the same in the case of Reverend Dimmesdale, who cannot find the sense of freedom in the woods that Hester enjoys because he has not confessed and expiated his sin. The woods for Hester, on the other hand, "set her free" and help her to an "estranged point of view" from which she can be critical of the Puritan settlement. "Her intellect and heart had their home, as it were, in desert places, where she roamed as freely as the wild Indian in his woods." Hawthorne, however, cannot let Hester go all the way, as far as Thoreau, for example, in his vantage point at Walden Pond: wandering "in a moral wilderness" strengthened her character "but taught her much amiss."

James Fenimore Cooper was able to respond more positively than Hawthorne to the wilderness. His knowledge of upper New York State and his acquaintance with some real woodsmen were supplemented by the influence of landscape painters like Thomas Cole and the Burkean aesthetics of sublimity.[50] These he found it possible to combine with Christian piety, seeing the immense expanse of American forest lands as "gifts of the Lord" that are capable of inducing virtue as long as they remain in a pristine condition, "untouched by the hands of man." But, while Cooper could create a single character, Leatherstocking, who combined wilderness prowess with high moral quality, he could not discover any way to make civilized communities compatible with wilderness, and his Leatherstocking novels constitute a lament on the passing of the forest under the successive encroachments of white settlers. This does not constitute, as some critics have charged, an escape from reality but rather an attempt to preserve in the imaginative life one aspect of the American past and to question the future of a nation that had deformed the beauty of the wilderness in such a short period of time.

In preserving a nostalgic regard for life in the woods, Cooper must make his hero more Indian than European, for he is well aware that the white man has no wilderness calling. "I fear I have not altogether followed the gifts of my color," Leatherstocking admits at the end of his life in *The Prairie,* "inasmuch as I find it a little painful to give up for ever the use of the rifle, and the comforts of the chase." Having "a true wilderness heart," he is angered by "the waste and wickedness of the settlements and the villages," but he knows that taming the wilderness is inevitable and he has some consolation in the thought that civilization brings law into the areas it has had to transform. This is small enough consolation, however, when we consider the dominant feeling of the loss of wilderness, which is expressed so eloquently in the rhetoric and tragic situation of Leatherstocking and his Indian companions. Through their melancholy Cooper helps to create and keep alive both the sense of wonder over the original forest and the sense of guilt over its destruction.

Cooper's transcendentalist contemporaries refined upon Cooper when they turned the woods into a symbolic force in the imaginative life of individuals. "In the woods is perpetual youth," declared Emerson in *Nature,* "we return to reason and faith." The garden had long been considered an appropriate place for the restoration of spiritual wholeness, but drawing a spiritual value from a wild forest was a revolutionary principle that romanticism introduced to Western thought, or, perhaps more properly, romanticism reintroduced a kind of visionary experience of the primitive aspects of environment that the Judeo-Christian tradition had all but obliterated. With the remnants of a great forest all about them, it is no wonder that American writers have felt the attraction of the woods more immediately than the garden.

Living in remnant of the woods on the outskirts of Concord, Thoreau tried to supply Emerson's wilderness principle with a concrete image. Not a practical experiment in wilderness survival, as was the case with Leatherstocking, the two-year stay at Walden Pond was devised as a method of learn "the gross necessaries of life" by subjecting oneself "to live a primitive and frontier life." *Walden* appears to be a book in the pastoral tradition, since a civilized man sets out to find reminders of his essential relation to life in a simple environment. But Thoreau minimizes the role of agriculture—a few rows of beans and "pasture enough for my imagination"; prefers the company of a woodchopper, "cousin to the pine and the rock," to the farmer, who "leads a fool's life"; and lingers lovingly and at length over the minutest details of pond ecology. "I am convinced that my genius dates from an older era than the agricultural," Thoreau writes in his attack on agriculture in the essay "Sunday." "Gardening is civil and social, but it wants the vigor and freedom of the forest and the outlaw." As with Emerson, the wilderness for Thoreau is not a place to live in but a place where civilized man goes to retrieve lost knowledge that he needs for his spiritual renewal. In assembling forest data and living as simply as an Indian, however, Thoreau goes well beyond the vague tone that Emerson struck when he wrote in "Self-Reliance" that his essays "should smell of pines and resound with the hum of insects." What Thoreau sought in the forest Melville's Ishamel hopes to find at sea: "in landlessness alone resides the highest truth." The sea is the wilderness for Melville, and in a curious transposition of features he often sees the land in terms of sea imagery. Mount Greylock is the epitome of a land place in *Pierre,* but, in looking out at the peak from the piazza of his farm house in Pittsfield, Melville felt he was at sea:

> In summer, too, Canute-like, sitting there, one is often reminded of the sea. . . . The purple of the mountains is just the purple of the billows, and a still August noon broods upon the deep meadows, as a calm upon the Line; but the vastness and the lonesomeness are so oceanic, and the silence and the sameness, too, that the first peep of a strange house, rising beyond the trees, is for all the world like spying, on the Barbary coast, an unknown sail.[51]

Like Thoreau in the woods, Ishmael collects, as scientifically as he knows how, the innumerable facts of the sea-wilderness; and through his knowledge and love of the sea and its life he seems to deserve his escape from the deep and his rebirth.

Of all the major American writers of the twentieth century, William Faulkner presents the most eloquent statement on behalf of the wilderness. In *The Bear* particularly, the value of the wilderness is explicitly set over against farming, and the emphatic conclusion is that cotton culture was accomplished only at the price of shamefully exploiting both land and people, whereas wilderness experience is the source of true pride, humility, courage—the ultimate release of the sensitive Southerner, Ike McCaslin, from the accumulated guilt that farming had visited on the land and its owners. What Ike learns in the wilderness leads him to renounce his share of his family's farm, and he becomes a carpenter, preserving in that way an innocent relationship with the woods. The last remaining patch of wilderness in Yoknapatawpha County is Ike's college—as the sea was Ishmael's Harvard—and Old Ben, the bear, is the "epitome and apotheosis of the old wild life." So intense is Ike's awakening that some readers, like Thomas Merton, see in *The Bear* a profound religious experience.[52]

But wilderness has its limitations, both emotional and practical, for the American writer. Ike McCaslin's wilderness experience in *The Bear* cannot keep him from mouthing Nazi racist propaganda in its sequel, "Delta Autumn," and even in *The Bear* Sam Fathers, the true forest guide and hunter is offset by Boon Hogganbeck, a clown of the woods, and Ash, the camp cook, who plays out a little parody of the hunt in the last section of the book. Faulkner knew only too well that the American pioneer woodsman, even though he preferred living in the woods, ironically spent his life "turning the earth into a howling waste from which he would be the first to vanish."[53] Against the sentimentality of *The Bear* must be set Flannery O'Connor's *The Violent Bear It Away*, the story of a boy who feels compelled to return to a clearing in "the farthest of the backwoods" and set fire to the woods in order to rid himself of the influence his great-uncle, whose religious fanaticism was accentuated by the freedom he enjoyed in the wilderness.

Even its most enthusiastic champions cannot shake the traditional horror of the wilderness place. Melville's sea produces a man-destroying monster in *Moby-Dick*, and a mountain in *Pierre* is described as another monster "radiating hideous repellingness" and signifying "stark desolation; ruin, merciless and ceaseless; chills and gloom" (479). Hester Prynne's feeling for forest freedom is only "half-valid," writes Roy Male: "In the gloom of the wilderness is the blankness of space, nothing of temporal or moral significance can be seen."[54] Passing by woods on a dark night was a more comforting experience to Robert Frost than to Hawthorne, who wrote in his notebook, "How very desolate looks a forest when seen in this way—as if, should you venture one step within its wild, tangled, many-stemmed and dark shadowed verge, you would inevitably be lost forever" (82). In his essay "Walking" Thoreau could utter the brave words, "Life consists with wildness. The most alive is the wildest," but the bleak summit of Mount Katahdin gave him a rare moment of terror because it presented an aspect of nature he could not bear to face. While Melville associated the mountain in *Pierre* with the fallen Titan Enceladus, Thoreau saw in Mount Katahdin "the rock where Prometheus was bound": there man loses "some vital part" of himself; "Vast, Titanic, inhuman Nature has got him at a disadvantage."[55]

When the elements of Nature are no longer amenable to human survival and use, they cease to be Nature. Hawthorne comes to the same conclusion in "The Great Carbuncle" when his two "pilgrims" ascend naked rock in search of a fabled gem: "In this bleak realm of upper air nothing breathed, nothing grew; there was no life but what was concentrated in their two hearts; they had climbed so high that Nature herself seemed no longer to keep them company." Wilderness is reduced ultimately to matter, matter is opposed to mind, and without mind existence is impossible. "What is this Titan that has possession of me?" Thoreau asks. "Think of our life in nature,—daily to be shown matter, to come in contact with it—rocks, trees, wind on our cheeks! The *solid* earth! the *actual* world! the *common sense! Contact! Contact!*" (93). Mountain tops, Thoreau concludes, are not places for mankind: "Only daring and insolent men, perchance, go there." *Walden* is not a book for mountain tops, writes Robert Pirsig: "The language structure is wrong for the mountain forest we're in. . . . The book seems tame and cloistered, something I'd never have thought of Thoreau."[56] Melville, however, did not draw away from the horror, and his Ahab dares to seek for something in the sea, as deep as the mountains are high. Likewise, Norman Mailer's two young hunters in *Why Are We in Vietnam?* climb an icy pinnacle in the Brooks Range of Alaska and find that "God was here, and He was real and no man was He, but a beast, some beast of a giant jaw and cavernous mouth," and the experience turns them into "killer brothers, owned by something, prince of darkness, lord of light, they did not know."[57] Thus, savagery and death may constitute the wilderness experience as well as freedom and rebirth. The "real history" of Americans, writes Thomas Wolfe, goes back "through solitude and loneliness and death and unspeakable courage, into the wilderness."[58]

Many years after the hunt for Old Ben, Ike, in "Delta Autumn," again goes on a hunting expedition, only this time he must travel two hundred miles to the site, and the hunting is not good. A doe is killed and the participants are not at all like those sanctified hunters of the past. At eighty years of age Ike has lived long enough to regret the change of topography and attitude. His distant kinsman scornfully asks, "I suppose the question to ask you is, where have you been all the time you were dead?" Like Rip Van Winkle, Ike has outlived the wilderness yet never forgets his wonderful experience there: "He seemed to see the two of them—himself and the wilderness—as coevals . . . the two spans running out together, not toward oblivion, nothingness, but into a dimension free of both time and space."

Just as competition between hunters and shepherds is a frequent theme in the early chapters of Genesis, so competition among the three principal images of land use has been a popular subject of American literature. The Eldoradan use of land always threatens the destruction of the garden and the wilderness because, being interested only in what may be immediately extracted from the land, it has no respect for the permanence of land. The farmer is essentially hostile to wilderness because he feels he must destroy all vestiges of wild life before he can be secure in his control over land. Wild life once included the Indian as well as the wolf and eagle. The Indian was exterminated because he could not adapt himself to an exclusively agricultural use of the land; he may have been "a natural expression of the place," as William Carlos Williams describes him, but the place he expressed was not what the white man wanted it to remain. Pushing the Indian off the land was rationalized on the assumption that land had no value as "the haunt of game" and received value only through the labor expended on it by Europeans who farmed it. Indian agriculture, perhaps because it was subsistence agriculture, was conveniently overlooked. The black man, on the other hand, could be made to take part in the white man's farming, first as a slave, then as share-cropper and even landowner, if he were only given the chance.

American wilderness writing ignores the black, because of his association with agriculture, and honors the Indian guide and hunting companion. The Indian is the white man's link with the wilderness spirit. Hemingway's black gun-bearers are Africans who are uncorrupted by planters; the hunt staged by the black cook, Ash, in Part V of *The Bear,* is a parody of the great bear hunt conducted by Indians and whites in Part I. For D. H. Lawrence even the ghost of the red man will be effective, for "no place exerts its full influence upon a newcomer until the old inhabitant is dead or absorbed," and to save himself the American "must embrace the great dusky continent of the Red Man."[59] There are innumerable instances of the Indian leading the white man to the redemptive secrets of the wilderness: Cooper's Chingachgook, Sam Fathers in *The Bear,* Lewis Moon in Peter Matthiessen's *At Play in the Fields of the Lord,* the mesa dwellers in Willa Cather's *The Professor's House,* Joe Sam in Van Tilburg Clark's *The Track of the Cat.* Ken Kesey provides a reversal of this motif in *One Flew Over the Cuckoo's Nest,* in which a white man, McMurphy, makes it possible for an Indian to leave the madhouse of white civilization and return to his wilderness homeland.

Washington Irving's "The Legend of Sleepy Hollow" owes some of its power as myth to the dramatization of the conflict of farmer, treasure hunter, and woodsman. The garden image is represented by the prosperous farm of Baltus Van Tassel and his daughter Katrina, "a blooming lass" who is described in terms of farm products—"plump as a partridge; ripe and melting and rosy cheeked as one of her father's peaches." Both farm and daughter are desired by Ichabod Crane, the daughter less for normal sexual purposes than for the good things to eat that she represents, and the farm because it can "be readily turned into cash, and the money invested in immense tracts of wild land" in the West. For Ichabod is neither farmer nor lover, but a seeker of riches in the form of land that can be converted through speculation into cash, a true Eldoradan. Even his personal appearance announces his symbolic opposition to the garden ideal: "One might have mistaken him for the genius of famine descending upon the earth, or some scarecrow eloped from a cornfield." Fortunately Katrina has another suitor, Brom Bones, "a burly, roaring, roystering blade" who is fond of disturbing the rural quiet with his roughneck antics. While Ichabod has a horror of the woods, fed by "large extracts from his invaluable author, Cotton Mather," Brom Bones is at home in the woods around Tarry Town: "In cold weather he was distinguished by a fur cap, surmounted with a flaunting fox's tail." He uses his knowledge and Ichabod's fear of the woods to scare off his competitor, thus winning the maiden. The garden bounty goes to the man who is not himself a farmer but who has proved himself in the wilderness, while the Eldoradan, who has no real knowledge of the land he covets, goes empty-handed.

The Eula section of Faulkner's *The Hamlet* adapts the Irving story with appropriate changes for the Southern setting. The prosperous farmer is Will Varner, a crafty landholder; his daughter Eula, like Katrina, is a figure of exaggerated fertility—"honey in sunlight and bursting grapes." She, too, has a manly suitor, Hoake McCarron, although her ill-favored suitor is split into two characters: the schoolteacher Labove, a young man of "fierce and unappeasable appetites," and the passionless store-clerk Flem Snopes. None of Eula's suitors is interested in farming, though McCarron acts as overseer on the family plantation to oblige his mother. Labove is studying law and hopes someday to be governor of the state. "Aint no benefit in farming," says Flem. "I figure on getting out of it soon as I can." McCarron seduces Eula, Labove flees the village in panic, like Ichabod, and Flem gets to marry her. But Flem is the Ichabod type, the speculator who turns land and people into cash so that he can proceed to more speculations in the town. He is the very kind of man Labove was afraid Eula would end up with: "He would be a dwarf, a gnome, without glands or desire . . . the crippled Vulcan to that Venus, who would not possess her but merely own her by the single strength which power gave, the dead power of money" (119). Flem cannot serve Eula or the land she brings to him, "the fine land rich and fecund and foul and eternal and impervious to him who claimed title to it." In fact, Flem terminates his stay in the farmland when he sells the old plantation he was given as a reward for marrying Eula; he tricks three buyers into believing that gold is buried there, and the last we see of Old Frenchman Place is the garden being dug up by a demented gold-seeker. In *Sanctuary* it is further degraded when it becomes the scene of a bootlegging operation, a murder, and particularly sordid rape.

Faulkner's version of the story omits the suitor who is devoted to the wilderness. Mink Snopes frequents a Gothic forest, a place of foul murder and concealment, not certainly the mythic forest Faulkner was to do later in *The Bear*. Mink stands in contrast to Ike Snopes, who is the center of a grotesque pastoral idyll played out in a beautiful creek-side meadow. *The Hamlet* reflects a sceptical time when farm, wood-land, and mine are possessed by madmen. Irving's earlier treatment clearly finds an accommodation of the garden and the wilderness. After winning the maiden the wilderness man will settle down to farming, much like the Western story's cowboy surrendering his wild ways to join the ranks of the settlers after he has won the heart of the genteel woman he has rescued. In the system of nineteenth-century American ideals, wilderness experience prepares a man to assume special roles in civilized society. But Eldoradan aims, especially the quest for gold, invariably spell disaster for the farm-garden. A popular motif in fiction has one son remaining on the farm and eventually prospering while another son goes off to the mines in the West and is lost forever.[60] Later the quest for gold is replaced by business interests, with the entrepre-neurial son going off to the city in search of some get-rich-quick scheme. In Rawlings' *The Sojourner* Asa Linden is the devoted farmer while his brother goes West to find his fortune in gold and timber; in the next generation, Asa's own son actually enriches himself in the West through crooked real estate dealing, and Asa elects to turn the farm over to a Polish couple, no kinsmen of his, because he knows "they would cherish the land and not despoil it." To Asa only farmland is good: "Mountains were jumbles of sterile stone. Cities were already ruins. . . . Only the farms and fields were beautiful. Green and red and golden and violet squares and rectangles spoke of man's sole kindness to the earth" (325). In Willa Cather's *O Pioneers!* the three land images come across very clearly: Alexandra labors to turn the prairie into a blooming garden, her brothers prefer to go into business in the town, while Crazy Ivar tries to preserve the wilderness quality of the land— "Ivar had lived for three years in the clay bank without defiling the face of nature any more than the coyote that had lived there before him had done" (36). In B. Traven's *The Treasure of Sierra Madre,* of the three adventurers who go off together in search of gold, only one holds to his purpose, surrendering his honor and eventually his life for it; another gives up the quest and is content to live with Indians in the wilderness, and the third plans to get a wife and farm.

Jack London's *Burning Daylight* is the story of a very capable man who discovers over a lifetime that being a successful gold-miner, stock speculator, and real estate developer—all prime Eldoradan occupations—is simply a matter of winning at gambling games, whereas being a farmer is reality and contentment. So committed does he become to farming that Elam Harnish covers up an outcropping vein of gold ore he accidentally discovers rather than spoil his new life and land as a farmer. This theme is continued in *The Valley of the Moon* for members of the working class, a teamster and a laundress who reject both the city life and prospecting in favor of farming: "We're not looking for gold but for chickens and a place to grow vegetables. Our folks had all the chance for gold in the early days, and what have they got to show for it?"[61] London's couple resembles the pair in Hawthorne's "The Great Carbuncle" who give up the search for "the wondrous gem" with its unnatural lustre in order to live in simple enjoyment of the "green earth . . . the blessed sunshine and the quiet moonlight."

Compromise has been the American way to resolve conflicting ideals of land usage. An Audubon or a Boone, while deeply respectful of the wilderness, could still engage in its exploitation. A fully committed wilderness man himself, Cooper's Leatherstocking yet generously risks his life to help settlers survive in a wilderness that they will one day destroy. A happier and less ironical compromise is to be found in the figure, like Thoreau and Ishmael, who fashions for himself the role of a detached observer of the natural environment without garnering any of its material rewards. Their solution is to establish themselves on a middle ground. Thoreau's retreat is a middle landscape, the region between the town and the woods where agriculture can be practiced on a very small scale, yet where the trees come up to the door of the hut. Huck Finn delights in another kind of middle landscape, the river, which helps him keep a safe distance from both farm and town, though at the end of his adventures even the river fails him and he must "light out for the Territory" to avoid being civilized. In the Western film the cowboy on a horse moves back and forth between the wilderness—vast jumbles of rocky terrain—and the ranch and town on the plain.

The most popular form of compromise has been that between farm and forest. American farmers have always known that good agricultural practice requires the proximity of wilderness, and the hunter-farmer is a figure reaching heroic proportions in American legend.

"Wild Pastoral" is the apt term John Seelye uses to differentiate the American version of the pastoral from, with its accommodation of wildness, from the Virgilian.[62] In books like *Wyandotte* and *The Red Rover,* for example, Cooper makes a much broader assimilation of farm to wilderness than he does in the Leatherstocking series; and in spite of his harsh statements about his farmer neighbors Thoreau could eulogize the "noble work" of plowing.[63]

To reconcile the pastoral with the wilderness, the constraints of farming with the freedom of the woods, was the task Robert Frost set himself. A favorite character of his is the mower who spares the wild flower, the farmer who makes some concession to "unharvested" nature. It is a lucky farmer, in "Blueberries," who spends time picking berries with his children:

> He has brought them all up on wild berries, they say,
> Like birds. . . .
> It's a nice way to live, . . .
> Just taking what Nature is willing to give,
> Not forcing her hand with harrow and plow.

When chores cannot be lightened in some way, the farm becomes a burden and the farmhouse a place of terrible fears and hopeless alienation between man and woman. The woods are then a refuge to flee to and a reminder of a value that bears remembering. In the very first poem of his first volume of poetry, Frost expresses a wish to "steal away" into the vastness of the forest. Duty forbids yielding to the spell of woodlands, but at least the poet-farmer is always aware of their presence on the edge of his fields or close to his dwelling, as in "Tree at My Window":

> Tree at my window, window tree,
> My sash is lowered when night comes on;
> But let there never be curtain drawn
> Between you and me.

and "The Sound of Trees":

> I wonder about the trees.
> Why do we wish to bear
> Forever the noise of these

> More than another noise
> So close to our dwelling place? . . .
> They are that that talks of going . . .

Frost's woods are thus quite tamed, more like Wordsworth's comforting groves than Faulkner's dense, semi-tropical growth or Cooper's Indian-infested wilds.

The latest compromise has been the growth of suburbs, particularly since the end of World War II when many Americans have had the old feeling of making a new start in life. In this version of the American dream the ideal dwelling-place is located between the commercial, money-making place—city, industrial complex, retail markets—and the farm and forest. But precious little landscape of this sort survives near suburbs, and the ritual cultivation of lawn and foliage is no substitute for the real thing. The suburb fails to supply a home on the land, the suburban home being a place almost without surroundings; consequently, suburbanites spend a surprising amount of time indoors, where, through communications technology of all sorts, they make contact with a wide and abstract world beyond their doors. The wilderness, if it is still sought on land and sea, must be reached by complicated and expensive travel. F. Scott Fitzgerald foresaw the folly of suburbanism in *The Great Gatsby,* in which there is graphically represented the dreamland of Long Island estates, the hot and oppressive city, and the wasteland between created by this artificial separation of functions. It is appropriate that the ash heaps between East Egg and New York City are described in terms of a fallen garden: "This is a valley of ashes—a fantastic farm where ashes grow like wheat into ridges ahd hills and grotesque gardens." The sea lies just beyond Gatsby's lawn, and a green light on the shore, on the dock of Daisy's estate, beckons Gatsby as the American coastline once beckoned Dutch explorers; but Daisy is no virgin continent, and Gatsby dies miserably in his swimming pool. Writing on John Cheever, another writer who portrays the failure of suburbia, Eugene Cheswick observes that American life has gone "from ocean side to pond side to pool side."[64] In Cheever's "The Swimmer," the hero's progress through a series of suburban pools leads him finally to his own house, where he finds that "the place was empty."

Important as they have been in the imaginative life of Americans, it must be conceded that the preconceptions of the New World we have been examining have not been prime movers in the motivation of Americans, for behind them there was always an ideal standing high and free above the details of place, the conviction that a new way of life could be attained in the new land. The imagery of garden, Eldorado, and wilderness merely gave this driving force the appearance of fact and reality. The efficient ideal was political, not spatial, not limited by the horizon of a specific locality. The error Columbus made—that he had discovered a *passage* to a lucrative trade route to the East rather than a great landmass—is an ironical anticipation of the still prevailing view of America as an opportunity for individual achievement rather than a place, a means rather than an end. More feeling has been generated by the ideal than by the actual occupation and possession of the land itself. Being an American, Archibald MacLeish seems to be saying in "American Letter," has nothing at all to do with geography:

> America is a great word and the snow,
> A way, a white bird, the rain falling,
> A shining thing in the mind and the gulls' call.

In a speech at an American Legion convention in 1952, Adlai Stevenson said:

> When an American says that he loves his country, he means not only that he love the New England hills, the prairies glistening in the sun, the wide and rising plains, the great mountains and the sea. He means that he loves an inner air, an inner light in which freedom lives and in which a man can draw the breath of self-respect.

Having such idealistic preconceptions and such abstract motivations, Americans appear not to feel much attachment to the land they live in. The charge is often made by hostile observers, but it is not altogether true, for many Americans have displayed a true love of their land through the extensive knowledge they have acquired about it and the painstaking work they have done to preserve and improve it. The wilderness has been the most deeply cherished place in our history. Although from a practical point of view agrarianism for a long time succeeded in binding more Americans to farmland, their feelings toward it, as we have seen, have always been ambivalent. The large city has never commanded respect, though the early towns, created by the needs of merchants and artisans in the eighteenth century, are still highly valued.

It is not that Americans have no profound feelings for the land, or wanted none, but that they have wavered between appreciation of the unspoiled wonders of a virgin land and determination to transform it for the uses of civilization they inherited from the European past. They experienced several possible relationships to the land in a relatively short period of time. A strong relationship with the environment is not easy to establish when the environment itself is being rapidly changed by man's works and when people move frequently from one home to another so that places never have the chance to acquire a history. "Our past is effaced almost before it is made present," complains a character in William Styron's *Set This House on Fire*. In "A Cabin in the Clearing" Frost tells about cabin dwellers who

> have been here long enough
> To push the woods back from around the house . . .
> And still I doubt if they know where they are,
> And I begin to fear they never will.

Asking the Red Man where they are probably would not help:

> If the day ever comes when they know who
> They are, they may know better where they are.

In using the land of the New World as a means of attaining ideal ends, Americans more easily abused the land. Because there was nothing sacred, or inviolable, about an adopted land—except to native Indians whose notions were either ignored or misunderstood—it was more readily transformed to realize ends that were deemed worthwhile. From the beginning land acquisition in the New World was accomplished through considerable violence and theft. A popular theme in American melodrama, it is treated in Hawthorne's *The House of the Seven Gables*. Possibly this is true of all original settlements in the history of mankind, but the American experience rankles because it is so recent and well documented. Violence and theft to gain possession of the land, wastefulness in its use—these characterized the American's relationship with the land in the past and still influence his relationship with the land in the present.

Running counter to these tendencies, however, were the efforts of settlers to sacralize the land, first when religious groups saw it as their God-given destiny and later, in the early nineteenth century, when the vogue for nature worship was imported from Europe and found abundant material in the wild landscape of America. Later, as settlers

moved out of the forested Eastern seaboard, which bore reassuring
resemblances to European landforms, they sought to endow the more
forbidding landscape of the West and Southwest with meaning by associating it with ancient Indian civilizations. Cooper in *The Prairie* and
Cather in *The Professor's House* draw on this material, but the sentiment has had no appreciable effect and it still remains difficult for the
American to think of his land in terms of the past event and the past
inhabitant. When Robert Frost was invited to read a poem at the Kennedy Inauguration in 1961, he chose "The Gift Outright," the ending of
which reads:

> Such as we were we gave ourselves outright . . .
> To the land vaguely realizing westward,
> But still unstoried, artless, unenhanced,
> Such as she was, such as she would become.

President Kennedy asked the poet to replace *would* with *will* in the last
line, a change that made the enhancement of the land through story and
art something to be achieved in the future rather than something that
had already been accomplished.

The recentness of the American occupation of the land and the
speed with which Americans have changed its face account for the
profound force of land in the life of the nation. That force is a mingling
of at least three feelings: love of the land when it represented the
symbol of American aspirations for a new life, hatred of the land as an
obstacle in the way of survival and material progress, and guilt over
misuse of the land, or guilt inspired by recognition of the gap between
love and hatred of the land. How people use the environment they live
in has an influence on how they feel about themselves. Harming the
environment amounts to harming oneself. In the American case the
harmful results of occupying the New World are all the more aggravated because the original aspirations were so high.

It may be that movement across seemingly unlimited space, more
than attachment to place, expresses the American's relation to his
land. "Thank fortune, we are not rooted to the soil," Emerson wrote in
his Journal, "and here is not all the world."[65] Displacement is the order
of American history, starting with the migration from Europe, followed
by the westward movement across the continent, and continuing with
the flight from farms and towns to the cities and, presently, the removal
of job-hunters from city to city. Ironically, Americans of European
origin in their turn have had to suffer what they had imposed upon
others—the dispossession and relocation of Indians and the forced
migration of blacks.

But not all movement was compelled, for movement may be preferred to remaining fixed by people in search of new life opportunities. To stay or to go has been the most common, and not necessarily unwelcome, decision for Americans to make. Jimmy Durante was hardly uttering nonsense when he sang:

> Did you ever have the feeling that you wanted to go
> And then had the feeling that you wanted to stay?

The prime hero of American literature is the man in motion, and he moves best through the wilderness because there is no stopping-place there. Leatherstocking travels West with the moving frontier, just ahead of the settlements; Ahab crosses seas, never making a landfall; Huck runs with the river, stopping only when occasion demands; the cowboy hero is master of the distances between frontier outposts. But motion cannot forever satisfy, and there have been stopping-places in the American experience. As well as those Americans who practiced quick exploitation of the land and removal to other sites, there were those who remained behind out of timidity or contentment with their lot. These may have suffered a sense of guilt over their failure to meet American standards of success, but they also developed a sense of devotion to the old place and its history. Hawthorne and early local colorists made literary capital of the guilt and the attachment of New Englanders, Faulkner of Southerners. It is ironical, but perfectly understandable, that those people who failed to realize American ideals of success are those who are most attached to the land. The process continues today, only now, with the sharp decrease in the amount of space to expand in, there is an even broader awareness of the gap between expectations and the actual results of land use. Radical changes in countryside and city since World War II visibly brought home this realization. Agribusiness, or the industrialization of agriculture, has reduced the farm-garden to a given volume of marketable soil; the passion for travel and recreation must now be added to extractive industries as rabid consumers of wilderness. Americans of the twentieth century, more than any other generation, suffer from the Rip Van Winkle syndrome, the disquieting discovery that a place has been transformed almost beyond recognition. This disorientation may not be lasting, however; the sense of failure and guilt may possibly do more to strengthen ties with the land than the pride of achievement. The old images of the land no longer apply, but new expectations, more reasonable than the old, may be forming from their ruins.

6

PLACELESSNESS
*The Concern of
Twentieth-Century Literature*

Romanticism taught literature to respect the creative influence that places in the natural environment could have on the life of the individual. Attuned to both exterior and interior space, romanticism developed a method for the use of place in the representation of an inwardness that could be ecstatically at home either in the universe or beyond it. Naturalism took an opposite direction when it documented the findings of biological and social sciences with demonstrations of the absolute power of environment and the disorientation of the individual in a world being transformed by industrialism and war. It set itself the task of showing the painful results on people of a vast change from a traditional, relatively natural environment to an artificial, hastily improvised one. The naturalistic version of the influence of environment saw place, among other factors, victimizing man rather than nourishing or restoring him. It reflected the decline of earth as the home of mankind, the loss of cherished places, and the despair of placelessness. This view had already dawned in the romantic era, but naturalistic writing developed a persuasive, though dull, method to present the effects of a depreciated world. Through massive accumulations of place details laid out side by side without differentiation, the naturalistic novel contracted space, an effect quite the opposite of the romantic techniques that produced a feeling of expansiveness by means of the poet's passionate identification with places. One might disagree with the theory of environmental determinism that naturalism put forward but not with the record it compiled of its time, for recent history has confirmed the impression that the quality of traditionally honored places has deteriorated, if the places themselves have not entirely disappeared, and a whole new set of questionable places is being created by new social and economic forces.

The centralization of governing power and economic process, the development of transportation and communication, the radical redistribution of dwelling places are among the new conditions that have diminished the importance of place and increased the importance of movement in twentieth-century life. Mass media—radio, television, the press—dissolve the differences between peoples that space once supported, and location is no longer of crucial importance in bringing people and things together. In his immensely influential *Future Shock,* Alvin Toffler speaks of the demise of geography:

> Never in history has distance meant less. Never have man's relationships with place been more numerous, fragile and temporary. . . . We are witnessing a historic decline in the significance of place to human life. We are breeding a new race of nomads, and few suspect quite how massive, widespread and significant their migrations are.[1]

The "concomitant of mobility," Toffler points out, is "the shorter duration of place relationships" (93). Another result of mobility and the worldwide spread of common technologies is that every part of the world is beginning to look like every other part. The growing uniformity of places alarms those who see the impoverishment of life in the loss of variety. Theodore Roszak warns that within a few generations "worldwide technological coalescence" will create "an oppressive urban-industrial uniformity over the earth," leaving no place worth visiting since "Almost every place is becoming Anyplace."[2]

The disappearance of familiar places and the proliferation of a more and more limited set of uniform places have caused a peculiarly modern malaise called *placelessness.* What poets and novelists have been observing for the past hundred years now comes to the attention of sociologists and geographers. It is particularly painful for geography, the study of places, to take placelessness into account. One geographer who does is Edward Relph in a book entitled *Place and Placelessness:*

> Placelessness describes both an environment without significant places and the underlying attitude which does not acknowledge significance in places. It reaches back into the deepest levels of place, cutting roots, eroding symbols, replacing diversity with uniformity and experiential order with conceptual order. At its most profound it consists of a pervasive and perhaps irreversible alienation from places as the homes of men.[3]

Assaults on the certainties of place are reflected in literature by frequent expressions of loss and regret over the passing of old places and bitter disaffection with new places. Place loss, place devaluation, has been without question one of the principal motifs of literature over the last one hundred years, and from one point of view modern literature is a dialogue of opposed positions regarding the individual's relation to the emerging new world as a place. The despair of deracination is countered with the hope of restoring attachments to remnant places, expatriation alternates with return to the impaired homeland, disaffection is answered with accommodation to the new places of our time. Writers for whom neither alienation nor recommitment is acceptable turn to other choices: escape into nostalgia, distortions of place through fantasy and hallucination, and the rejection of place altogether in favor of other dimensions of existence such as time and motion.

LOST PLACES

The Garden

Was this garden, then, the Eden of the present world?—
Hawthorne, "Rappaccini's Daughter"

Lingering romanticism has filled literature with a sense of loss of once-cherished places—the pastoral countryside, the greenwood, the garden, the village, the country house, the city street and square. Particularly keen has been the regret over the lost garden and lost love in the garden.

Because the garden is the epitome of all earthly delights, it is especially susceptible to loss and destruction. It offers material ease, harmony with nature, love's pleasures and virtue's rewards, but these may be snatched away through human error or natural catastrophe. Living in Eden carries with it the possibility of disaster by reason of the tabu that is attached to its proper use. With proper care England could be "this other Eden, demi-paradise," says Gaunt in *Richard II,* but with lapse of care it may be "full of weeds, her fairest flowers choked up." Every age has availed itself of the double garden theme of possession and loss. Losing the garden leads to feelings of guilt and the hope of return, which may be accomplished geographically, as in the return to Zion or migration to America, or spiritually, as in the restoration of political forms in *Richard II* or moral regeneration in Dante and Milton. There is no question for Milton of a return to Eden in the physical sense—at least not for his Adam, though it may be possible for Eve, who is allowed to make Adam her paradise:

> with thee to goe,
> Is to stay here . . . thou to mee
> Art all things under Heav'n, all places thou.
> (*Paradise Lost* XII.615–8)

The progress from an actual garden in the original creation to a spiritual garden at the end of creation is annunciated in *Paradise Lost* ("A paradise within thee, happier far") and confirmed in *Paradise Regained*. The return is a return of God to man, not a return of man to place, which is a matter of indifference, theologically speaking. On the Day of Judgment the "True Image of the Father" is enshrined "In fleshly Tabernacle, and human form" (IV. 596–9). All that remains of Eden is a vivid memory adding piquancy to the sense of loss and imagistic form to the eventual spiritual rehabilitation of man. With God's return man's inner moral strength in the midst of worldly temptations is *like* a walled garden in the wilderness. With his resistance to Satan in *Paradise Regained* Christ himself has revealed the true paradise:

> Infernal Ghosts, and Hellish Furies, round
> Environ'd thee, some howl'd, some yell'd, some shriek'd,
> Some bent at thee thir fiery darts, while thou
> Satt'st unappall'd in calm and sinless peace. (IV.422–25)[4]

It is this Christian, transcendent Eden that T. S. Eliot employs in *Four Quartets*. At first the garden in "Burnt Norton" is the rather explicitly described scene of an incipient, or perhaps only imaginary, love affair in a time of innocence; when the poet returns to the garden at the end of the poem, it is the Day of Judgment,

> When the last of earth left to discover
> Is that which was the beginning.

But now the garden is transformed into a metaphor of spiritual health; its "hidden waterfall" and "children in the apple-tree" cannot be known but only "heard, half-heard in the stillness," for now paradise is

A condition of complete simplicity
(Costing not less than everything)
And all shall be well and
All manner of thing shall be well.

Highest among the costs that must be paid to gain this inner paradise is
the renunciation of human love, a surrender of the woman in the garden that Eliot anticipates in "Ash-Wednesday":

The Single Rose
Is now the Garden
Where all loves end. (II.32–4)

In *Four Quartets* a "tongue of flame" is added to the rose: "And the fire
and the rose are one." As in Dante, the rose appears first as the symbol
of human love in a real enough place and then as the object-symbol of
human love transformed into divine love by a process of growing ab-
stractionism.[5]

Eliot's traditional treatment of the garden is certainly not typical
of the majority report of his time, which finds in the fallen garden a
symbol of earth's actual decline as a suitable environment for man and
his aspirations. For Christianity and Eliot the garden is God-given and
is lost through defective faith; the modern view, beginning in the eighteenth century, sees the fall of the garden in more naturalistic—we now
say, ecological—terms as a result of the harmful effects wrought upon
countryside and city by industrialism and war. These have fed literature's obsession with the degradation of the earthly paradise, the failure of love in the garden, and the doubtful return.

Intimations of the lost garden begin with the romantic poets,
whose favorite theme was the separation of the child from Nature, or
wild garden, and his eventual return as an adult by one means or
another—poetry, love, memory. Bossey was Rousseau's childhood
Eden, lost through a false accusation of wrong-doing and regained
when Rousseau settled down with Madame de Warens at Les Char-
mettes. The "wild wood" Poe knew as a child is temporarily regained in
a "calmer hour" when the adult poet takes time out to write poetry.
Coleridge's poetry is full of "the way back" to lost paradises.
Wordsworth attempts to make a return to the childhood paradise
through the recollection of past feelings if not the re-possession of
places.

Of all the English Romantics Byron is most concerned with the fall from Eden and the attempt to regain it through love, and his pessimistic mood is closest to the modern mood. For Byron, as one of his readers put it, love "*is* paradise regained."[6] But Byron was able to offer only one rather weak example of Adam and Eve being permanently restored to Eden. In "The Island" the native girl Neuha, "gentle savage of the wild," and the European Torquil, "a truant mutineer" from the *Bounty*, flee her South Pacific island home, a "guilt-won paradise" occupied by the mutineers. After Christian Fletcher and his companions die at the hands of British marines, the lovers return to the island, now "no more polluted with a hostile hue," and presumably live there happily ever after. The Haidee episode in *Don Juan* does not turn out as well. The lovers remain tainted because, like the ill-fated maidens and suitors in the *Odyssey*, they have enjoyed their guilty love while the master of the island has been absent: "Haidee forgot the island was her sire's." Upon his return the lovers are separated and "the isle is now all desolate and bare." Don Juan's travels end in London, which is described as a parody of paradise: his chariot passes

> Through Groves, so call'd as being void of trees
>   (Like *lucus* from *no* light); through prospects named
> Mount Pleasant, as containing nought to please,
>   Nor much to climb; through little boxes framed
> Of bricks, to let the dust in at your ease,
>   With 'To be let' upon their doors proclaim'd;
> Through 'Rows' most modestly call'd 'Paradise,'
> Which Eve might quit without much sacrifice. (XI.21)

For Childe Harold, we recall, the ultimate place, "the scene/Which is his last," is the sea, which cannot be ravaged by man:

> Dark-heaving;—boundless, endless, and sublime—
> The image of Eternity—the throne
> Of the invisible. . . ." (183)

But Byron could imagine a condition of earth in which even that refuge is denied to the Pilgrim seeking an earthly paradise: In "Darkness" the sea itself is desolate as the world comes to an end:

> The rivers, lakes, and ocean all stood still,
> And nothing stirr'd within their silent depths . . .
> The waves were dead; the tides were in their grave . . .

Needless to say, there is no Adam and Eve in this end-of-the-world scene; two survivors die when they see "their mutual hideousness" by the "dying embers of an altar-place" fire:

> No love was left;
> All earth was but one thought—and that was death.

Brooding over the unrecoverable garden paradise was voiced occasionally by Victorian writers—the Arnold of "Dover Beach" and the Tennyson of "Lockesley Hall Sixty Years After." Tennyson's return to a place and Arnold's, in "Resignation," are certainly not as happy as Wordsworth's in "Tintern Abbey." The place endures changeless for Arnold, but it "seems to bear rather than rejoice," and Tennyson is struck with the recognition that "All the world is ghost to me," a latter-day prospect of a forlorn world corresponding to Arnold's in "Dover Beach" and Browning's in "Childe Roland to the Dark Tower Came"—

> and now mere earth
> Desperate and done with.

Ruskin felt that England was a paradise ruined by "turning flower-beds into heaps of coke," but was hopeful that woman might redeem it since "female power" is the guardian of earth's fruits.[7] In *The King of the Golden River* a valley laid waste by economic greed is made fertile again through love.

The lost paradise theme is particularly strong in American literature because the disillusionment is greater, America having been considered the site itself of a new Eden. Herman Melville, like Byron, sought island paradises and found instead a succession of infernos. Hawthorne presaged the twentieth-century theme of the fallen garden and the failure of love as he tested in one work after another the capability of modern man to accept an Eve who has been tainted by a fallen environment. Giovanni, the young lover in "Rappaccini's Daughter," fails the test because he mistakenly assumes that Beatrice's heart is as false as the poisoned garden her father has brought her up in, "the Eden of the present world." Donatello, in *The Marble Faun,* for a long while abandons his sinful Eve in Rome and retreats to his ancestral Arcadia in Tuscany; finally he rejoins Miriam, not to walk with her in a garden as he had done formerly but to be together in prison to pay for the murder they had committed. Holgrave and Phoebe, in *The House of the Seven Gables,* are Hawthorne's most hopeful pair as they make the best of a guilt-ridden world that is symbolized by the haunted house and the decaying garden behind it.

Thomas Hardy worked out similar but more realistic tests in his novels. His settings are symbolic of the forlorn world of his time, early modern wastelands that crush the human spirit and forbid love and life. The second stanza of "The Darkling Thrush" presents a striking image of cosmic desolation:

> The land's sharp features seemed to be
> The Century's corpse outleant,
> His crypt the cloudy canopy,
> The wind his death-lament.
> The ancient pulse of germ and birth
> Was shrunken hard and dry,
> And every spirit upon earth
> Seemed fervorless as I.

A more specific wasteland image, a setting suitable for characters in a novel to play out their lives in, is "the vast tract of unenclosed wild known as Egdon Heath" in *The Return of the Native*. Like Hawthorne and Melville, Hardy substituted infernal for paradisal places to represent the world. "Haggard Egdon," he writes in the first chapter, "appealed to a subtler and scarcer instinct, to a more recently learned emotion, than that which responds to the sort of beauty called charming and fair." It is a matter of satisfying the mood of the time, he continues:

> Indeed, it is a question if the exclusive reign of this orthodox beauty is not approaching its last quarter. The new Vale of Tempe may be a gaunt waste in Thule: human souls may find themselves in closer and closer harmony with external things wearing a sombreness distasteful to our race when it was young. The time seems near, if it has not actually arrived, when the chastened sublimity of a moor, a sea, or a mountain will be all of nature that is absolutely in keeping with the moods of the more thinking among mankind.[8]

Though written earlier, *The Return of the Native* represents a more advanced stage in Hardy's conception of the modern world as a wasteland than *Tess of the D'Urbervilles* and *Jude the Obscure,* in which the flaws of seemingly paradisal places, such as Froom Valley and Christminster, have to be discovered by innocents who search for a new home in a world they have not entirely despaired of.

Tess is a product of the new agrarianism of industrialized farm labor, more specifically a victim of the abuse of the land's fertility by male domination. She is seduced by her upper-class landholder kinsman in "the oldest wood in England," and she is abandoned by another man in the fertile Valley of the Dairies. All of the traditionally good features of the garden are turned to evil results. After her failure to continue in the old country ways, Tess is again sexually abused, this time figuratively, by the harvest machinery that transforms the rural scene into an inferno. Tess, her mother, and sisters—a family whose ancestors dwelt in one place for five hundred years—become migrant farm laborers, experiencing the same kind of rural displacement that John Steinbeck was to picture much later in *The Grapes of Wrath*.

While it is the failure of fertility in the countryside that undoes Tess, it is the inadequacy of England's towns that denies Jude his chance to realize himself. Jude is cruelly deceived by the town of Christminster, which, in the distance, appears to his young eyes as "the heavenly Jerusalem" and the "place which he could call admirable," where he could "set himself to some mighty undertaking." But Christminster simply does not correspond to "the poetized locality he dwelt in" in his untutored imagination; the medievalism he worshipped remains only in the decaying architecture of the college buildings and the pedantry of the dons. Jude has no interest in the actual contemporary life of the town that has moved to "a spot called the Fourways in the middle of the city." Just as Tess was at her best as an oldstyle milkmaid and out of tune with mechanized agriculture, so Jude, a stonecutter with a passion for Gothic church-building, is out of touch with modern means of production. Both find it hard to adjust to the changes made by new technology and to surrender their notions of the ideal countryside and town; both are victims of class and sexual mistreatment that seems to thrive among dislocated people.

Turned out of places that once could have nurtured them, Tess and Jude must "enter on a shifting, almost nomadic, life," wandering miserably from one place to another, each succeeding place worse than the last. In a tragic declension, Tess goes from the teeming dairyland of Talbothays to larger and less fertile farms, to "higher and drier levels" of land, until she reaches Flintcomb-Ash, "a starve-acre place." After being rejected by the college in Christminster, Jude lowers his sights somewhat and removes to Melchester, then to Aldbrickham, a city that has none of the associations with church and medievalism that Jude so fervently desires. There follow two years of roving from town to town in search of small stone-cutting jobs. The lowest point in his effort to maintain his superannuated craft is reached when, in reverting to his first trade, the baking business, he bakes gingerbread cakes in the form of Gothic buildings—"Christminster cakes" are hawked in the streets by his wife Sue.

Ironically, the homelessness of Tess and Jude is played out against the backdrop of an ancient land where intense life and spirit throbbed in many generations of men. Now barrenness and dessication reign. Jude directs his steps wherever he can find the remnants of England's medieval past. Tess sometimes moves among the ruins of her once noble family's estates, and her final refuge is the altar stone at Stonehenge: "The stone was warm and dry, in comforting contrast to the rough and chill grass around." Death, not life on earth, is her lot. "So now I am at home," she says resignedly.

The tragedy of Tess and Jude is that they remain sensitive to places when the activity of the modern world is no longer tied to places but to processes and motions. This truth occurs to Jude, though he is powerless to act on it:

> He saw what a curious and cunning glamour the neighborhood of the place had exercised over him. To get there and live there, to move among the churches and halls and become imbued with the *genius loci,* had seemed to his dreaming youth, as the spot shaped its charms to him from its halo on the horizon, the obvious and ideal thing to do. . . . It would have been far better for him in every way if he had never come within sight and sound of the delusive precincts, had gone to some busy commercial town with the sole object of making money by his wits, and thence surveyed his plan in true perspective.[9]

Tess, too, wanted to be æn integral part of the scene" she inhabited. But, unable to support their lives in the places of their choice, Tess and Jude are forced to maintain life through constant movement; in searching for a place to dwell in they are committed to endless journeying. Against their will they are thrown into a predicament that has become all too familiar to their twentieth-century successors, the substitution of motion for place.

In *Return of the Native* the world has reached a condition of universal bleakness; there is no variety to explore in travels, no paradisal retreats, no further disillusionment, only the will to accommodate oneself to a diminshed world or perish. To Eustacia Vye, a lightsome creature brought up in a seaside resort, Egdon Heath is hell and she an imprisoned Eurydice waiting for an Orpheus to deliver her.

The first scene finds her on the highest point of the heath, telescope in hand, seeking out the window of Wildeve, the man who seems at the present to be her best means of escape. In returning to the "airy perch" where she lives with her grandfather, a mishap occurs that symbolizes her relationship to her surroundings: "A bramble caught hold of her skirt, and checked her progress. Instead of putting it off and hastening along, she yielded herself up to the pull, and stood passively still. When she began to extricate herself it was by turning round and round, and so unwinding the prickly switch. She was in a desponding reverie" (80). Eustacia yearns to escape but must submit to the place. For Clym Yeobright, however, Egdon Heath is the place he has elected to return to after having experienced the freedom of living abroad. The perspective of distance has proved to him that he is a product of the home place, that he is "permeated with its scenes, with its substance"; he prefers its deprivation to the indulgent materialism of the world beyond the heath, the world Eustacia thinks she must have in order to live. Hardy leaves no doubt that Clym is a man of the future, one of the "advanced races," because he can turn away from the "old-fashioned revelling" in the happier conditions of earlier times and face up to the grim operation of natural law that now makes life "a thing to be put up with." Clym revels in the untamable wildness of Egdon Heath as he views it from the heights, "indulging in a barbarous satisfaction at observing that, in some of the attempts at reclamation from the waste, tillage, after holding on for a year or two, had receded again in despair, the ferns and furze-tufts stubbornly reasserting themselves" (192).

The Return of the Native looks forward to a good deal of twentieth-century literature that explores the adjustment of characters to a diminished world. Making do with the wasteland is not the choice of D. H. Lawrence, however. Having learned from Hardy that love as well as environment fails people like Tess and Jude, that a terrible sense of placelessness goes with disillusionment with love, Lawrence yet maintains the hope of removal to another place where the spirit of lovers may be restored.

In Paul Morel, the hero of Sons and Lovers, is incorporated the experience of both Tess and Jude. His affair with Miriam takes place in an idyllic English countryside, where for a week Paul and Miriam play the part of lovers in a "small and cosy" cottage near "a bright little brook that ran into a bog at the foot of a very steep bank. Here they wandered, picking still a few marsh marigolds and many big blue forget-me-nots" (301). The setting transfigures the pair: "she sat on the bank with her hands full of flowers, mostly golden water-blobs. As she put her face down into the marigolds, it was all overcast with a yellow shine." Paul's affair with Clara has a much different setting, the industrial town of Nottingham, which is within commuting distance from his home in the colliery town. The River Trent is the place where Paul and Clara first make love, and to reach the spot the couple must make a perilous descent down a "steep bank of red clay" until they reach a place where "two beech-trees side by side on the hill held a little level on the upper face between their roots. It was littered with damp leaves, but it would do." Beside them "the river slid by in a body, utterly silent and swift, intertwining among itself like some subtle, complex creature." After they arise, Paul "saw suddenly sprinkled on the black, wet beech-roots many scarlet carnation petals, like splashed drops of blood; and red, small splashes fell from her bosom." Later on in their affair, when love-making had become "mechanical," they return to the same spot to see if they can renew the satisfaction they once had: "They would be very near, almost dangerously near to the river, so that the black water ran not far from his face, and it gave a little thrill" (378).

Clearly, the brook and the flowers in the scene with Miriam constitute a pastoral place for innocent, idealized love, whereas the River Trent is the setting of an affair made preternaturally passionate by the frustrating industrial environs in which it occurs. But Paul is typical of the modern hero who cannot find love in either countryside or town; innocence, in keeping with an abstract pastoral ideal, keeps him from giving himself wholly and Miriam from receiving him wholly, while guilt leads Paul to restore Clara to her husband. At the close of the novel, with both affairs over and his mother dead, Paul is truly forlorn, having been stripped of relationships to people and places—the home, the farm, and the town. He suffers the despair of placelessness that echoes so often twentieth-century literature following Lawrence:

> The town, as he sat upon the car, stretched away over the bay of railway, a level fume of lights. Beyond the town the country, little smouldering spots for more towns—the sea—the night—on and on! And he had no place in it! Whatever spot he stood on, there he stood alone. From his breast, from his mouth, sprang the endless space, and it was there behind, everywhere. (435)

Paul is almost persuaded to join his mother in death, in the darkness that surrounds him, just as he has been drawn to darkness many times before in his walks with Miriam in the woods around Willey Farm. But Paul is not Gerald Crich, who succumbs to the attraction of a deathly place after he loses Gudrun and his father; Paul is strong enough to reject the image of himself as "infinitesimal, at the core of nothingness." Like Bunyan's Christian he has passed through the country of Beulah, or the experience of woman's love, and is rewarded with the vision of the Heavenly Jerusalem:

> But no, he would not give in. Turning sharply, he walked towards the city's gold phosphorescence. His fists were shut, his mouth set fast. He would not take that direction, to the darkness, to follow her. He walked towards the faintly humming, glowing town, quickly. (436)

Ursula at the end of *The Rainbow* has a similar hopeful view of a shining place to be found in the future: "She saw in the rainbow the earth's new architecture, the old, brittle corruption of houses and factories swept away, the world built up in a living fabric of Truth, fitting to the over-arching heaven." The same image occurs in the report of a dream Lawrence had in which the colliery town where he was born is seen "rising from the hill-top in the afternoon light like the walls of Jerusalem."[10] A pattern emerges in Lawrence's works as well as in his personal travels: after disillusionment with people and places in a certain situation, a vision of a new place arises, and the cycle begins anew with a journeying out to the world in search of it. Hardy's Jude sees the "city of light" at the start of his career and, disillusioned and crushed, dies in Christminster at the end. Paul, on the other hand, has a vision of the golden city after a course of disillusionment; he is then ready for reincarnation in other heroes, in the person of Birkin in *Women in Love,* for example.

Willey Farm, the English Eden in *Sons and Lovers,* becomes Willey Water in *Women in Love,* and this time the idyllic place turns out to be what its name suggests, a Will-o'-the-wisp or *ignis fatuus.* It is the culminating image in the decline of English pastoralism that Lawrence traces in *Sons and Lovers, The Rainbow,* and *Women in Love.* Willey Water and its immediate surroundings dominate the entire long first part of the novel. It is the place where the Crich manor house, Shortlands, is located, the center of traditional English country life with its round of public occasions; it is the place where lovers meet, where "water-plants rose up, thick and cool and fleshy, very straight and turgid." But Willey Water is one of those pastoral places that incorporates death as well as life *(et in Arcadia ego).* At a Crich party for the people of the region a daughter of the family and her young doctor friend are drowned in a boating accident; the water of the pond is drained to discover at the bottom the bodies of the lovers in deathly embrace. The people disperse, and Willy Water is never the same again.[11] In his dying hour Gerald Crich's father learns that the lake will have to be drained again because the water is leaking into one of the coal pits; the beautiful pond must be sacrificed to industry, a consequence the father deplores and the son presides over.[12] The old man dies and Gerald is left "alone with death, facing the winter-black landscape"; he feels "suspended on the edge of a void."

Willey water is representative of pastoral England, of a world that is polluted in its physical features, obsolete in its social forms, and fallen spiritually. Shortlands may have been a desirable goal for a Jane Austen heroine but not for Lawrence's.[13] Another manor house in the neighborhood, Breadalby, is described as looking "like an English drawing of the old school. . . . as final as an old aquatint." Birkin flees the house and its mistress. What has replaced the past is even less tolerable. The middle-class home of the Brangwen sisters in the town of Beldover is a horror. "Can you believe you lived in this place and never felt it?" Gudrun asks her sister as they return to close up the house that had been their girlhood home. "Everything was null to the senses, there was enclosure without substance"; the drawing room was "another piece of shut-in air; without weight or substance, only a sense of intolerable papery imprisonment in nothingness" (382). The region in which these houses are located is "defaced"; the colliery towns are "like a country in the underworld," "warrens of meanness," "a vision of hell"; going to London is a "real death." The whole earth has been despoiled by man:

> The sea they turned into a murderous alley and a soiled road of commerce, disputed like the dirty land of a city every inch of it. The air they claimed too, shared it up, parcelled it out to certain owners, they trespassed in the air to fight for it. Everything was gone, walled in, with spikes on the top of the walls, and one must ignominiously creep between the spiky walls through a labyrinth of life. (193)

The romantic association of love and place comes to an end in *Women in Love*. Escape from the sordid middle-class environment into the upper-class ambiance does not ensure success for Ursula and Gudrun; the lovers are turned out of the paradisal place, which, like Eden, has fallen, and must "wander about the face of the earth," as Birkin

puts it. The tasteful apartment Birkin had set up in the Old Mill at
Willey Water seemed to Ursula a perfect place for them to set up
housekeeping, and it would have satisfied many an ordinary couple.
But Birkin would not have it, and Ursula must learn about the new
dispensation for lovers, placeless wandering:

> "We must get out," he said . . .
> "I should be perfectly happy at the Mill," she said.
> "It's very near the old thing," he said. "Let us wander a bit . . ."
> "Where will we wander to?" she asked.
> "I don't know. I feel as if I would just meet you and we'd set off—
> just towards the distance." (321)

The consummation of their love occurs in a clearing of Sherwood
Forest, to which they had driven in Birkin's new automobile: "The
green lane widened into a little circle of grass, where there was a small
trickle of water at the bottom of a sloping bank." After making love,
"they slept the chilly night through under the hood of the car." The
clearing in the forest we shall see again in "a secret little clearing,"
"one of the unravished places," where Lady Chatterley and the gardener make love. The remnants of the ancient English forest make the
only place where true love may thrive, and even that refuge is gone in
E. M. Forster's *Maurice,* which tells a story of homosexual love that
"belongs to the last moment of the greenwood. . . . There is no forest or
fell to escape to today" (254)

Homelessness is a lesson Ursula never quite takes to heart, any
more than Lawrence himself, who spent a lifetime travelling around
the world, as Mark Schorer puts it, "to discover a place where the vital
connections could be maintained intact."[14] Upon leaving England for
the continent with Birkin, Ursula looks forward to "the unknown paradise towards which she was going, a sweetness of habitation, a delight
of living quite unknown, but hers infallibly" (397). Wherever she goes
she pines for the places of her childhood as these were earlier described in *The Rainbow;* a cowshed in the Alps, for example, reminds
her of Marsh Farm. When she gets Birkin to flee with her from the
Alpine hotel, she comforts herself with the thought that Italy is not far
away:

> Now suddenly, as by a miracle she remembered that away
> beyond, below her, lay the dark fruitful earth, that towards the
> south there were stretches of land with orange trees and cypress,

grey with olives, that ilex trees lifted wonderful plumy tufts in
shadow against a blue sky. Miracle of miracles! this utterly silent,
frozen world of the mountain-tops was not universal! One might
leave it and have done with it. One might go away. (446)

With Birkin, however, Lawrence is much more uncompromising,
for Birkin half knows there is no ideal place in the world and he is
accordingly intent only on the trip, which signifies to him a "transit out
of life" into the unknown, or out of the customary life of his time into
mysterious areas of human behavior involving possibly a new order of
relations with women and men. Earlier in his career Lawrence had
created an Ursula who wanted to leave the homeplace, unlike her
mother, Anna, for whom her husband and sons "staked out and
marked her horizon." The Brangwen men were content to stay on the
farm at Cossethay, even though it was beginning to suffer from the
inroads of industrialism. At the close of the book Ursula has no "al-
located place" but looks forward "into the undiscovered land before
her." In *Women in Love* Lawrence returns to the traditional split between the home-seeking woman and the night-journeying man. Ursula
everywhere sees places that remind her of Marsh Farm, Birkin sees
only the adventures of new human relationships. In his new conception
of love the life of lovers cannot be pinned down to places. It is essential
"to be free, in a free place . . . It isn't the locality, though . . . It's a
perfected relation between you and me, and others" (322). Ursula pro-
tests:

> "But one must live somewhere."
> "Not somewhere—anywhere," he said. "One should just live
> anywhere—not have a definite place. I don't want a definite place.
> As soon as you get a room, and it is *complete,* you want to run
> from it. Now my rooms at the Mill are quite complete, I want them
> at the bottom of the sea. It is a horrible tyranny of a fixed milieu,
> where each piece of furniture is a commandment-stone." (365)

The journey of lovers into the unknown land begins with the sexual
encounter; Birkin's body becomes the mysterious realm for Ursula to
discover: "There were strange fountains of his body, more mysterious
and potent than any she had imagined, or known . . . She had thought
there was no source deeper than the phallic source. And now, behold,
from the smitten rock of the man's body, from the strange marvellous
flanks and thighs, deeper, further in mystery than the phallic source,
came the floods of ineffable darkness and ineffable richness" (320).

Ursula and Birkin learn the lesson of lovers in the modern world: They leave the fallen garden and face the journey into the unknown courageously, she with hope to find a new paradise, he with wonder only for the journey itself. Gudrun and Gerald are likewise turned out of the garden, which Gerald has helped to despoil through his mining operations, but, failing to find love for each other, they succumb to the place of death, the Alpine resort where the two couples had come to spend a holiday. Through their love Ursula and Birkin are able to withstand "the stillness, the cold, the frozen eternality"; they are able to leave that place and continue their wandering. To Gerald and Gudrun, however, the Alpine scene is the final, sterile world itself and, being committed to the world, they cannot leave the resort. Gerald willfully dies there, and Gudrun falls under the influence of Loerke, with whom she plays a game in which, paradoxically, to express their worldliness they imagine all sorts of catastrophes that will bring the world to an end. Gerald had come to be Gudrun's world, and with his death "the world was finished now, for her. There was only the inner, individual darkness." She is left like Paul facing death, but she sees no golden city in her future, only Dresden in the company of Loerke. Gudrun "wanted to gather the glowing, eternal peaks to her breast, and die." The world has turned to ice, garden flowers are covered with snow. Gudrun conceives the notion that the Schnapps she and Loerke drink when they go tobogganing has been distilled from "the bilberries under the snow. . . . It is exactly as if one could smell them through the snow." Loerke dismisses the remark as one of Gudrun's "verbal extravagances." The implication of the Alpine episode, the transformation of Eden into a frozen inferno, is more explicitly drawn out in Pynchon's *V.* In digging a cache in Vheissu, a wasteland country in Antarctica, Hugh Godolphin makes the same discovery as Gudrun:

> Two or three feet down I struck clear ice. . . . Staring up at me through the ice, perfectly preserved, its fur still rainbow-colored, was the corpse of one of their spider monkeys. . . . I think they left it there for me. . . . A mockery, you see: a mockery of life, planted where everything but Hugh Godolphin was inanimate. With of course the implication. . . . If Eden was the creation of God, God only knows that evil created Vheissu. . . . Vheissu itself, a gaudy dream. Of what the Antarctic in this world is closest to: a dream of annihilation.[15]

Pipit's husband in Eliot's "A Cooking Egg" ask the question, "Where are the eagles and the trumpets?" The answer, like Lawrence's and

Pynchon's comes back, "Buried beneath some snow-deep Alps." April is the cruelest month because its signs of reviving life are so ironically pitiful in the midst of universal lifelessness.

England is a fallen paradise for Lawrence's lovers, who are forced out into the world to search for other places. Is it possible for lovers to remain in the ruined garden? Lady Chatterley and the game-keeper try this solution but must give it up when they realize that their love is becoming infected by degradation of their surroundings. Mellors must admit "that the seclusion of the wood was illusory." He considers emigrating to America, but nothing comes of it. Anyway, the exotic place offers no better chance than the outworn home place and the lovers who seek it invariably become permanent wanderers.

Samburan is an island in the Java Sea, but, like England, it too has been tainted by coal mining. Still, to Conrad's fleeing lovers in *Victory*, it seems preferable to the "garish, unrestful hotel" that the world has become. Samburan is a short sail from Sourabaya, the center of whatever civilization there is in the Java Sea archipelago, and though it is no longer paradisal it is at least a place apart, a border place between civilization and jungle wilderness. Heyst and Lena take up residence in the "abandoned settlement" made by the now defunct Tropical Belt Coal Company, of which Heyst was once the engineer. He regrets now his part in the attempt to exploit the island's resources, "a great step forward, as some people used to call it with mistaken confidence." Heyst and Lena are people defeated by civilization who want now only to live in peace among the ruins it has left. "This seemed to be an inexpugnable refuge," says Heyst, "where we could live untroubled and learn to know each other." But the experiment fails. Civilization in the form of three desperadoes seeks out Heyst for gain. The couple are denied asylum in the jungle by the natives, who want no further contact with civilization: a pile of "fresh-cut branches" in the path makes "a barrier against the march of civilization." On the seaward side of the island there is the ocean, transformed into an "abomination of desolation" by the glare of the sun. The unfortunate lovers cannot establish a lasting middle condition between the two elemental wildernesses.

Heyst is a kind of reformed Gerald Crich and his Samburan is the kind of "free place" that Birkin sets out to find with Ursula, a place where the relationship between a man and woman can be perfected. This cannot be the usual place, house, or middle-class environment. "No. We've got to live in the chinks they leave us," says Birkin. An island in the Java Sea is the chink Heyst has chosen, a place abandoned in the "march" of civilization, but it is rediscovered by civilization and Heyst's hopes go up in the fire he sets. This is better than the icy end of

Gerald's and Gudrun's love—at least "fire purifies everything." And the love of Heyst and Lena has been heroic: She sacrifices her life for him and he, too late, recognizes the importance of love and life: "Ah, Davidson, woe to the man whose heart has not learned while young to hope, to love—to put its trust in life!"

Nostromo has a similar theme in a much more complex social setting. Charles and Emilia Gould try to make a worthwhile life in Costaguana, a country between the high mountains of the Cordillera and the "immense indifference" of the sea. Their fortunes, too, are involved with an abandoned mine, which, upon being brought back into production, opens up the whole country to materialistic values that eventually consume life and love. The materialistic appropriation of earth makes a wasteland of Conrad's and Lawrence's worlds.

Love may compensate Antony for a lost empire and Byron for a lost Eden. Matthew Arnold is willing to settle merely for loyalty between lovers. In a world once "so various, so beautiful, so new" and now "a darkling plain," at least lovers can be "true to one another." But what is the result when love fails, too? Lawrence gives one answer in the case of Gudrun and Gerald. However, a world turned to ice is not the only way that deep alienation from one's surroundings may be expressed. The desert will also do as a symbol of cosmic desolation. This is well illustrated in Gide's *The Immoralist,* a novel in which the protagonist, Michel, is a Birkin become satanic in his weariness with the traditionally valued places of the world and his quest for a new place that will restore his life force. This turns out to be the desert of North Africa. A geographical contest is dramatized through Michel's relations with his ailing wife, Marceline, whom he drags from one place to another until her death. He avoids the civilized places of Europe, preferring desert landscape. On their itinerary Sorrento, Palermo, and Naples yield to places called Chegga, Kefeldorh', M'reyer—"dreary stages of a still more dreary road." Once in North Africa he prefers the desert to the oasis, for the desert is the "land of mortal glory and intolerable splendor. Man's effort here seems ugly and miserable." Particularly repulsive to him is the pastoral, fertile place, best represented in the book by his mother's estate "in the greenest of green Normandy." Here the couple resides for a while in "a large and very pleasant house standing in a garden watered by running streams." In this feminine landscape of "narrow coombes and gently rounded hills," Marceline tells her husband that she is expecting a child, and for a time he is tender with her, "with a will that seemed softened, as though by harkening to the counsels of that temperate land." But he soon reverts to his old habits, which are homosexual and criminal, and abets the efforts of poachers who steal game from his own land. Turning away from fertile Normandy, they set off again on their travels. Marceline dies in North Africa, where "the hostile landscape crushes her," and Michel fares little better. In spite of his easy access to both male and female Arab lovers, he is discontent and succumbs to the desert in the same way that Gerald succumbs to the Alpine landscape. In the end it renders him helpless. "Take me away," he implores friends paying him a visit, "I can't move of myself."

A simplified version of Gide's moral and philosophical tale is Paul Bowles's *The Sheltering Sky*. In this American novel Port Moresby travels the North African desert because he must have "the proximity of infinite things," he must "be able to penetrate to the interior of somewhere." Woman does not serve this purpose and, like Michel, he is alienated from his wife and repulsed by feminine landscape. Typical is his putting off the exploration of "a small valley that lay between two gently graded bare hills. At the end was a steeper hill, reddish in color, and in the side was a dark aperture." His ambition lies beyond landscapes; he lives in the hope that in the sky a "split would occur, the sky draw back, and he would see what he had never doubted lay behind advance upon him with the speed of a million winds." The poor man never achieves this transcendent end, of course, and dies in a miserable, tiny room in a desert town infirmary; his last vision is of excrement and "his bleeding entrails open to the sky." Directly, his wife abandons herself to the enclosed places she always preferred, chiefly the dark tents and rooms of an assortment of Arab lovers.

The Immoralist and *The Sheltering Sky* illustrate the use of cosmic ambition as a means of transcending the usual forms of existence. When romantic love fails, when attachment to customary places weakens, the male hero shifts his affection away from woman and earth to cosmic sexuality and abstract space. In addition to his homosexual affairs, Michel engages in a kind of sun worship which nearly produces orgasm, and Port requires "proximity to infinite things." In self-defense the women turn the other way, Marceline to the "narrow coombes" of Normandy and Kit to the crowded quarters of the Arab world.

Geoffrey and Yvonne Firmin in Malcolm Lowry's *Under the Volcano* are another pair of lovers who fall from the paradisal garden to inferno. Mexico, with its potential of being a heaven or hell, is the place where the twentieth-century lovers repeat the sad story of the Emperor Maximilian and Carlotta, whose effort to make a paradise for themselves and the Mexican people failed in the nineteenth century. Their lovely palace and gardens, now in ruins, act as a warning:

> The broken pink pillars, in the half-light, might have been waiting to fall down on him; the pool, covered with green scum . . . to close over his head. The shattered evil-smelling chapel, overgrown with weeds, the crumbling walls, splashed with urine, on which scorpions lurked—wrecked entablature, sad archivolt, slippery stones covered with excreta—this place, where love had once brooded, seemed part of a nightmare.[16]

The Firmins' house and garden in Quauhnahuac (Cuernavaca) also was once "like a Paradise," but their marriage founders on his alcoholism and impotence and her infidelity; the result is that the house and garden fall into disrepair. Moreover, being strangers in Mexico they are regarded by the natives as two more in the succession of conquerors who have spoiled the original Eden of Mexico. This idea is brought out by means of a sign in a public garden next to Firmin's:

> ¿Le Gusta Este Jardin?
> ¿Que es Suyo?
> ¡Evite Que Sus Hijos Lo Destroyan! (128)

Firmin mistranslates the last line to mean "We evict those who destroy," when it should be "See that your children don't destroy it," but both meanings apply: the mess Geoffrey and Yvonne make of their marriage leads to their removal, by death, from Mexico. The Biblical penalty for moral failure is eviction from Eden. Quauhnahuac and its environs, an "Earthly Paradise" under one aspect, becomes an inferno, dominated by a barrance, a ravine running through the center of the region—a "frightful cleft," a "general Tartarus and gigantic jakes" where people throw their refuse. For Geoffrey the end comes in a miserable bar, the Farolito, "the paradise of his despair," where he is mortally wounded in an altercation with Mexican fascists and thrown into the ravine along with the body of a dog. Yvonne dies at about the same time as her horse tramples her to death in a storm. Ironically, that same morning she and her lover had ridden over the same ground, which then wore the aspect of Eden. They had been accompanied by the two foals of the mares they rode and a white dog that went ahead "to detect snakes" in their path: "they were a company, a caravan, carrying for their greater security, a little world of love with them as they rode along . . . the countryside on either hand smiled upon them with deceptive innocence" (107).[17] As Yvonne dies she has a vision of the destruction of her house and garden: "The fire was spreading faster and faster, the walls with their millwheel reflections of sunlight on water were burning, the flowers in the garden were blackened and burning, they writhed, they twisted, they fell, the garden was burning" (336). For Yvonne, the private dream of paradise, based on love, perishes; for Geoffrey the world itself dies as he falls into the barranca: "The world itself was bursting, bursting into black spouts of villages catapulted into space, with himself falling through it all, through the inconceivable pandemonium of a million tanks, through the blazing of ten million burning bodies, falling, into a forest, falling" (375).

From antiquity the city has been regarded as a sexual trap for the hero. Modern literature has come to the point where the garden or pastoral paradise becomes another trap and no longer the refuge where love and vitality are restored. Melville's Pierre, Hardy's Jude, and Lawrence's Paul Morel are unable to find love in either city or countryside. The age-old commitment to the redemptive garden ceases and there develops a horror of vegetation and a perverse inclination toward sterility among male characters. In spite of the progress he makes in country things, Angel Clare in *Tess of the D'Urbervilles* can never quite identify with the rank vegetation of the Valley of Froom, "that green trough of sappiness and humidity." In a manner so similar as to suggest the influence of Hardy and Conrad, Faulkner also yokes fertile earth women and sterile men.[18] But Faulkner cannot take as unambiguous a view of this kind of tragedy as Hardy does; Eula Varner, Lena Grove, Dewey Dell are fertile and wholesome but they are done in a low comic mode, while Temple Drake, Caddie, Joanna Burden, and Rosa Coldfield are as sterile as male characters. The final scene of *Sanctuary,* showing Temple and her father listening to band music in Luxembourg Gardens, is a striking image of that sterility:

> Temple yawned behind her hand, then she took out a compact and opened it upon a face in miniature sullen and discontented and sad. Beside her her father sat, his hands crossed on the head of his stick, the rigid bar of his moustache beaded with moisture like frosted silver. She closed the compact and from beneath her smart new hat she seemed to follow with her eyes the waves of music, to dissolve into the dying brasses, across the pool and the opposite

semicircle of trees where at sombre intervals the dead tranquil
queens in stained marble mused, and on into the sky lying prone
and vanquished in the embrace of the season of rain and death.[19]

The House

My house is a decayed house—Eliot, "Gerontion"

The failure of love in the garden leads to a feeling of revulsion
against garden and love altogether. A more hopeful result seems to
flow from the image of the house as a stay against the deterioration of
place and civilization. Eliciting public rather than private themes, the
house represents family, class, and society more than nature and the
individual. The rehabilitation of the decayed country house became a
favorite subject for British novelists of conservative mind who deplored the transformations brought about after World War I. They used
the country house as the symbolic center of a pre-industrial society
consisting of a wealthy land-owner's extended family, his tenants and
neighbors, the local clergyman and his parish, and the town with its
artisans and shop-keepers. The effective principle of this kind of material depends on the association of a well-ordered way of life with a well-
defined place that is blessed with natural as well as man-made beauty.
Time also lends its authority and charm in the form of ancient buildings, religious observances, and community occasions. All this offered
an attractive alternative to the new kinds of social and spatial organization created by the new economics in city and suburb.

The country house was an alternative of the mind, however, not of
reality, for writers must have known that they were embracing a cozy
image of the past rather than a program of action for the present.
Consequently, irony touches most country house fiction of the twentieth century. Tony Last in Evelyn Waugh's *A Handful of Dust* is more
than a little ridiculous in trying to reestablish the former glory of Hetton Abbey. The building itself is imitation nineteenth-century Gothic,
and the estate life Tony tries to maintain there is proved very fragile
when it topples with the death of his son and the infidelity of his wife.
Tradition should withstand such blows, but nostalgia is weak-minded
and runs the risk of childish regression, and there is much that is
childish at the present Hetton Abbey—naming rooms after figures in
the Arthurian legend, for example. We note the same slightly ludicrous
association of adult values with the sentimentality of childhood
memories of houses in Waugh's Nanny Hawkins, for whom the only

reality is the childhood years of the Flytes in *Brideshead Revisited;* in the fascination for tales about the wych-elm in *Howards End;* in the instructions the quester receives in Robert Frost's "Directive" to use a child's toy cup to dip water from an old house spring in order to "Drink and be whole again." Hetton Abbey eventually falls into the hands of Tony's cousins, who turn the estate into a silver fox farm while Tony himself still seeks his glorious place, which appears for the last time as a Heavenly Jerusalem hovering over the jungle in Brazil.

Succession is the most serious problem of the country house in a free, not feudal, society. Who can be recruited to maintain the old place after the present faithful occupant dies and his family does not honor his values? Waugh offers a kind of solution in *Brideshead Revisited.* After all of the members of the ancient family are corrupted and dispersed, a successor of sorts is found in the British Army troops who are quartered on the estate. Most essential, the family chapel has been sanctified again and is serving a "surprising lot" of troops: "The art-nouveau lamp burned once more before the altar." But the military are war-makers, and they have succeeded the family, who, though weak-willed, were saints. The idyllic landscape will be destroyed: "The valley has great potentialities for an assault course and a mortar range," observes the commanding officer. The role of Charles Ryder as an architectural painter is the same as the novelist's, preserving the memory of places that can no longer survive in the modern world: "I was called to all parts of the country to make portraits of houses that were soon to be deserted or debased; indeed, my arrival seemed often to be only a few paces ahead of the auctioneers, a presage of doom."[20]

The break-down of the family endangers the continuity of the great houses in *A Handful of Dust* and *Brideshead Revisited.* A bad succession seems likely at the end of *Sword of Honour,* too. E. M. Forster, however, in *Howards End,* is willing to put his faith in recruits to the tradition of the English country house, just as Jane Austen had made middle-class girls the champions of upper-class estate culture in the eighteenth century. The conversion of a variety of middle-class people to an upper-class ideal of the past is Forster's political theme, which is based on the assumption that a loss of contact with the earth, specifically that English countryside which was the creation of the country-house economy, perverts the life of the nation. The unhappy plight of his characters before their conversion is the plight of England, and a return to the land and to the country-house community is necessary to restore the nation's torn fabric of love and morality. Living in London, the working-class Leonard Bast is practically imprisoned in the grey city from which "nature withdrew"; the Schlegels are intellectuals of whom it is said that they have "accreted possessions without taking root in the earth"; businessmen like Mr. Wilcox buy and sell land and houses without the slightest feeling for either; and the upper class itself has "no part with the earth and its emotions." Upper-class gentility and commercialism breed the "Imperialist" type or "cosmopolitanism," a word Forster loads with almost as much evil connotation as it bears in Communist polemics. The Imperialist "is a destroyer. He prepares the way for cosmopolitanism, and though his ambitions may be fulfilled, the earth that he inherits will be grey."[21] All has turned to greyness in England, Margaret Schlegel complains.[22] Cosmopolitanism is not associated with permanency but with motion, which is represented in *Howards End* by the importance the motor car has for the younger generation. The worst effect of motion is nomadism, and the city is its harbinger: "London was but a foretaste of this nomadic civilization which is altering human nature so profoundly."

There is redemption, however, for erring people in the salutary influence of a country house in the middle of fields still being actively farmed. The importance of the house has been kept alive by two women: the owner, Ruth Wilcox, a natural aristocrat with a love of the past and nature; and Mrs. Avery, an old servant with a superstitious regard for the house. Mrs. Wilcox selects Margaret Schlegel as a worthy heir of Howards End, firmly believing that "a wych-elm tree, a vine, a wisp of hay with dew on it—can . . . be transmitted where there is no bond of blood"; and after Mrs. Wilcox's death, Mrs. Avery draws Margaret into a close relationship with the house. The spell works so well that the intellectual Margaret reaches a point where her mind can dwell with satisfaction on things alone—"on ruddy bricks, flowering plum-trees, and all the tangible joys of spring." At Howards End the Schlegel sisters end their nomadism by coming to love an old English place; at Howards End Mr. Wilcox ends his business career, which had dealt so destructively with English towns and country sites. Conversion is not as direct for the lower-class Leonard Bast, for whom the country house, appropriately, cannot have as decisive an influence as it does for people who have been accustomed to costly things. A chance association with the intellectual Schlegel sisters and a number of literary texts presenting a back-to-earth point of view stir in Bast deep dissatisfaction with the greyness of the city and prepare the ground for a visionary experience. This occurs in an unusual night walk he takes from the Underground station at Wimbledon out into the countryside of Surrey. Bast had been reading *The Ordeal of Richard Feverel,* and his walk is like that taken by Richard when he learns of the existence of his son and experiences "something of a religious joy—a strange sacred pleasure" as he "sallied into the air, and walked on and on." Bast's walk liberates him from the confinement of his city room through the rediscovery of space outside and "ancient night." Although Bast does not live to enjoy Howards End, his son will, for Margaret Schlegel, who has inherited the estate by reason of the "fanciful" wish of Mrs. Wilcox, intends to leave it in her will to "her nephew, down in the field."

In the characterization of Margaret Schlegel, Forster summarizes the significance of Howards End as a symbol of all England:

> She recaptured the sense of space, which is the basis of all earthly beauty, and, starting from Howards End, she attempted to realize England. She failed—visions do not come when we try, though they may come through trying. But an unexpected love of the island awoke in her, connecting on this side with the joys of the flesh, on that with the inconceivable. (204)

Put to the test, however, the redemptive power of the English country house cannot succeed. It had not worked in *The Longest Journey,* either; Sawston, the old manor housing a prep school, fails to wean Richie away from his dell, an infantile reversion to the womb. At Cadbury Rings, though, an ancient, mythic place, Richie is helped to a feeling of love for his mother and brother. But the mythic place is also subject to doubt later in *Passage to India,* in which the venerable Marabar Caves are made to represent the utter indifference of place in the affairs of men and the mischief false inferences from places may inspire. Mrs. Moore has an experience quite the opposite of Margaret Schlegel's; she flees India in horror when she discovers that the caves "robbed infinity and eternity of their vastness." As for the other characters in the novel, they are hopelessly drawn apart rather than brought together in India; the subcontinent cannot be a "meeting place" for different races, and in the last scene Aziz and Fielding cannot stay together as they ride their horses—"the earth didn't want it, sending up rocks through which riders must pass single file." This bleak ending must be compared with the harmony of the diverse people who come finally to live at Howards End; they are the "spiritual heirs" of the house whom Mrs. Wilcox, the counterpart of Mrs. Moore, had sought. Yet harmony comes at a price of emasculating the male, for at the close we find the Schlegel sisters in control, Henry Wilcox invalided, his son in jail, and Leonard Bast murdered and now represented by his infant son. "The house symbolizing England has become a feminine sanctuary," writes Wilfred Stone.[23] The sexual limitation of the country house comes out again in Forster's *Maurice*. In that work the country house, Penge, in a state of serious decay, harbors the assignations of stealthy homosexual lovers, and at the end it is the image of "the greenwood," "forest and fell," that serves Forster's turn for a place of love. But it is a question in Fosrter whether place, in the final analysis, should be of crucial importance in the relations of people. In *Howards End* love of place supersedes love of people, but this is regrettable, as Margaret Schlegel reflects: "It is sad to suppose that places may ever be more important than people" (130).

The nearest approach to the European country-house ideal in America has been the Southern plantation and the Western ranch. The Civil War and its aftermath made the plantation available only to sentimental history, and the ranch house, borrowed from the Mexican hacienda, seems fit only for melodramatic films about cattlemen. Henry James had to go to England for his country houses, and then he proceeded to treat them as part of a "lovely but lost" world. The ancestral house in American literature is a place harboring only guilty feelings and seeds of destruction. There may be, as Richard Poirier declares, "an obsession in American literature with plans and efforts to build houses,"[24] but, once built, almost all of our great houses are either excrescences on the land, such as Judge Temple's house in *The Pioneers* and Gatsby's house on Long Island, or places destined to be destroyed—Poe's House of Usher, Silas Lapham's new house, and almost every Southern plantation house from George Washington Cable to Faulkner and Walker Percy. Instead of venerable bastions, the ideal American house is a small affair, indistinguishable from its natural surroundings—like Leatherstocking's and Thoreau's huts in the woods—or at best, as Hawthorne suggested, simple structures that can be easily torn down after forty years of service.

The Wilderness

> and all the grief of wood—of its own murdering.—Faulkner,
> *The Hamlet*

The return to the country house in British fiction is part of a larger wave of nostalgia for the land that has taken many forms in this century: agrarian back-to-earth movements, primitivistic wilderness cults, suburbanism, and the immensely popular diversions of touring, camping, hunting, and hiking. In America a group called the Southern Agrarians launched "a national agrarian movement" for the purpose of countering the evils of industrialism and serving as a source of cultural revival. In his contribution to their manifesto, John Crowe Ransom speaks of a mystical attachment to the land: "Out of so simple as respect for the physical earth and its teeming life comes a primary joy, which is an inexhaustible source of arts and religions and philosophies."[25] But agrarian dreams were never realized. Farming, as we have noted, does not really excite the American imagination even though the nation's economy was for a long time based on agricultural production. For some reason the return to the land in America has been by way of the wilderness rather than the farm or country house.

Agrarian back-to-earth movements are based on the conviction that the lost garden can be restored, but once the wilderness goes it is practically impossible to bring it back to its original quality. Since the end of World War II half of the earth's forests have disappeared. Attempts to preserve the remaining forests must be accounted commendable moral exercises rather than practical measures since it is no longer possible to set aside tracts of land large enough and isolated enough from the deleterious effects of modern technology to maintain wild vegetation and animals in any variety. In a time of ecological sensitivity, even industry tries to coexist with natural places without destroying them utterly. When only extractive processes are involved, and not the settlement of a large population, it is sometimes possible for a power plant or mine to eliminate the deleterious effects of their operations on wilderness and farmland. But compromise with wilderness is still most difficult to accomplish because of the fragility of its ecosystems. Having wilderness experiences is entirely out of the question for the vast majority of people. For the intrepid few there are simulated exercises in survival, such as crossing the ocean in a raft, reaching the North Pole by dog-sled, or crossing the Australian "outback" with four camels and a dog.[26] For many others there is the enjoyment of remnant wilderness by means of expensive hunting, fishing, and hiking expeditions. But only utopian dreamers may speculate on a large-scale return of civilization to pre-agricultural conditions; Paul Shepherd, for instance, lays out a plan for a "cynegetic world" in which the interiors of the continents would be kept in a permanent wilderness condition while mankind would live only on the coasts and nourish itself with microbial food products.[27] Eventually mankind will have to be content with the traditional substitute for the wilderness, the zoo, where a sampling of animals is kept alive as a symbolic reminder of the kind of earth they once inhabited.

The practical difficulty of preserving an actual wilderness for the benefit of any considerable number of people makes it necessary for the relation of mankind to the wilderness to take a symbolical rather than literal form. This was as true for the ancient world as it is for the modern, the wilderness having disappeared quite early in all civilized portions of the globe. Art has always had to assume some of the burden of preserving the wilderness experience, whether it be the bas-relief of an Assyrian king killing a lion or the stylized representation of vegetation and animals in a Persian rug. Art is an elegy for the departed wonders of the world, and for the civilized man art conveys primitive experience more acceptably than any other way.

American literature has been particularly adept at this task, probably because the disappearance of the actual wildnerness is so recent in American history. The sense of guilt over the ugly consequences of settling the western hemisphere is palliated a little by the evocation of its wilderness condition when the white man first arrived in the New World. The elegiac tone is best struck at the very moment when the wilderness disappears: when the Indians and the white frontiersman Leatherstocking are pushed off the land by settlers, just before "the lumber company moves in and begins to cut the timber" in *The Bear,* and just before a wild river is drowned by the water backing up behind a new dam in James Dickey's *Deliverance* or an island is drowned by the backed up waters of a lake in Margaret Atwood's *Surfacing.* The wilderness and the hunt live on in Cooper, Melville, Hemingway, Faulkner, and many others, who, like epic poets celebrating a heroic age long since dead, preserve "the image of the irrevocable past," as Francis Parkman described his own contribution to the memory of the West, *The Oregon Trail. The Bear* outlives the Mississippi forest it was modelled on, and fiction may fill the void of non-experience. In his book on Faulkner's Indians, Lewis Dabney points out that N. Scott Momaday, a Cherokee, depends on Faulkner for the account of a hunter's initiation in *House Made of Dawn:* "Faulkner had shaped the Indian writer's vision of the ritual of his people."[28] What the novel does for the forests of the East, film does for the wide open spaces of plains and mountain ranges in the West.

If the garden is Nature perfected by God or by man, the wilderness—forest, desert, mountain, sea—is unperfected Nature only slightly removed from uncreated, formless matter. Resorting to the wilderness is the furthest step one may take away from civilization and history without being engulfed altogether by chaos, and the primitivist is of the opinion that to take this step, backward in time and outward in space, is to return to the health and sanity of mankind's original condition on earth. Perhaps the most important reason the primitivist has for maintaining wilderness experience is freedom from the abstractions of

civilization and immersion in the materiality of environment, the ultimate of which is the hunting and killing of wild animals. This view of
hunting has been defended even by the philosopher Ortega y Gasset in
an essay claiming that "only the hunting ground is the true countryside."[29] American literature is noted for the high value it places on the
hunt, and it has become almost a tradition for writers following
Hemingway to do at least one hunting novel—*The Bear* of Faulkner,
Henderson the Rain King of Saul Bellow, *Why Are We in Vietnam?* of
Norman Mailer. The degradation of the hunting motif occurs in the
manhunt, a subject with a long history in America beginning with the
revengeful hunt for marauding Indians, such as Robert Montgomery
Bird's *Nick of the Woods,* and continuing with the hunt for runaway
slaves. Contemporary versions are to be found in John Hawkes's *The
Cannibal,* Davis Grubb's *The Night of the Hunter,* and James Dickey's
Deliverance.

A spectrum of twentieth-century responses to the wilderness-as-
salvation notion is presented in William Golding's *The Lord of the
Flies.* Jack Merridew and his "hunters" represent the false primitivism
of civilized people who kill for pleasure and are opposed to any social
organization not based on brute force. The wilderness setting does not
inspire in them the healthy instincts of aborigines but simply affords
them the opportunity to exercise their sadistic and destructive impulses. The destruction of the ecology of the whole island by the fire
they set in the pursuit of war is a fitting symbol of the only possible end
their way of life can have. Simon is Jack's exact opposite. Mystical and
poetic, he thoroughly identifies himself with the wilderness place, its
plants and animals. He spurns the shelters the other boys have built on
the beach and discovers a tiny opening in the jungle "where more
sunshine fell. . . . The whole space was walled with dark aromatic
bushes, and was a bowl of heat and light.[30] At night his "little cabin" of
vegetation was transformed into a womb of life:

> Now the sunlight had lifted clear of the open space and with-
> drawn from the sky. Darkness poured out, submerging the ways
> between the trees till they were dim and strange as the bottom of
> the sea. The candle-buds opened their wide white flowers glimmer-
> ing under the light that pricked down from the first stars. Their
> scent spilled out into the air and took possession of the island. (72)

The boy Ralph tries to maintain a position between Jack's brand of
primitivism and Simon's romanticism. He never gives up the hope of

being rescued and returning to civilization because he knows that the wilderness cannot support a life worthy of being lived: "He found himself understanding the wearisomeness of this life, where every path was an improvisation and a considerable part of one's waking life was spent watching one's feet" (95). But, unlike Piggy, who cannot progress beyond the idea of a return to civilization, Ralph knows he must accommodate himself to the primitive in order to survive, and for all of the boys to survive he knows that a society must be formed to deal effectively with their forlorn condition. A Promethean boy Crusoe, he uses fire to raise man above his earthly limitation, specifically to make smoke signals that might attract a passing ship. In the meantime he is forced to resort to jungle ways when is viciously hunted by Jack's "tribe." Like a wild pig he goes to earth in a place that is the opposite of Simon's even though it is in the same jungle: "Here, bushes and a wild tangle of creeper made a mat that kept out all the light of the sun." It was the "right place" only because of his desperate attempt to escape his would-be murderers.

Madman, dreamer, realist are tested by Golding in the wilderness setting. Jack Merridew can only seek to destroy whatever world he lives in, and he finds it easier to destroy the wilderness island than England; in losing himself in nature Simon renders himself incapable of coping with social problems that destroy the nature he loves. Only Ralph deals with the wilderness in a rational manner, accommodating himself to its demands and yet withholding some part of his humanity from the temptations offered by selflessness on the one hand and barbarous violence on the other.

James Dickey's *Deliverance* is another novel that examines the responses of civilized men to wilderness experience. In this case the adventure of four men in a wild river gorge in northern Georgia is not enforced by accident but chosen for a variety of reasons. Lewis, their leader, rationalizes his primitivistic fetishism on both personal and social grounds on the grounds that wilderness prowess proves one's manhood and may well save the remnant of mankind after a nuclear war. Ed Gentry appreciates neither of these reasons and is moved rather to join Lewis out of a vague feeling for the popular romance of the hunt. His encounter with the wild terrain and with the degenerate inhabitants of the place opens his eyes to the true nature of wilderness: The wild place is beautiful but not altogether assimilable. The problem of wilderness experience is what one does with it upon returning to civilization. The beauty of a river becomes an inspiration to Gentry, as it was to Huck Finn; it delivers him from the stultification of routine job and home: "In me it still is, and will be until I die, green, rocky, deep, fast, slow, and beautiful beyond reality." But what one must do there in order to survive—adapt one's body to a cliffside, kill, see one's friends die—cannot be countenanced, even in memory. Ed Gentry's survival in his wilderness ordeal also delivers him from the primitivist's false notions of the wilderness. Other examples of ambiguous deliverance may be found in Faulkner's Ike McCaslin, who outlives in "Delta Autumn" the influence of the forest he felt in *The Bear;* in Bellow's Henderson, who declines to offer a kingship in the deepest Africa; in Mailer's Tex and D.J., whose secret hunting experience seems to lead only to Vietnam. Only Hemingway seems never to have surrendered his vision of the hunter as the complete hero. Most writers yield only temporarily to the powerful attraction of the wilderness, knowing that its use in literature is but a reminder of a passing time and an experience mankind cannot hope to continue, however meaningful it has been. To expect more is to be sentimental. Nowhere is Faulkner more sentimental than in *The Bear,* but he had the good sense to admit that the book presents a world that hardly exists: "There's a case of the sorry, shabby world that don't quite please you, so you create one of your own."[31]

THE CONDITION OF PLACELESSNESS

> O that she may live like some green laurel
> Rooted in one dear perpetual place.
>   —Yeats, "A Prayer for My Daughter"

The loss of traditional places—garden, forest, country house, city—has resulted in a universal recognition of a new condition in the history of mankind: the dwindling importance of fixed places in the lives of individuals, or the change from a life influenced by locations to a life governed by mobility and communications. This recognition, long in coming and rather painful to face, underlies a good deal of the thought of our time. Much of the material and tone of a piece of twentieth-century writing depends on whether the writer accepts or deplores the diminishment of place. *Dépaysment* and Heidegger's conception of being not-at-home *(Unheimlichkeit)* are points of departure for existentialists. From another direction popular conservative thought points an accusing finger at uprootedness as the cause of decay in civilization since World War I. Rootedness, on the other hand, is considered necessary to keep alive the traditions that support society, attachment to place being one of the ingredients of tradition. As Simone Weil states it in her aptly titled *The Need for Roots*, rootedness *(enracinement)* "is automatically brought about by the place, conditions of birth, profession and social community," from which the individual draws "the whole of his moral, intellectual and spiritual life."[32] An admirer of Weil, Robert Coles, comes to the same conclusion in another pointedly titled book, *Uprooted Children:* "It is utterly part of our nature to want roots, to need roots, to struggle for roots, for a sense of belonging, for some place that is recognized as *mine,* as *yours,* as *ours*" (120). He goes so far as to say that "learning about one's roots, one's place, one's territory" is "perhaps *the* central fact of existence."[33]

The sociological view holds that commonly shared places unite people, that the natural environment serves to orient primitives while the city acts as a focal point for advanced civilizations. Susanne Langer observes that "the displacement of the permanent homestead by the modern rented tenement—now here, now there—has cut another anchor-line of the human mind."[34] Siegfried Giedion fears for the equilibrium between organism and environment when man separates himself too drastically from earth and growth.[35] Damage to the psyche is Carl Jung's concern for the person who "loses touch with the dark, maternal, earthy ground of his being."[36] The ancestral spirits of that part of the earth we inhabit go to make up the unconscious, and "alienation from the unconscious and from its historical conditions spells rootlessness." Charles A. Reich is similarly worried over the "loss of the land, of weather, of growing things. . . . Man used to spend a thousand years in the same place, his roots went down deep; he built his life around the rhythms of the earth and his mental stability upon the constancies of nature. Can a hundred years change his physiology enough so that the need for these rhythms and certainties no longer exist?"[37] Even a venturesome writer like Norman Mailer fears that "some part of us is aware that to uproot the past too completely is a danger without measure. . . . To return to an old neighborhood and discover it has disappeared is a minor woe for some; it is close to a psychological catastrophe for others, an amputation where the lost nerves still feel pain."[38] It is from a religious point of view that Mircea Eliade deplores the "desacralization of the cosmos," particularly the loss of a sacred central place to serve as an *imago mundi*, without which, he feels, man cannot "attain to a properly religious experience and vision of the world."[39]

Conservatives have evolved a formula in which rootedness stands for civilization, social stability, traditional beauty of place; uprootedness and mobility for barbarism, radical change, universal bleakness. The United States is offered as a prime example of rootlessness. The high mobility of Americans is easily demonstrated by statistics, in Vance Packard's *A Nation of Strangers,* for example; and the conclusion seems inescapable that many Americans have lost any sense of relationship to places and to other people. Rootlessness is an American illness, writes William Cass in a review of Gertrude Stein.[40] Comparisons with other nations are invidious. "The human life of the English provinces long ago came to terms with nature, fixed its roots. . . . But it is the character of our urbanized, anti-provincial, progressive, and mobile American life that it is in a condition of eternal flux." At about the same time that John Crowe Ransom wrote this in his contribution to *I'll Take My Stand* in 1930, the most extreme wing of reactionary criticism, New Humanism, damned modern writers because they had "no sense of anything fixed or permanent either within or without themselves that they may oppose to the flux of phenomena and the torrent of impressions."[41] Not having felt the effects of industrialism until rather late, the South escaped the general proscription, and its writers were praised for their brilliant use of place. In her essay on place in fiction, Eudora Welty deplores novels "with no roots struck down . . . unfixed, unconnected, and not so much sensitive to the world as vulnerable to it." For her, as well as for Simone Weil, characters in literature and people in real life must have a "base of reference" to establish identity. "Being on the move is no substitute for feeling. Nothing is. And no love or insight can be at work in a shifting and never-defined position, where eye, mind, and heart have never willingly focused on a steadying point."[42] The conservative-minded assume that a break with familiar places leads to a break with the past; they fear mobility because it may expedite social change.

Whether or not these formulations are tenable will be examined later, but no matter what the result the idea of an absolute relationship between human values and fixed place underlies the literary theme of regret over the passing of traditional places. Impressions derived from cultural heritage are more important than realities in the way most people react to places. In the twentieth century we are caught between a lingering attachment to places and a new condition of life that minimizes the role of place, and it is quite natural that some writers regret the change. One of the most common clichés of twentieth-century writing is the comparison of a place as it was in the past, when civilization supposedly flourished, and the same place now sadly degraded by some form of modern barbarism—the Venice Canaletto painted and the Venice of Bleistein in Eliot's poem, Bostom Common of the Civil War monument and Boston Common on the parking lot in Robert Lowell's "For the Union Dead," the glowing Greek world of antiquity and the "plain without feature" of the present world in Auden's "The Shield of Achilles." Writers who can no longer honor the traditional places, who are denied strong emotional attachment to places, experience an acute sense of psychic damage. Especially prone to the syndrome of uprootedness were the American writers known as the "lost generation." Malcolm Cowley, the chronicler of the expatriates, attributes this special character to "a long process of deracination. Looking backward, I feel that our whole training was involuntarily directed toward destroying whatever roots we had in the soil, toward eradicating our local and regional peculiarities, toward making us homeless citizens of the world."[43] The work of these writers, from one point of view, is an attempt to develop stratagems to cope with the modern condition of placelessness. Hemingway, Fitzgerald, Faulkner, and many others depict the predicament of people who, because they have been uprooted by events in the twentieth century, have lost their feeling for traditionally honored places and spend their lifetime searching for new places to act in. The customary return of the hero to his homeland does not work for this set of writers. When economics finally forced their return to America, the expatriates, Cowley points out, had no place to return to because they, as well as their home places, had changed so much: "they could go back to Iowa, but only as alien observers, and back to Wisconsin, but only as Glenway Wescott did, to say good-by." The characters they created make a mess of reorienting themselves; Hemingway's returned soldier, Krebs, and Fitzgerald's Nick Carraway, like Wescott, return to homes in the Midwest but not to live there. A few expatriates thought return was possible, notably Louis Bromfield in *Pleasant Valley* and other back-to-earth statements, but the exceptions were not very convincing. Dick Diver's return to America in *Tender Is the Night* is an admission of defeat; Jack Burden's return to the South after his flight to the West in *All the King's Men* is motivated only by the lack of anything else to do since "any place to which you may flee will now be like the place from which you have fled, and so you might as well go back, after all, to the place where you belong, for nothing was your fault or anybody's fault, for things are always as they are."[44]

Thomas Wolfe announced the theme and explored the consequences of the expatriate syndrome in *You Can't Go Home Again*. His Odyssean wanderer, George Webber, thinks he sees a way out of the despair of homelessness, for, if he cannot go home again, he can go "outward, outward toward the rich and life-giving soil of a new freedom in the wide world of all humanity. And there came to him a vision of man's true home, beyond the ominous and cloud-engulfed horizon of the here and now, in the green and hopeful and still-virgin meadows of the future."[45] Wolfe died before he could explore this future, and his hopeful mood was certainly not shared by his contemporaries, even by those who admired him. Although places are brilliantly realized by these writers and setting is of crucial importance in the conception and execution of their works, the despair of placelessness pervades their characters. It is true that "few writers have been more place-conscious" than Hemingway, as Carlos Baker claims; that there are landscape descriptions in Hemingway that rank with the greatest—the ride into Spain in *The Sun Also Rises;* that Hemingway was a stickler for the precise representation of settings—"Unless you have geography, background, you have nothing," he is reported to have said.[46] But Hemingway's strong sense of place is his means of emphasizing the disappearance of place among the good things people once enjoyed. He is intent on showing how terribly war has scarred the world, and though the few remaining unspoiled places may be savored by his knowing heroes, they can only be briefly tasted, like rare wine and women. Among his initiates there is a touch of touristic snobbery in frequenting out-of-the-way places, though in their best light these are places of refuge for people who can no longer bear the common life of the time.

In the Hemingway system of values the chosen place really has less effect upon the hero than the activity, usually sport, that it affords: fishing a trout stream, skiing in the Alps, hunting in Africa.[47] Roncesvalles is notable not for its historical significance as the place where Roland made his heroic stand but because of the good fishing there for Jake and his friends. The ritual of sport in Hemingway has the redemptive power that the romantic poets once found in the contemplation of place alone. The fishing site in "Big Two-Hearted River" is "the good place" because of the fishing; the land itself is "burned-over country," or the world damaged by war, and the river itself has bad spots where fishing would be "a tragic adventure." Nick's river is as ambiguous as Huck's river. The good place has its limitations and can be enjoyed only for a short time. the Burguete fishing idyll and swimming at San Sebastian are cut short by the importunity of restless friends; the romantic interlude of Jordan and Maria in the mountains lasts but three days in *For Whom the Bell Tolls;* the Swiss Oberland hideout of Lieutenant Henry is ended by Catherine's death in hospital.

Motion, not place, is the dominant mood of Hemingway's masterpiece, *The Sun Also Rises.* The frequency of verbs of motion in this text is not as high as that in the passage from Ecclesiastes from which Hemingway took the title of the book—over a dozen in seven and a half lines—but the overall impression of movement is unmistakably there: the walking, taxiing, and bussing of Jake Barnes on a typical day in Paris (dining out requires three movements: an apéritif in one place, dinner in another, coffee in a third) and the constant pleasure-seeking travel of Jake's crowd of friends. The motion is circular, accomplishing nothing for either Jake or Lady Brett. It may start in Paris and end in Madrid, but the cities are interchangeable and the kinds of movement are always the same. In the last chapter Jake takes the night train from San Sebastian to Madrid, taxis to Brett's hotel, takes Brett for a drink to another hotel and dinner at a restaurant followed by a ride through town in a taxi. All of this is meticulously chronicled. The book ends with the cab stopped in traffic, but we can be sure that the ride will be resumed, probably in Paris, and will last forever. The earth may abide, but this generation cannot know that because it is always frantically moving across it.

   Farewell to Arms is a retreat from the position taken by Hemingway in *The Sun Also Rises* since it deals with the purposeful flight of a hero and heroine across war-torn Europe to a good place. Lieutenant Henry's plunge into the River Tagliamento is a symbolical death, or a release from soldiering; crossing Lake Geneva is a purgation of war for both lovers, a means of escape to the high country of Montreux where they expect to begin a new life as a family. *For Whom the Bell Tolls* is a still further retreat since it has little motion, none at all for the lovers who are closely bound to earth, and it is closely organized around a single place, a bridge over a ravine in the mountains, a narrow place to be defended in the manner of the epic tradition. In both of these books Hemingway, after seizing the spirit of modern placelessness in *The Sun Also Rises,* slips back into the romantic lovers' search for the paradisal place.

   With age, however, love ceases and sport falters; sentimental trust in the contribution of place to the healing process is difficult to maintain in Hemingway's older heroes. The title of Hemingway's last work. *The Old Man and the Sea* suggests the ultimate reduction of the struggle of man against his environment; Santiago is the stripped-down man-like Ahab "cut away from the stake"—and the sea is that place which, in its immense sameness and its total lack of the works of man, is almost an abstraction and no place at all. Places exist only in the old fisherman's dreams: "He only dreamed of places now and of the lions on the beach"—a vision of the distant beautiful coast of Africa, not the horrible reality of the interior. After the last great struggle there is only "a clean, well-lighted place," a midnight bar, the ultimate reduction of environment to the basic components of place that seem appropriate to a man facing death.

Hemingway devised a "code of loss" for his heroes so that they could face the confusion of disintegrating values with some degree of honor. For them the disease of placelessness could be eased by constant motion, though ultimately the true hero must make a stand against the world as it is reduced to its basic elements. No heroic code, except that of the scrupulous observer, is to be found in Scott Fitzgerald; and his sense of loss depends more on the historical decline he notes in the American homeland from an innocent paradise to a wasteland of corruption and violence. *The Great Gatsby* ends with the terrible realization that the beautiful land once beheld by Dutch sailors has now become an uninhabitable "valley of ashes." No one in the book is attached to place, American or otherwise. Having returned from the War "restless," the narrator, Nick Carraway, finds it impossible to stay in the Midwest where his family had lived for three generations; "Instead of being the warm center of the world, the Middle West now seemed like the ragged edge of the universe."[48] Nick's friends, the Buchanans, do not live permanently in the East but "drifted here and there unrestfully"; their house, though elaborate, is not quite differentiated from Nature; "the fresh grass outside . . . seemed to grow a little way into the house," a breeze blowing through the open windows "rippled over the wine-colored rug, making a shadow on it as wind on the sea" and created the illusion of the furniture being not quite stationary. Gatsby's many guests are of no particular place, though their shadowy occupations are hinted at. Only Gatsby makes a great effort to maintain permanence in the land by establishing an immense mansion in the suburbs and from that base attempting to regain the affections of an old sweetheart, Daisy Buchanan, who in his mind is associated with the ideal of success. In this ambition Gatsby is representative of the historical American dream of a paradisal existence in the New World Eden, though naturally the dream is colored with the materialistic extravagances of the 1920s: "a vast, vulgar, and meretricious beauty . . . a universe of ineffable gaudiness spun itself out in his brain." But the actuality he creates is hardly more real than his dream. He builds his mansion in the ideal American border place, the area between the wilderness and the city which we now call the suburbs; yet in spite of immense size and expensive appointments it is all unreal, "a new world, material without being real." The house does nothing for Gatsby, making him unsubstantial too, particularly at the end of his notorious parties when the guests have departed: "A sudden emptiness

seemed to flow now from the windows and the great doors, endowing
with complete isolation the figure of the host, who stood on the porch,
his hand up in a formal gesture of farewell" (56). This picture of the
forlorn plutocrat may have been inspired by H. G. Wells's description
of the uncle of George Ponderevo, an English tycoon, in *Tono-Bungay:*
"There he stands in my memory, the symbol of this age for me . . . the
current master of the world. There he stands upon the great outward
sweep of the terrace before the huge main entrance, a little figure,
ridiculously disproportionate to that forty-foot arch. . . . On either
hand the walls of his irrelevant unmeaning palace rise."[49] George goes
on to say that it is typical of contemporary financiers to build such a
house "to bring their luck to the test of realisation." The last line of
Fitzgerald's novel ("So we beat on, boats against the current, borne
back ceaselessly into the past.") verbally echoes the ending of Wells's.
Sailing down the Thames is the same as "to run one's hand over the
pages of the book of England from end to end," and as his boat leaves
the river and pushes out to sea, George observes, "Out to the open we
go, to windy freedom and trackless ways." The book ends with this
line: "We are all things that make and pass, striving upon a hidden
mission, out to the open sea."

    The Great Gatsby confirms what Fitzgerald had discovered earlier
in two lesser novels, *The Beautiful and Damned* and *This Side of
Paradise:* that life in the American scene is oppressive and that forays
into the American countryside—of Connecticut and Maryland—are
disastrous. Perhaps Europe could furnish satisfactory places for his
distressed characters; at least this was part of the "system of ideas"
fashionable in American Bohemian circles of the 1920s. *Tender Is the
Night* explores the possibility, and at first it seems to work. Walking on
"the substantial cobble-stones of Zurich" rather than the "scarcely
created grass" of West Egg, the young hero, Dick Diver, makes close
contact with both land and sea in Europe. To be even closer to the
Swiss landscape he takes long bicycle rides—instead of racing around
in motor cars—climbs mountains, makes friends with the natives.
Whereas Gatsby gets his death by water, Diver is revived by his associations with the sea and lakes. At Gausse's Beach on the Riviera he
experiences young love again—"This is his place—in a way, he discovered it."[50] It seems to him that Lake Geneva is "the true centre of
the Western World." The villa where Dick and Nicole live for some
time has a lovely garden and is located on a ledge between a village and
the sea. And yet Diver's appreciation of European landscape turns to
bitterness because though Nicole is supposedly cured of mental illness,
their marriage fails in spite of all the lovely places they live in and Dick

accomplishes nothing in his profession. Indeed, the natural beauty, the "pastoral delight," of Switzerland makes an ironical contrast with Dick's failure and the corruption of his set of friends. The place and the Americans staying there are simply not related in any normal way. Switzerland is "a postcard heaven," not quite real, the "home of the toy and the funicular, the merry-go-round and the thin chime." Switzerland, finally, is part of "the world of pleasure" dreamed up by the very young: "the incorruptible Mediterranean with sweet old dirt caked in the olive trees, the peasant girl near Savona with a face as green and rose as the color of an illuminated missal . . . the Isles of Greece, the cloudy waters of unfamiliar ports, the lost girl on the shore, the moon of popular songs" (195–96). Dick Diver has come to realize, as Margaret Schlegel does too, that in real life places matter only because of the people in them: "He cared only about people; he was scarcely conscious of places except for their weather, until they had been invested with color by tangible events" (220). Without the love of Nicole Lake Geneva is not the center of the world but a place of ambiguous appearances: "Upon it floated swans like boats and boats like swans, both lost in the nothingness of the heartless beauty" (147). For Dick there remains only the all-too-real Geneva, New York, one of the last towns "in the heart of the Finger Lakes Section" he is heard from.

Insubstantiality of place is pathologic in Fitzgerald's characters. Gatsby's "scarcely created world" leaves Dick Diver in despair. All of the houses at West Egg are "inessential," like "a night scene by El Greco"; the whole East, for that matter, seems haunted to Nick. But the Midwest to which Nick may return is also an illusion, a memory of holiday seasons in his youth, "not the wheat or the prairies or the lost Swede towns, but the thrilling returning trains of my youth, and the street lamps and sleigh bells in the frosty dark and the shadows of holly wreaths thrown by lighted windows on the snow."

As in Hemingway, endless motion both eases and expresses the despair of placelessness for Fitzgerald's people. The circular motion of the ferris wheel, merry-go-round, and funicular in *Tender Is the Night* symbolizes the fruitless "life progress" of the ill-fated Dick and Nicole Diver. In *The Great Gatsby* the automobile is the instrument of destiny. It makes possible the geographic structure of the contemporary metropolis—the city center, the outlying suburbs, and the wasteland of service industries between; the relationships of characters are formed by their racing from one of these places to another, and the accident at the end is the efficient cause of the tragic dénouement. The automobile is the new technological detail among the more customary images of motion, of which wind and water are the most striking: people and things are said to ripple, flow, float, flutter, drift, swirl, eddy, hover. Against these liquid effects are set abrupt gestures of jumping and darting, often violent—as for example, "Making a short deft movement, Tom Buchanan broke her nose with his open hand"—and frequent pairs of opposed directions, such as "up and down," "back and forth," "here and there."

Although most of his works are organized around a locale specific enough to be modelled on a geographical region, a county in Mississippi, the fiction of William Faulkner eventually proves to be more concerned with time and motion than with place. Yoknapatawpha County functions as symbol rather than environment. It is a dull, flat land; its exhausted farms hardly support the inhabitants, its forests are no longer good for hunting, its rivers flood in the spring and are dry in the summer, its towns are dilapidated. Outside of Ike McCaslin in *The Bear,* there is no other character in all of Faulkner with the slightest feeling for natural places, unless we count the idiot Ike Snopes in his meadow, where he pursues a cow for the purposes of sodomy. Faulkner characters relate not to the land but to people and history. Faulkner's emphasis is not on the lack of suitable place, as it was in Hemingway and Fitzgerald. There is no place nostalgia in him: "I don't hold to the idea of a return," he once said in an interview; "we mustn't go back to a condition, an idyllic condition."[51] Place is a negative factor in the consciousness of Faulkner characters, a force to contend with though not to be really aware of or have feelings about. The reader, of course, is made acutely aware of the overwhelming presence of a deteriorated place of massive proportions, but the characters who spend their lives in this miserable setting either attempt to flee it or succumb to it. Those who succumb to it are doomed to self-imprisonment and self-torture, witness the plight of Reverend Hightower, Rosa Coldfield, and Joanna Burden. The most prominent indigenous structure, the plantation house with its "rotting portico," is the scene of but two possible outcomes: tragic horror, as in the houses of Sutpen and the Old Frenchman, or comic absurdity, as in the houses of the McCaslin brothers and the Beauchamps. The effect of the degraded environment upon people in Faulkner is so bizarre that details of place often take on an air of unreality, called by one commentator the "oneiric quality of the landscape."[52] Even the Negroes, who fit into the environment a lot more comfortably than whites, inhabit an unreal world. The church Dilsey visits at the end of *The Sound and the Fury* is the ultimate expression of the Negro community she has walked through on Easter morning, but it is "like a painted church, and the whole scene was as

flat and without perspective as a painted cardboard set upon the ultimate edge of the flat earth."

If remaining motionless in a limited place is a form of death, then it
follows that "life is motion" in the Faulknerian logic.[53] Characters moving through a still scene, like Joe Christmas and Lena Grove in *Light in
August,* impart motion to others. Yet one should not conclude, as some
critics do, that motion is a good in itself, for it is usually the case in
Faulkner that the life won through motion is not much better than the
life wasted in immobility. As in the case of place-bound characters,
those who are in motion meet either tragic or comic ends, tragic when
the movement is obsessive, comic when the movement is casual. There
is no optimum movement; we have either the frantic flights of Joe
Christmas or Lena Grove's leisurely pursuit of the father of her child.

One of the structural principles of a Faulkner novel is the interrela-
tionships between one set of people who have confined themselves to a
single place and another set of people who are in motion. In *Absalom!
Absalom!* the Sutpen males move frantically between the outside world
and Sutpen's Hundred, while the Sutpen females remain fixed at the
plantation house; in the Snopes Trilogy all of the highly mobile Snopes
people swirl around the hapless residents of village, town, and farm. In
The Sound and the Fury the tormented movements of the three Compson brothers—Benjy hunting Caddy, Quentin roaming Cambridge, Ja-
son chasing his niece—are opposed to the fixed reign of Dilsey in her
kitchen, ending finally with her stately promenade to church on Easter
Sunday. *Light in August* is a story of people in motion coming in
contact with people tied to places. The fortunes of two pairs of lovers,
a tragic pair and a comic pair, are presented in contrasts of place and
motion. From the "street" where he has been running for thirty years,
Joe Christmas finds brief refuge on the grounds of an old plantation
house occupied by a spinster-recluse who is wedded to that place
through the memory of her abolitionist father and brother. After a
violent sexual affair and murder, Joe takes to the road again, "doomed
with motion"; his flight comes to an end in the cottage of Reverend
Hightower, where he is killed. Like Joanna, Hightower is a futile recluse trying to maintain an ideological as well as physical stronghold in
the midst of an alien country; hers was the heritage of Northern
abolitionism, his the memory of Confederate heroism, equally ill-suited
to the modern South. Each is stirred out of isolation through contact
with a perpetual traveller, Joanna by Joe Christmas, Hightower by the
influences of Joe and Lena Grove that are conveyed to him by Byron
Bunch. But the extent of Hightower's stirring is his walk to Joe's hut to
assist Lena in childbirth, a generous act that has no lasting effect on

him, any more than love can rescue Joanna from her house and her obsession with past ideals. In the end we find Hightower in his cottage again: the faces of those real people who had so recently been in his life "rushed out of him, leaving his body empty and lighter than a forgotten leaf and even more trivial than flotsam lying spent and still upon the window ledge which has no solidity beneath his hands that have no weight." In the meantime, to console us, we have the progress of a pair of comic lovers. After having her baby at the same place where Joanna was murdered—redeeming the sterile land with new life—Lena Grove resumes her placid wandering over the land, only now she is accompanied by her would-be lover, Byron Bunch. Devotion to Lena has moved Bunch out of his fixed place, the saw mill. As survivors of the book's hectic action, though, Lena and Byron are hardly heroic or even serious lovers. Lena travels in a vacant, bovine mood, and the last we see of Byron he is chastised for attempting to make love to Lena on the floor of a furniture salesman's wagon.

ESCAPES FROM PLACELESSNESS

> the going round
> And round and round, the merely going round
> Until merely going round is a final good.
> —Wallace Stevens, "Notes Toward A Supreme Fiction"

Motion

Narrative requires movement away from static situations, but movement in modern literature, when it comes at all, is aimless and often destructive. If there is movement, it arrives nowhere; the usual alternative is absolute lack of movement, or stasis in an indifferent place. We have seen that sets of distressed characters in Hardy, Lawrence, Gide, and Lowry, as well as those in the American group, set out on the road for relief and find nothing but further aggravation of their problems. For the ultimate reduction of motion we must turn to Samuel Beckett. As the world diminishes, becomes flat and featureless, so the movements of the multi-named hero of Beckett's Trilogy become more and more limited. Molloy first sets out on his travels riding a bicycle and ends up crawling. Malone cannot even walk, "for he was incapable of picking his steps and choosing where to put down his feet"; he resorts to rolling himself along like a cylinder. Finally immobile in bed and unable to move toward things, he must use a stick to move things to himself. In the last part of the book, "The Unnamable," he does not even have a stick.

The generation of writers between the wars tried to compensate for the malaise of place-loss by throwing themselves into motion; in the words of Tom in Tennessee Williams's *Glass Menagerie* they attempted "to find in motion what was lost in space." But it was done in a mood of despair, a mood that was caught in one work after another. Thomas Wolfe gets it into the title of *You Can't Go Home Again* and then elaborates:

> Perhaps this is our strange and haunting paradox here in America—that we are fixed and certain only when we are in movement. At any rate, that is how it seemed to young George Webber, who was never so assured of his purpose as when he was going somewhere on a train. And he never had the sense of home so much as when he felt that he was going there. It was only when he got there that his homelessness began. (56)

The taxi ride of Jake Barnes and Lady Brett at the end of *The Sun Also Rises* is very much like the taxi ride of Gumbrill and Mrs. Viveash in the earlier *Antic Hay,* and what Charles Rolo wrote of the Huxley novel may equally apply to the Hemingway piece: "The book is a dance, which progresses with a demonic acceleration culminating in an utterly pointless nocturnal taxi ride, round and round London."[54] The ride accomplishes nothing for Gumbril and his lady, most of their friends either not being at home or refusing to receive them. "I like driving for driving's sake," says Mrs. Viveash, "a road which goes on for ever."[55] The last stop is the laboratory of Professor Shearwater, who, conducting a scientific experiment on fatigue, is found pedalling a stationary bicycle in a wooden box. To the scientist, as well as to the couple who come to watch him through the window of the chamber, place is a matter of indifference and motion is travel on a "nightmare road":

> He must have travelled the equivalent of sixty or seventy miles this afternoon. He would be getting on for Swindon. He would be nearly at Portsmouth. He would be past Cambridge, past Oxford. He would be nearly at Harwich, pedalling through the green and golden valleys where Constable used to paint. (345)

Literature of the first half of the twentieth century reflected the pain of placelessness. The mood continues, but there is detectable among some writers coming to their prime after World War II less regret over the loss of place and more willingness to experiment with ways to discover substitutes for place. Interest in motion goes on but without the reservations of their predecessors. Perhaps new life experiences account for the change. The War itself was an experience in mobility rather than the tedium of fixed positions of World War I, and the post-War period saw a vast increase in the means of travel and communication. Modern painting anticipated the new feeling for motion when it enticed the eye away from landscape to space and movement; cubism, it is said, is a "research into space" and futurism a "research into movement."[56]

American writers have a special proclivity for motion because their literary tradition long ago reflected the conquest of space in the migrations westward. Exhilaration over automotive travel in recent American writing is but the latest form of a passion that goes back to the spirit of Melville's perpetual sea journeys and Whitman's preference for the open road to the "dark confinement" of the house. "To know the universe itself as a road" was Whitman's ideal, a road that offered only fleeting glimpses of places along it. Jack Kerouac's *On the Road* introduced another "great time of traveling" to a generation that has seen the construction of an unbelievably extensive national highway system and the record-breaking mass production of highspeed vehicles of all sorts. Travel is in the blood of his principal characters, Sal and Dean, who drive an assortment of cars back and forth across the country, not to migrate but simply for the joy of movement and companionship. Dean is an ideal hero because of his prowess in handling a car at high speeds and over long periods of time. Influenced by Kerouac, Tom Wolfe elaborates the automotive journey in *The Electric Kool-Aid Acid Test*. The vehicle is now an old school bus, the only thing a group called Merry Pranksters consider worth saving out of their childhood past; it serves as their home as well as their transportation on an extended journey around the United States. Hallucinogenic drugs and loud music produced by a hi-fi system in the bus are added to motion for kicks, and the whole experience is preserved in the art of the movie camera. The destination sign on the bus is not a place, but simply a promise to move: "Furthur." In the film *The Last Chance,* the hero defies a totalitarian society's ban on automobiles by driving his old racing car to California, where he is jubilantly welcomed by a society that is still free.

From being an instrument of tragedy, as it was with the earlier

group, the automobile has become a source of pleasure, and the highway of earlier disasters has become "the holy road." If there is any
place at all in the lives of this new breed of character, it is the highway
itself, the same wherever it is (thanks to national standards of construction), a universal place like space itself in that its only use for man is to
be traversed, and it must be traversed by means of an automobile. The
highway makes motion in space available to everyone without special
preparations or prohibitively costly equipment; it is there for instant
use, not merely contemplation. The highway exists for the automobile
and the automobile for the highway, one being useless without the
other, in spite of the advertisements that fondly picture the automobile
in natural settings where only the walker and horseman can go. To
those who truly appreciate the automobile it is driving on the highway
that alone counts; "the-rapture-of-the-freeway" is the phrase of Joan
Didion, a writer who understands these things as well as anyone. "The
freeways become a special way of being alive," she writes, "the extreme concentration required in Los Angeles seems to bring on a state
of heightened awareness that some find mystical."[57] Driving the freeway is the one emotional release possible for the troubled heroine of
Didion's *Play It as It Lays:* "She drove it as a riverman runs a river,
every day more attuned to its currents, its deceptions . . . just as a
riverman feels the pull of its rapids."[58] The assimilation of a totally
mechanical operation, driving an automobile on a highway, to a semi-
natural operation, piloting a boat on a river, is a token of the new
constructiveness in attitudes about the automobile. Didion shares
these with other western Americans, with Reyner Banham, for example, a writer on architecture, who also speaks of skillful drivers as
"freeway-pilots" and of the Los Angeles highway system as "a single
comprehensible place, a coherent state of mind, a complete way of life,
the fourth ecology of the Angeleno."[59]

But the transition from place to motion is not complete in Didion,
who admits being a member of "the last generation to carry the burden
of home," the generation in their thirties in 1968. "Some nameless
anxiety colored the emotional charges between me and the place that I
came from. The question of whether or not you could go home again
was a very real part of the sentimental and largely literary baggage with
which we left home in the fifties."[60] Freeway driving is desperate relief
for Maria in *Play It as It Lays,* and she still suffers terribly from a lack
of orientation as she faces the specter of nothingness in Las Vegas:
"Two or three times a day she walked in and out of all the hotels on the
Strip and several downtown. She began to crave the physical flash of
walking in and out of places, the temperature shock, the hot wind

blowing outside, the heavy frigid air inside. . . . By the end of the week she was thinking constantly about where her body stopped and the air began, about the exact point in space and time that was the difference between *Maria* and *other*" (170).

Motion, it must be concluded from literary works that explore it, cannot be an entirely acceptable substitute for place. Man's deep-seated need to orient himself in space by means of familiar locations cannot be altogether neglected, and there is consequently always some despair in an exclusive diet of motion. "Place is a pause in movement," writes the geographer Yi-Fu Tuan.[61] One must pause occasionally, and periodically the yearning for Zion must be satisfied. Although Didion's heroine poetically relates driving a car to piloting a boat on a river, her fascination for the freeway remains essentially a study of death and nothingness. After all else has failed—marriage, lesbianism, drugs, Las Vegas—Maria "imagined herself driving, conceived audacious lane changes, strategic shifts of gear, the Hollywood to the San Bernardino and straight on out, past Barstow, past Baker, driving straight on into the hard white empty core of the world" (162). Maria is no Ahab or Taji of Melville, who saw the plunge into the great whiteness as the supreme heroic act; she suffers instead the despair of Poe's A. Gordon Pym or Twain's distraught father facing the Great White Glare in "The Great Dark."

"To travel is better than to arrive" is a sentiment concealing no despair in Robert Pirsig, whose *Zen and the Art of Motorcycle Maintenance* attempts to present the case for a compromise between motion and place, between technology and humanity, between the individual and society. The automobile is replaced by the motorcylce, a vehicle that can get one closer to places and things and still satisfy the need for motion. The motorcycle can open up "secondary America" to its devotee: "back roads, and Chinaman's ditches, and Appaloosa horses, and sweeping mountain ranges, and meditative thoughts, and kids with pinecones and bumblebees and open sky above us mile after mile, all through that, what was real, what was *around* us dominated." After the individual's need for concrete reality is served, the motorcycle can bring one into the abstract flow of the "primary America," the freeway at the end of the book, "the freeway that grows wider and fuller now, swelling with cars and trucks and buses full of people, and soon by the road are houses and boats and the water of the Bay."

The growing popularity of the recreation vehicle, or van, seems to suggest that some people have worked out a practical if limited compromise between motion and place, for the van is not only "the wheels" to keep one in motion but the fixed home in the midst of a variety of places. One of Walker Percy's characters defends, with only a slight touch of irony, the camper van as "a good way to live nowadays . . . mobile yet at home . . . in the world yet not of the world, sampling the particularities of place yet cabined off from the sadness of place, curtained away from the ghosts of Malvern Hill, peeping out at the doleful woods of Spotsylvania through the cheerful plexiglas of Sheboygan."[62] Such a vehicle may serve to compensate for the destruction that the automobile and highway have wrought upon places, particularly in the city, since the home on wheels gives one the opportunity to live in a place outside of the city at least some of the time.

Tourism

Being in motion is an alternative for staying put in a disagreeable place. Another way to satisfy the need for engaging places is to seize upon the few unique places that are still to be found. The passion for tourism is the attempt of people to acquire a commodity in short supply, unspoiled and truly distinguished places. And truly distinguished places, for many people, are those that are associated with a supposed golden past in distant lands. Catering to these needs is a lucrative business in a world becoming more and more uniform in appearance. "There is a mystic and beautiful place still left, it's called India," reads a travel advertisement that perfectly exploits the dearth of places. Ironically, tourism itself destroys the very places it seeks out, the Acropolis perishing not from neglect, as once was the case, but from excessive use. When notable places cannot be made available, they may be faked in the construction of primitive, antique, and futuristic sites: wildlife compounds, Disney World amusement parks, and business establishments that masquerade as exotic wonderlands. Literature, too, supplies the demand with historical novels, detective stories in glamorous settings, and with what Eudora Welty calls "the Isle of Capri novel."

Hallucination

Distorting places through hallucination is another way to escape.[63] The French symbolists set the literary pattern for this practice, which is well adapted to the modern problem because the deterioration of places offers no obstacle to, and may even help, the results. "I saw quite plainly a mosque where a factory stood," writes Rimbaud in *A*

Season in Hell. After Joyce, the distortion of places becomes a regular feature in fiction using the stream of consciousness technique. Just as chronological time is broken, so place is wrenched from normal perspective and presented in unrelated fragments. More recent drug-induced hallucinations of places add little to the effects already achieved by the unaided imagination. Gary Snyder believes that "peyote and acid have a curious way of turning some people in to the local soil . . . to follow the timeless path of love and wisdom, in affectionate company with the sky, winds, clouds, trees, waters, animals and grasses."[64] Two pipes of kif throw the hero of Bowles's *Let It Come Down* into a mood of ecstatic identification with earth and sky: "Walking became a marvelously contrived series of harmonious movements, the execution of whose every detail was in perfect concordance with the vast, beautiful machine of which the air and the mountainside were parts."[65] A piece of majoun stirs him to sexual intercourse that is accompanied by the traditional imagery of earth and woman: "The soft endless earth spread out beneath him, glowing with sunlight, untouched by time, uninhabited, belonging wholly to him. How far below it lay, he could not have said. . . . Yet he could touch its smooth resilient contours, smell its odor of sun, and even taste the salt left in its pores by the sea in some unremembered age" (226).

The drug-taking culture has undoubtedly revived the back-to-earth feeling among young people, but it is also to be observed that no matter what earth-bound convictions hippies had, everything, including natural landscapes as well as city streets and grotesque living quarters, was material to be consumed in the constant search for the kicks that may be had from distorting reality. A redwood forest is wired for sound and sprayed with Day-Glo paint by the Merry Pranksters in Tom Wolfe's *The Electric Kool-Aid Acid Test:*

> *Dusk.* Huge stripes of Day-Glo green and orange ran up the soaring redwoods and gleamed out at dusk as if Nature had said At last, Aw freak it, and had freaked it. Up the gully back of the house, up past the Hermit's Cave, where Day-Glo face masks and boxes and machines and things that glowed, winked, hummed, whistled, bellowed, and microphones that could pick up animals, hermits, anything, and broadcast them from the treetops, like the crazy gibbering rhesus background noises from the old Jungle Jim radio shows. (124)

Another "happy forest" is to be found in Robert Stone's *Dog Soldiers,* in which loudspeakers, lights, and baubles are strung over a mountain top. Tourism, drugs, and the traditional pastoral place all come together in a revealing scene in Stone's novel when a drug pusher treats his girlfriend to an especially pure does of heroin, a dab of which he puts on a postcard of Marine World, a famous tourist attraction in California:

> He pared away a tiny mound of the stuff with the cardboard funnel and eased it onto the postcard's glossy blue sky. . . .
>
> She crouched over the stuff like a child and drew it into her nostril. . . .
>
> "Better than a week in the country, right?" Holding to him, she stood up and he helped her to the bed. She lay across it, arching her back, stretching her arms and legs towards its four corners.
>
> "It's a lot better than a week in the country," she said. . . .
>
> "It's its own poem," she said, when the lift came. "Very serious elegant poem."[66]

APOCALYPSE—THE END OF ALL PLACES

> and now mere earth
> Desperate and done with.
> —Browning, "Childe Roland to the Dark Tower Came"

The feeling of place-loss may be allayed by indulging oneself in premonitions of a universal catastrophe when all places will be obliterated. The same imagination that is attracted to places of the past—the forest, the country house—may also be haunted by dire prognostications of the future. E. M. Forster, we have seen, yearned for the greenwood of Old England, but in "The Machine Stops" he foresees a time when civilized man will abandon altogether the earth's surface and move into an underground world where life-supports are supplied by a gigantic machine technology. Those who will not bend to this way of life are banished to the surface of the earth, now terribly polluted and degraded; they are thought to be "homeless," since the machine has become the place man inhabits, not Nature. But the machine breaks down, stops, and all who live underground perish while those who have been banished to the earth's surface become, ironically, the saving remnant who will carry on the species. The separation of a completely mechanized world from a deteriorating natural world is

also to be found in Franz Werfel's *Star of the Unborn* and Eugene
Zamiatin's *We*.

There is nothing new, of course, in the fear of the world's ending,
since what has been created may as easily be destroyed. "The earth is
an uncertain habitation," goes a line in an anonymous fifteenth-century
poem. Legends of disappearing countries, like Atlantis, are common
and always fascinating. The mood of mankind wavers between despair
and hope for the world's survival. The medieval belief in its imminent
demise gradually gave way to ideas of progress in the seventeenth and
eighteenth centuries. Faltering faith in progress in the second half of
the nineteenth century, however, inspired some notable end-of-the-
world visions: Melville's *Moby-Dick,* Twain's *The Mysterious Stranger* and "The Great Dark," Hardy's heath, Tennyson's "The Passing of
Arthur"—

> A land of old upheaven from the abyss
> By fire, to sink into the abyss again.

The strong return to the apocalyptic mood in the twentieth century
may be caused by new forms of anxiety taking over from Christian
theological guilt. The world political situation looks toward the finality
of nuclear warfare, but a more constant alarm is the growing knowledge that man's environment is being destroyed at an accelerated rate
by technological means in the service of commercial appetite and national defence. The consolation of earlier dogmas in a cyclical rebirth—
the subsiding of the Flood, the New Jerusalem—is denied to the
modern mood, which must face either total annihiliation of a radical
diminution of life as end-results of the process of environmental damage. Thus in Forster's short story mankind may not altogether perish,
but its continuation lies in the hands of wraith-like creatures "hiding in
the mist and the ferns" of an earth turned brown with pollution. If there
is hope of survival in apocalyptic fiction, it is a terribly forlorn one,
with mankind caught in a process of "devolution." Idiots inherit the
fallen South in Faulkner, whose Yoknapatawpha novels seem uni-
formly devoted to portraying the dissolution of man and earth.[67] The
survivors of cosmic catastrophe in science fiction are savages and sim-
pletons leading deprived lives amid the ruins of civilization: apes in *The
Planet of the Apes,* monstrous "half-angels, half-beasts, but no man" in
Walker Percy's *Love in the Ruins,* diminutive men taking to the trees in
Richard Aldiss' *The Long Afternoon of Earth,* bewitched children in
Arthur Clarke's *Childhood's End,* simple-minded worshippers of trout

in Brautigan's *In Watermelon Sugar,* drugged half-people in Vonnegut's *Slapstick.*

The moment of earth's destruction is attempted by few writers, probably because it is not easily imaginable in its totality. Synecdoche is the safest way. Popular films use particular disasters to satisfy the apocalyptic mood that has now become quite general: a ship turned upside down in *The Poseidon Adventure,* a high-rise apartment on fire in *Towering Inferno.* A small island completely carried away by a storm on the Chesapeake Bay makes an ominous preview of the end of the entire Delmarva Peninsula in James Michener's *Chesapeake.* A hotel is the world in *Self Condemned* by Wyndham Lewis, who perhaps took a clue from the opening of Conrad's *Victory* in which the world we live in is compared to "a garish, unrestful hotel." Lewis's hotel in Canada burns and then freezes into an iceberg after being flooded with the water used to extinguish the fire; not to lose the point, Lewis reminds us that "the destruction of a microcosm gives one a foretaste of the destruction of the world." The sudden destruction of buildings was a motif growing naturally out of World War II; its continued use decades later is ominous. In Heinrich Böll's *Billiards at Half Past Nine,* a man who was a demolitions expert in the war blows up, for no reason he can discover, an abbey that his architect father had built; and in Graham Greene's "The Destructors," an architect's young son leads a gang of his playmates in cutting away the supports of a neighbor's house so that the whole interior instantly collapses leaving the external shell of the building deceptively standing. The bombing of a city, Dresden, is Kurt Vonnegut's model for the world's end in *Slaughterhouse-Five.* To emphasize the difficulty of approaching the subject, Vonnegut makes the whole book a series of evasions on the part of his chief survivor, Billy Pilgrim. More direct is the final scene of *Cat's Cradle* in which the entire world turns to ice: "the moist green earth was a blue-white pearl." In *Slapstick* Vonnegut gives up the notion of total and immediate destruction and turns to gradualism, which reflects better the feeling of the 1970s that there is much less chance of nuclear holocaust than of creeping deterioration of the earth's environment. In this latest version, tampering with gravity by Chinese Communists has serious but not yet fatal consequences; breaks in the smooth functioning of an advanced civilization begin to crop up ominously. Thus the opening scene in New York City presents some disturbing anomalies: "Smoke from a cooking fire on the terrazzo floor of the lobby of the Empire State Building on the Island of Death floats over the ailanthus jungle which Thirty-fourth Street has become." Novels dealing entirely with the accumulation of details pointing to the gradual deterioration of mankind's whole environment are Harry Harrison's *Make Room! Make Room!* and John Brunner's *The Sheep Look Up.*

Post-apocalyptic landscape, or what the world will be like for survivors, offers opportunities for the exercise of the modern taste for a combination of satire and horror. After the Great Burning and Destruction, the few remains of Manhattan are taken to be "The Place of the Gods" in Stephen Vincent Benet's shory story of that name. An ironical veneration of the old dead places is also found in Walter Miller's *A Canticle for Leibowitz,* which presents a circumstantial history of the world and its landscape for six centuries following the Flame Deluge—mankind simply repeats the steps that led up to the last holocaust. Satire is served from a different perspective when post-apocalyptic societies reject the intellect and technology that made the earth what it was in the past and eventually led to its destruction. *The Planet of The Apes* films make this point very emphatically. In George R. Stewart's *Earth Abides* a geologist's hammer, pulling the arm downward, becomes a sacred symbol of authority to the handful of people still living in the enduring hills around San Francisco, while the great Bay Bridge rusts away and unused books lie mouldering in the University library. The same situation occurs in Richard Brautigan's *In Watermelon Sugar:* the broken-down remains of the old world are locked away in a place called the Forgotten Works, and the new world is made of watermelon sugar, has rivers that are a half-inch wide and a capital city that seems to be a house. The reader is vaguely disturbed by the queer physical qualities of the post-apocalyptic environment and by the grotesque psychology of its inhabitants, who are not bothered about violence and death nor moved by feelings of love and joy.[68]

Since the city has often served in the history of literature as a symbol of the civilized world in its glory, the destruction of the city is a familiar image in modern apocalyptic writing to represent the fall of civilization. The nineteenth-century realism of Balzac, Dickens and Dostoevsky detailed the city's rooms and streets, concentrating on their function as traps for naive characters. The street was the favored detail to represent the city, and reporting the dull and sometimes vicious life of the street was a common device to be found in such naturalistic fiction as Zola's *L'Assommoir,* Arthur Morrison's *Tales of Mean Streets,* and Frank Norris's *McTeague.* With twentieth-century literature streets became a bewildering maze filled with the grotesque horrors of a world dying of war, crime, and racial hatred. The transition is conveniently marked in the course of T. S. Eliot's poetry: the streets of "Preludes" and "Rhapsody on a Windy Night" are characterized by the tedium and sordidness of the naturalistic mode, while in the later "Little Gidding" of *Four Quartets* the "disfigured" street of war-torn London is figuratively a place in purgatory where the poet and the ghost of "some dead master" walk "the pavement in a dead patrol." Juxtaposing contemporary cityscapes with scenes out of the heroic past gave Eliot and Joyce the means to make very damaging comments on the decay of civilization. After Eliot's "Unreal City" and Joyce's Dublin, the city as Dantean inferno became a commonplace image in twentieth-century literature. There is the Valley of Ashes bounded "by a small foul river" dividing the suburbs and New York City in *The Great Gatsby;* Harlem torn by race riots in Ralph Ellison's *Invisible Man;* the grotesque streets of wartime Rome, into which Yossarian, like some hero out of Greek mythology descending into Hades to rescue a maiden, ventures in order to find "Nately's whore's kid sister" in *Catch-22;* London under attack of V-2 bombs in Thomas Pynchon's *Gravity's Rainbow;* Chicago and New York in a number of Saul Bellow's works.[69] It is in the city subways that Bellow's heroes see most dramatically the analogy of the city with hell. The hero of *Herzog,* after taking note of the debris from a burning building, descends from the street to the subway station and is struck by the thought that "innumerable millions of passengers had polished the wood of the turnstiles with their hips," a reflection Leventhal has earlier in *The Victim*— "innumerable millions, crossing, touching, pressing"—and Wilhelm in *Seize the Day*—"The great, great, crowd, the inexhaustible current of millions of every race and kind pouring out, pressing round . . . much faster than any man could make tally." These are the souls of the departed as they are imaged in the long epic tradition of hell in Virgil, Dante, and Milton; with Eliot they inhabit the city:

> A crowd flowed over London Bridge, so many,
> I had not thought death had undone so many.

In Anthony Burgess's *The Clockwork Testament or Enderby's End,* New York appears as "a vicious but beautiful city, totally representative of the human condition." The subway entrance at Times Square is a "hellmouth," and the train stopping unaccountably between stations is "a fair simulacrum of the ultimate misery," an echo of Eliot's lines in "East Coker:"

Or as, when an underground train, in the tube, stops too long
   between stations
And the conversation rises and slowly fades into silence
And you see behind every face the mental emptiness deepen
Leaving only the growing terror of nothing to think about.

After emerging from the subway, Enderby walks "through the deserted streets full of decayed and disaffected and dogmerds." The subway scene in "Burnt Norton" is introduced with the line: "Here is a place of disaffection."

Details of the ultimate destruction of the city are pictured in a number of horrifying projections, some science fiction, some not. In Nevil Chute's *On the Beach,* the last Americans behold a perfectly intact but lifeless and uninhabitable San Francisco, while a handful of survivors, in Stewart's *Earth Abides,* manages to hang onto life in the same city. New York seems to be coming apart in Bellow's *Mr. Sammler's Planet;* Denver is near death in Brunner's *The Sheep Look Up;* rat-dogs and monkeys wage vicious war on each other in a ruined city in Doris Lessing's *Briefing for a Descent into Hell.*

ACCOMMODATION WITH PLACELESSNESS

The question that he frames in all but words
Is what to make of a diminished thing.
              —Robert Frost, "The Oven Bird"

Those who anguish over the condition of placelessness probably overemphasize the importance of place in human affairs. There is no proof, as Wyndham Lewis reminds us, "that *to have roots* (as if one were a vegetable or a plant) is a good thing for a man: that to be *rootless* is a bad thing for a man."[70] The maturation of an individual is not possible without the successive abandonment of places, and a society may die for lack of contact with societies in other places. Nations dislodged by catastrophe or need have resumed a successful existence elsewhere; migration is the common experience of all peoples. Indeed, traditions may thrive without localization among groups of people having an especially intense common interest, and many of the more civilized activities of the world have been carried on by groups less identified by shared places than by shared interests. Judaism and Christianity first owed their strength and value to the mobility that dislocation forced upon them; later, their striving for fixed geographic positions led them into uncharacteristic barbarisms. The English nation may have "fixed its roots" in an island, as Ransom says, but the English have also been well-traveled people and their great civilization probably owes more to their disposition to roam and live abroad than to their staying at home.

People who have the greatest need for place are those who have failed, for one reason or another, to keep pace with history or with the movement of society around them. Much of the fear of placelessness stems from resistance to the accelerated rate of change that does not allow sufficient time for some people to adapt themselves to the alteration of places. Often the change is in some accidental detail or some related social perquisite that has been temporarily suspended or modified. Technology is accounted the villain, but it is the change in place and behavior caused by technology that is really unacceptable; few complain about technologies that have made changes to which we have become accustomed. In the world today it is possible for technology of communication to replace shared locality as the principal means of maintaining a high degree of community life. Marshall McLuhan finds support for his belief that "our new electric culture provides our lives again with a tribal base" in the pages of none other than Pierre Teilhard de Chardin, whom he quotes approvingly: "Thanks to the prodigious biological event represented by the discovery of electromagnetic waves, each individual finds himself henceforth (actively and passively) simultaneously present, over land and sea, in every corner of the earth."[71] Some geographers are willing to admit the inadequacy of the old "location theory." In an anthology devoted to the consequences of a shrinking world, Allen K. Philbrick writes:

> The single most important consequence, however, will be that the perception of place that has dominated us since pre-history will be lifting. We will increasingly understand that objects and established patterns of things are not just relatively located objects in a culturally defined concept of space. We will regard things and the patterns of things as events in time-space. We will witness increasing negation of the significance of place—we will overcome the tyranny of place.[72]

Regret over the loss of places is not a theme that literature can continue profitably. Disgust with a changing world has been the dominant note since the middle of the nineteenth century, but there is also another and more promising effort, which is to seek accommodation

with a diminishing world rather than its depreciation through nostalgia
or its destruction through despair. This point of view recognizes that
the earth has always been on a downward course and that the condition
of the environment is a relative thing. Thoreau had the good sense to
realize that Walden was fallen even before he found it a paradise.

Fiction of the nineteenth century began to explore the possibilities
of accommodation when it examined the impact of environment on
character. Female characters were especially good subjects because
women could serve as the prime victims of an environment that a male-
dominated society had created for them. (In the following century
Negroes and Jews would assume this role.) Emma Bovary is destroyed
by provincial surroundings that forbid romantic dreams; Hester
Prynne, however, learns to thrive in a community even more hostile to
romantic love. Something in the cultural background, perhaps Puritanism, gives English and American heroines the power to contend with
the harsh conditions forced on them by false lovers, tyrannical husbands and fathers. Hester and Jane Eyre are succeeded by Dorothea
Brooke and a number of Henry James's heroines, who study ways to
cope with the suddenly diminished opportunities of their lives. Isabel
Archer is a young woman who wants to "roam through space," to
assert her personal prerogatives to the fullest extent, but she finds
herself the victim of an unhappy marriage to a husband who is revealed
as a vulgar opportunist of the worst sort. Like her Gothic-novel
forebears Isabel is trapped, but only figuratively, in "a kind of domestic
fortress," the Italian palazzo of her husband. Her real tragedy is that
the life that once seemed to stretch before her like "a long summer
afternoon" full of wonderful people and places is now terribly
shrunken:

> . . . she had suddenly found the infinite vista of a multiplied life to
> be a dark, narrow alley with a dead wall at the end. Instead of
> leading to the high places of happiness, from which the world
> would seem to lie below one . . . it led rather downward and
> earthward, into realms of restriction and depression . . . (II. 189)

Disillusionment with the seemingly bright and various world is
Arnoldian, though James himself thought that the case was especially
American: "To be the heir of all the ages only to know yourself . . .
balked of your inheritance."[73] Isabel's decision to accept her lot is
anticipated by a conviction she has at the time of her marriage that "the
desire for unlimited expansion" must be succeeded "by the sense that
life was vacant without some private duty that might gather one's

energies to a point." Resigning herself out of a sense of duty to her husband and his young daughter, Isabel chooses to restrict her own freedom of movement and begins to see the European countries that once delighted her as "strange-looking, dimly-lighted, pathless lands." London, which once "loomed large and rich to her" now is terrifying. At the peak of her freedom, before her marriage to Osmond, Rome was a city "she went about in a repressed ecstasy of contemplation"; she was especially impressed by the "splendid immensity" of St. Peter's: "her conception of greatness rose and dizzily rose. After this it never lacked space to soar." After her disillusionment she could cherish only the ruins of Rome "through the veil of her personal sadness," as James puts it—but the use of settings to symbolize Isabel's plight makes James's portrait stand as an early exemplar of the modern alienation of person and place, of the denial of the world's variety to the deprived character. Because of her commitment to her husband, Isabel, at the very end of the novel, must reject Caspar Goodwood's offer of the world to her: "The world's all before us—and the world's very big." She replies, "The world's very small," but she is not telling him her true thought: "The world, in truth, had never seemed so large; it seemed to open out, all round her, to take the form of a mighty sea, where she floated in fathomless waters. She had wanted his help, and here was help; it had come in a rushing torrent" (II, 435). This is a rare outburst of passion for Isabel; her chance to possess the world is also her chance to be possessed, but she must reject this spatial and sexual consummation in order to honor her commitment to her husband, to whose restricted world and false love she presently returns. "There was a very straight path." In a similar scene in *The Scarlet Letter,* the roles are reversed. Hester Prynne, having earned the right to leave her husband, offers the wide world and herself to Reverend Dimmesdale: "Is the world, then, so narrow? . . . Doth the universe lie within the compass of yonder town?" she asks. But the minister cannot accept "the broad pathway of the sea" that Hester offers since he has not yet fulfilled his commitment to his religious faith; even the woodland pathway he takes back to the town is fraught with satanic temptations leading to damnation.

Isabel Archer is but one of many Jamesian heroines whose spatial scope is tragically circumscribed. Catherine Sloper in *Washington Square* is almost rescued from imprisonment in her father's house, as the force of her first and only love affair moves her from the back parlor to the front parlor and even out to the balcony; but once there she can only weep over her lost chance to go out into the world at large. Because of the treachery of a kinsman, Caroline Spencer in

"Four Meetings" must be content with a thirteen-hour stopover in LeHavre as her total experience of Europe. The frustrated movement of James's heroines is in sharp contrast to the successful movement of heroines of an earlier age: Fanny Price, for instance, moves from the outside of a noble house to its center.

What a Jamesian character loses through spatial limitation he gains in the range of his consciousness. Strether compels himself to return to a small New England town, but he carries with him a glowing consciousness of potential for life in the varied places of Europe. The interior point of view thrives when freedom to move in space is limited, for then it may explore in greater detail whatever has been left to it of the outside world, or elaborate its relationship to a diminished world. That James dealt more and more with less and less, as one critic puts it, is not a judgment against him but a recognition of the tendency of consciousness to be more intensively active when it has less data to work with. James's start in this direction was followed up by Proust, whose narrator's consciousness is developed in exquisite detail as compensation for his loss of mobility. The recovery of the past is Marcel's compulsive lifework and Proust's whole art, and to recapture the past the recreation of places is essential. The odor of madeleine pastries dipped in tea triggers the recollection of the places in Marcel's past. Georges Poulet observes that Proust's work is a search for lost places as well as past times and that without the recollection of places the people Marcel knew would remain abstractions, that it is the places that make their images precise ("Ce sont les lieux qui précisent leur image").[74] But the use of place goes beyond the rendering of characters through localization; Marcel's very being is dependent upon his realization of place in his life, a necessity established in the opening pages of *Swann's Way*. Only through experience of the place he is in and memory of the places he has been in can Marcel pull himself "up out of the abyss of not-being." The process is not only mental, for his body has a memory too:

> Its memory, the composite memory of its ribs, knees, and shoulderblades, offered it a whole series of rooms in which it had at one time or another slept. . . . And even before my brain . . . had collected sufficient impressions to enable it to identify the room, my body would recall from each room in succession what the bed was like, where the doors were, how daylight came in at the windows, whether there was a passage outside . . . (7)

From his bed, his grave at night, Marcel is reborn each morning along with the world he recreates—the bedroom, the hall, the staircase, the house, and "the whole of Combray and of its surroundings." The world Marcel creates upon waking is a subjective image of the real world and thus superior to the real world, which is "barren and devoid of the charm which they owed, in our minds, to the association of certain ideas" (121). Marcel's wonderfully elaborated imaginative world is compensation for one who has been deprived of the real world just as Proust's art was his compensation for the spatial restrictions caused by his poor health.

The spatial confinement of characters was a theme the nineteenth-century realist used to express the aggravated modern sense of environmental limitations. Henry James was not the first to recognize "the trapped, the caged, the excluded consciousness," as L. C. Knights claims.[75] Maggie Tulliver's effort to escape the mill and Lizzie Hexam's to escape the river come to mind. Dickens was certainly prolific in depicting people suffering from enclosure and exclusion in the city; Dostoevsky, strongly influenced by Dickens, fixed the extreme type of isolation with his underground man. "Now I am living out my life in my corner," says the speaker in *Notes from Underground,* "burying myself for grief in the underworld."[76]

And Dostoevsky's underworld is not the traditional place for the punishment of sins but precisely the opposite, "that hell of unsatisfied desires." This corresponds to the situation of nineteenth-century heroines, with, however, the essential difference that their restriction derives from male domination—the tyranny of a father, the deceit of a lover—whereas Dostoevsky's prisoner suffers from the recognition that his own will has failed to bring his vicious desires to fruition. Coming to their fate from opposite directions—the female from restrictions placed upon the free exercise of her will, the male by the wrong use of will—they both end up in places that confine their movement. While a good number of the women make the best of their restriction, some even improving their characters within it, the men, starting with Dostoevsky's gentleman, accept it fatalistically and even collaborate with it. "Better to do nothing! Better conscious inertia! And so hurrah for the underground!" exclaims his diarist.

The predicament of characters drawn by realists in the nineteenth century becomes the universal predicament of man in the twentieth century. "Enclosure becomes a measure of the world," writes Frederick Karl, one among a number of critics who have observed the "spatial reduction," the "claustral atmosphere" of the modern novel.[77] The prison cell and underground room are but two of the places used by modern literature to objectify the sense of confinement that has been

forced upon the modern hero by society or by his own tragic predicament. "Today we have the lyricism of the prison cell," exclaims the
narrator of Camus's *The Fall,* whereas "a hundred and fifty years ago
people became sentimental about lakes and forests" (123–23). In Kafka's "The Burrow" the mole drives himself to more and more elaborate
precautions in the construction of his home, so that finally the *idea* of
security counts for more than security itself. He is so proud of his
handiwork (does he ever actually build the burrow?) that he wants to
"settle down somewhere close to the entrance, to pass my life watching
the entrance, and gloat perpetually upon the reflection—and in that find
my happiness—how steadfast a protection my burrow would be if I
were inside it." John Fowles's butterfly collector reverses the process
when he devotes all his energy to making a sub-basement room absolutely foolproof against escape. Ironically, he is free to come and go as
he pleases, though his mind is wholly absorbed with improving the
stronghold, while his prisoner imagines a sketch she will paint of the
out-of-doors. Thus the prisoner and the jailer in *The Collector,* between them, share the contemporary trauma of the place of
confinement. In Hubert Selby's *The Room* a prison inmate, who can
see only laundry baskets outside his cell, boxes the compass forward
and backward to pass the time. Since World War II the institutional
place of detention has been a prime subject—the lock-up for political
prisoners in Koestler's *Darkness at Noon,* the apartment slots in Za-
matian and Huxley's authoritarian dystopias, the concentration camp
and hospital of Solzhenitsyn, the old people's home of Updike's
Poorhouse Fair, the mental hospital in Kesey's *One Flew Over the
Cuckoo's Nest.* These attest to the writer's response to the encroachments political organizations having been making on private space and
freedom of movement.

In addition to shrunken space, the proliferation of inappropriate
places in modern literature emphasizes the breakdown of traditional
place values. Kafka struck this chord early, in *The Trial,* with his law
courts located in dwelling houses. An old plantation house is used by
moonshiners in Faulkner's *Sanctuary,* a fine old estate is used for
military training in *Brideshead Revisited.* A married couple in John
Steinbeck's *Cannery Row* make their home in an abandoned industrial
boiler, the hero of Thomas McGuane's *Ninety-two in the Shade* lives in
a grounded airplane fuselage, and the hero of Richard Brautigan's
Abortion in a public library. Holden Caulfield in J. D. Salinger's
Catcher in the Rye finds the Egyptian mummy room at the Metropoli-
tan Museum "the only dry, cosy place in the world." The bar and the
bathroom are settings for the most serious transactions in twentieth-

century fiction. The bathroom is the most important room for the Glass family in Salinger's *Franny and Zooey;* it is a place to read, to exchange confidences, to expound religious mysteries—"our little chapel."[78] From a place of temptation and corruption—as in Zola's *L'Assommoir,* Stephen Crane's *Maggie,* and Dreiser's *Sister Carrie*— the bar has been transformed into a curiously ideal refuge for the sensitive hero, a place where he can maintain some minimal contact with humanity. Hemingway's "A Clean, Well-lighted Place" is the prime example. Camus puts in words what Hemingway only implied when he says of Cardona in *A Happy Life* that in a bar he gets "the herd warmth which is the last refuge against the terrors of solitude and its vague aspirations" (51). In *The Fall* Clamence makes a café in Amsterdam the center of his operations as a "judge-penitent." Sharing the confessions of others, he says, "I pass from the 'I' to the 'we.'" The bar is so important to the alcoholic consul in Lowry's *Under the Volcano* that it comes between him and his wife when he tries to make love to her one morning; in his imagination the bar takes the place of "that jewelled gate" of his wife's body:

> It was one of those cantinas that would be opening now, at nine o'clock: and he was queerly conscious of his own presence there. . . . Now he wanted to go! Ah none but he knew how beautiful it all was, the sunlight, sunlight, sunlight flooding the bar of El Puerto del Sol, flooding the watercress and oranges, or falling in a single golden line as if in the act of conceiving a God, falling like a lance straight into a block of ice—(89–90)

The process begun by James and Proust—the subjective elaboration of a diminishing world—is carried to its logical extreme by Beckett. Environment is systemically diminished to the vanishing point in his works, and introspection grows as his characters search desperately for some ground of existence. But there is no discovery for them of the values or duties that restore the Jamesian character to some manner of life, painful though it may be. Cursed with endless talking about nothing at all, the unnamed voice in the last part of the Trilogy finally realizes the importance of a place to be in, for then there would at least be two objective things to talk about, the place and the person occupying it:

> Help, help, if I could only describe this place, I who am so good at describing places, walls, ceilings, floors, they are my specialty,

doors, windows, what haven't I imagined in the way of windows in
the course of my career, some opened on the sea, all you could see
was sea and sky, if I could put myself in a room, that would be an
end of the wordy-gurdy, even doorless, even windowless, nothing
but the four surfaces, the six surfaces, if I could shut myself up, it
would be a mine, it could be black dark, I could be motionless and
fixed, I'd find a way to explore it, I'd listen to the echo, I'd get to
remember it, I'd be home . . . (399)

Of course the wish is fruitless, because he has already had the chance
to locate himself but has failed to: "if only I could feel a place for me,
I've tried, I'll try again, none was ever mine." But consciousness goes
on as well as his art of literary construction—"nothing but this voice
and the silence all around"; there is "no need of walls" as long as he has
consciousness and utterance: "The place, I'll make it all the same, I'll
make it in my head, I'll draw it out of my memory, I'll gather it all
about me" (411). The character for whom the world ceases to matter or
exists only in a minimal way always has recourse to an alternate world
of imagination. Interior spaciousness substitutes for a world of depleted space and uninhabitable places. The cultivation of interior space
often appears to be absurdly solipsistic, and the inappropriate use of
places appears to be grotesque, but these are processes of accommodation that cannot be denied to the human spirit as it seeks to save itself
from complete disorientation and despair. "I'll go on," says the Unnamable in Beckett's Trilogy, "you must say words, as long as there
are any."

Rebuilding an imaginative relation to a diminished world and tem-
pering the expansionist and sumptuous habits of modern society have
been important functions of literature in the last hundred years. T. S.
Eliot's change from repulsion to a carefully qualified acceptance of
history and "this twittering world" in his metaphysical system is typical
of a major turn in twentieth-century literature. His depiction of the
world as wasteland may still be repeated in fiction and poetry—in the
"unforgivable landscape" of poets like Robert Lowell—but counter-
forces are more and more found among writers, including even Lowell
after 1957, who follow the example William Carlos Williams gave in
Paterson when he celebrated the very heart of the wasteland; or Allen
Ginsberg, who finds a "sermon" in the fact that a a sunflower, sending
"its withered roots below, in the home-pile of sand and sawdust," can
still have a beautiful form and existence: "We're not our skin of grime
. . . we're all beautiful sunflowers inside." Eliot's "dull roots" are
finally redeemed.

Literature dealing with the theme of place-loss and placelessness has performed a valuable service in calling attention to earth's deterioration and recalling the traditional respect for earth that began to suffer a decline with the start of the Industrial Revolution. Long before science sounded the alarm, literature reacted to the onset of a problem serious enough to threaten the survival of mankind and began to develop a new sensibility to environment in preparation for a time that appears now to be the start of the age of ecology. It is unreasonable to expect a return to Eden, the primal place, but respect for earth's remaining beauty and for the health of its soil, air, and water may be revived out of the heritage of the past and refined with the new knowledge of earth sciences. This will be a service for literature to perform in the immediate future.

NOTES

1—THE NEW CONCERN FOR PLACE

1. Frederic Jameson, "Metacommentary," *PMLA* 86 (Jan. 1971): 12.

2. Rev. of *The Poet in the Imaginary Museum: Essays of Two Decades,* by Donald Davie, *New York Times Book Review,* 26 Mar. 1978, p. 22.

3. *A God Within* (New York: Scribner's, 1972), p. 45.

4. *Cannibals and Christians* (New York: Dial, 1966), p. 235.

5. *Cosmos and History: The Myth of the Eternal Return* (1954; rpt. New York: Harper and Row, 1959), p. vii.

6. *The Writings of Henry David Thoreau,* ed. Bradford Torrey, Vol. 7 (Boston: Houghton Mifflin, 1906), p. 253. The idea is a familiar one in the transcendental repertoire; it is frequently expressed in Margaret Fuller: "As man has two natures—one like that of the plants and animals, adapted to their uses and enjoyments of this planet, another which presages and demands a higher sphere—he is constantly breaking bounds, in proportion as the mental gets the better of the mere instinctive existence. As yet, he loses in harmony of being what he gains in height and extension; the civilized man is a larger mind but a more imperfect nature than the savage," *The Writings of Margaret Fuller,* ed. Mason Wade (New York: Viking, 1941), p. 91.

7. *The Mansion* (New York: Random House, 1955), p. 435.

8. "The Old People," *Go Down, Moses* (New York: Random House, 1942), p. 186.

9. *William Faulkner: The Yoknapatawpha Country* (New Haven: Yale University Press, 1963), p. 46.

10. *October Light* (New York: Norton, 1971), p. 11.

11. For the distinction between Utopia and Arcadia, see Northrop Frye, "Varieties of Literary Utopias," *Utopias and Utopian Thought,* ed. Frank E. Manuel (Boston: Beacon, 1967). This essay first appeared in *Daedalus* (Spring 1965).

12. Joseph W. Meeker, in *The Comedy of Survival: Studies in Literary Ecology* (New York: Scribner's, 1974), studies the ecological attitudes implicit in various literary genres. Comedy encourages adjustment to environment whereas tragedy encourages defiance of environment leading to ecological disaster.

13. Walter Whiter, *Etymologicon Magnum* (Cambridge, 1800); *Etymologicon Universale,* Vols. I and II (Cambridge, 1811), Vol. III (Cambridge, 1825). For Whiter's influence on Thoreau see Michael West, "*Walden's* Dirty Language: Thoreau and Walter Whiter's Geocentric Etymological Theories," *Harvard Library Bulletin* 22 (April 1974).

14. *Walden* (New York: Rinehart, 1948), p. 29.

15. *Maine Woods* (New York: Crowell, 1966), p. 92.

16. *The White Tower* (Philadelphia: Lippincott, 1945), p. 121.

17. R. W. Stallman, *The Houses that James Built and Other Literary Studies* (East Lansing: Michigan State University Press, 1961). Some early and late studies of landscape painting and literature: Elizabeth Wheeler Manwaring, *Italian Landscape in Eighteenth Century England* (1925; rpt. New York: Russell and Russell, 1965); Christopher Hussey, *The Picturesque: Studies in a Point of View* (1927; rpt. Hamden Conn.: Archon Books, 1967); John Dixon Hunt, *The Figure in the Landscape: Poetry, Painting, and Gardening During the Eighteenth Century* (Baltimore: Johns Hopkins University Press, 1976); Blake Nevius, *Cooper's Landscape: An Essay on the Picturesque Vision* (Berkeley: University of California Press, 1975).

18. Giamatti, *The Earthly Paradise and the Renaissance Epic* (Princeton: Princeton University Press, 1966); Blackstone, *The Lost Travellers: A Romantic Theme with Variations* (London: Longmans, 1962); Beach, *Obsessive Images: Symbolism in Poetry of 1930's and 1940's* (Minneapolis: University of Minnesota Press, 1960); Auden, *The Enchafèd Flood* (New York: Random House, 1950); Gill, *Happy Rural Seat: The English Country House and the Literary Imagination* (New Haven: Yale University Press, 1972).

19. Nicolson, *Mountain Gloom and Mountain Glory* (Ithaca: Cornell University Press, 1959); Smith, *Virgin Land: The American West as Symbol and Myth* (1950; rpt. New York: Vintage 1961).

20. "Setting and a Sense of World in the Novel," *Yale Review* 62 (Winter 1973): 188.

21. Introduction, *The Two Gentlemen of Verona* (London: Methuen, 1969) p. lvi.

22. See Christopher Salvesen, *The Landscape of Memory: A Study of Wordsworth's Poetry* (Lincoln: University of Nebraska Press, 1965), p. 69; Karl Kroeber, *Romantic Landscape Vision: Constable and Wordsworth* (Madison: University of Wisconsin Press, 1975), p. 106.

23. Reed Whittemore, *William Carlos Williams: Poet from Jersey* (Boston: Houghton Mifflin, 1975), p. 172.

24. J. Hillis Miller, *Poets of Reality* (1965; rpt. New York: Atheneum, 1969), p. 313.

25. *Natural Supernaturalism: Tradition and Revolution in Romantic Literature* (New York: Norton, 1971), p. 321. The children in the garden are presumably playing a game of hide-and-seek: "Shall we follow?/Quick, said the bird, find them, find them,/ Round the corner." An echo of this is to be found in Kurt Vonnegut's *Mother Night*. From "a little private park, a little Eden formed by joined back yards," the narrator "often heard a cry . . . a child's cry that never failed to make one stop and listen. It was the sweetly mournful cry that meant a game of hide-and-seek was over; that those still hiding were to come out of hiding, that it was time to go home. The cry was this: 'Olly-olly-ox-in-free' " (30).

26. "Notes toward a Supreme Fiction," *The Collected Poems of Wallace Stevens* (New York: Knopf, 1973), p. 383.

27. *The Poetry of Experience* (1957; rpt. New York: Norton, 1963), p. 200.

28. *The Inclusive Flame; Studies in American Poetry* (Bloomington: Indiana University Press, 1963), p. 129.

29. Cambon, *The Inclusive Flame*, p. 162.

30. *Reactionary Essays* (New York: Scribner's, 1936), p. 41; David Weimer, *The City as Metaphor* (New York: Random House, 1966), p. 117.

31. Cary Nelson, *The Incarnated Word: Literature as Verbal Space* (Urbana: University of Illinois Press, 1973), p. 85.

32. John Vernon, *The Garden and the Map: Schizophrenia in Twentieth-Century Literature and Culture* (Urbana: University of Illinois Press, 1973), p. 37.

33. *Collected Poems*, p. 459.

34. *Spirit of Place: Letters and Essays on Travel*, ed. Alan G. Thomas (New York: Dutton, 1969), p. 163; originally published in the Magazine Section of *The New York Times*, 12 June 1960.

35. *The English Novel* (New York: Dutton, 1954), p. 100.

36. *The Craft of Fiction* (1921; rpt. London: Jonathan Cape, 1954), p. 220.

37. Watt, *The Rise of the Novel: Studies in Defoe, Richardson and Fielding* (Berkeley: University of California Press, 1967), p. 26; Tate, *On the Limits of Poetry* (New York: Swallow Press, 1948), p. 143.

38. *The Iliad of Homer*, tr. Richard Lattimore (Chicago: University of Chicago Press, 1951), p. 439.

39. A similar scene, testifying to the popularity of this kind of landscape description and perhaps suggesting a possible influence, is to be found in James Thomson's *Spring* (11. 951–62), first published in 1728 and finally revised in 1746.

40. *The Craft of Fiction*, pp. 222–23.

41. See Martin Price, "The Picturesque Moment," *From Sensibility to Romanticism*, ed. Frederick W. Hilles and Harold Bloom (New York: Oxford University Press, 1965), pp. 265–68.

42. See Ian Watt, *The Rise of the Novel*, p. 27; Michael Irwin, *Henry Fielding: The Tentative Realist* (Oxford: Clarendon Press, 1967), pp. 61, 98, 138. Both are of two minds as to Fielding's realism of place, Watt admitting that "Fielding is some way from Richardson's particularity" and Irwin conceding that Squire Allworthy's estate "never proves relevant."

43. *The English Novel: Form and Function* (1953; rpt. New York: Harper and Brothers, 1961), p. 203.

44. *The Ambassadors*, ed. S. P. Rosenbaum (New York: Norton, 1964), p. 69.

2—A RHETORIC OF PLACE I: *The Properties and Uses of Place in Literature*

1. *Science and the Modern World* (1925; rpt. New York: New American Library, 1948), p. 50. A good brief history of the philosophical discussion of space is Joseph A. Kestner, *The Spatiality of the Novel* (Detroit: Wayne State University Press, 1978), Chapter 1.

2. *The Philosophy of Symbolic Forms*, Vol. 2 (1955; rpt. New Haven: Yale University Press, 1972), Chapter 2, "Mythical Thought."

3. *The Poetics of Space*, tr. Mari Jolas (1964; rpt. Boston: Beacon, 1969), p. 47.

4. *Survival Through Design* (1954; rpt. London: Oxford University Press, 1969), Chapter 22.

5. *Space and Place: The Perspective of Experience* (Minneapolis: University of Minnesota Press, 1977), p. 54.

6. The term seems to have originated with E. Minkowski, *Le Temps Vecu* (Paris, 1933). See O. F. Bollnow, "Lived-Space," *Readings in Existential Phenomenology*, ed. Nathaniel Lawrence and Daniel O'Connor (Englewood Cliffs, N.J.: Prentice-Hall, 1967), pp. 178–86.

7. Bachelard, *The Poetics of Space*, pp. 103–04.

8. *Landscape in Poetry* (London: Macmillan, 1897), pp. 137, 51.

9. Preface to *Roderick Hudson,* reprinted in *The Art of the Novel,* ed. Richard P. Blackmur (New York: Scribner's, 1953), p. 9.

10. *Thieves of Fire* (New York: Oxford University Press, 1974), p. 135.

11. *Mythologies,* tr. Annette Lavers (New York: Hill and Wang, 1972), p. 74.

12. John Seelye, "Some Green Thoughts on a Green Theme," *TriQuarterly,* 23–24 (1972): 589.

13. Quoted in James Baird, *The Dome and the Rock: Structure in the Poetry of Wallace Stevens* (Baltimore: Johns Hopkins University Press, 1968), p. 241.

14. See especially Chapter 6 in Yi-Fu Tuan, *Topophilia: A Study of Environmental Perception, Attitudes, and Values* (Englewood Cliffs, N.J.: Prentice-Hall, 1974).

15. Henry James, *The Portrait of a Lady* (1881; rpt. New York: Random House, 1951), vol. 2, 393.

16. "The Pleasures of the Imagination," *Spectator* No. 412.

17. *Archetypal Patterns in Poetry* (1934; rpt. London: Oxford University Press, 1963), p. 115.

18. For the imagery of prisons among the romantics, see Victor Brombert, "The Happy Prison: A Recurring Romantic Metaphor," *Romanticism: Vistas, Instances, Continuities,* ed. David Thorburn and Geoffrey Hartman (Ithaca: Cornell University Press, 1973), pp. 62–79; William York Tindall, *The Literary Symbol* (New York: Columbia University Press, 1955), p. 134.

19. See Carl Jung, "Mind and Earth," *Civilization in Transition,* tr. R. F. C. Hull (Princeton: Princeton University Press, 1970), pp. 29–49.

20. *Anatomy of Criticism* (1957; rpt. New York: Atheneum, 1966), pp. 203–206; *Fables of Identity* (New York: Harcourt, Brace, 1963), pp. 58–61.

21. *Dostoevsky and Romantic Realism* (Chicago: University of Chicago Press, 1967), p. 173.

22. *The Wings of the Dove* (1909; rpt. New York: Dell, 1958), p. 106. The association with the New Testament may also be found in the title of the novel. See Psalm 68: "Though ye have lien among the pots, yet shall ye be as the wings of a dove covered with silver, and her feathers with yellow gold."

23. "Of Classical Landscape," *Modern Painters,* Vol. 3 (New York: Wiley and Halsted, 1856), p. 187.

24. *Mythologies,* p. 74.

25. Fuller, *Earth Inc.* (New York: Anchor Books, 1973); Neutra, *Survival Through Design,* p. 167.

26. *The Fall,* tr. Justin O'Brien (New York: Vintage, 1956), p. 72.

27. *Three Novels: Molloy, Malone Dies, The Unnamable* (1955; rpt. New York: Grove Press 1965), p. 40.

28. Vernon, *The Garden and the Map,* p. 72.

29. *Faulkner in the University,* ed. Frederick L. Gwynn and Joseph L. Blotner (1959; rpt. New York: Random House, 1965), p. 74.

30. *The Sacred and the Profane* (1959; rpt. New York: Harper and Row, 1961), pp. 42–43. The sacred central places of Moslems, Jews, Christians, and Hindus are the subject of Malachi Martin, *The New Castle* (New York: Dutton, 1974).

31. The role of sculpture in orienting people to places is discussed by F. David Martin, "Sculpture and Place," *Dialectics and Humanism* 2 (1976): 45–55; the role of architecture, by Yi-Fu Tuan, *Space and Place,* pp. 102–08.

32. *The Town* (New York: Random House, 1957), pp. 315–16.

33. *The Hamlet* (1931; rpt. New York: Random House, 1940), p. 321.

34. Graham Greene's use of place is discussed by Ron Walker, *Infernal Paradise: Mexico and the Modern English Novel* (Berkeley: University of California Press, 1978).

35. "Edge City" is the name of the chapter on Kesey in Tanner's *City of Words: American Fiction, 1950–1970* (New York: Harper, 1971); Wolfe's novel about Kesey is *The Electric Kool-Acid Test* (New York: Farrar, Straus, 1968).

36. *Romantic Agony* (London and New York: Oxford University Press, 1951), p. 19.

37. *The Maine Woods* (New York: Crowell, 1966), p. 92.

38. *The Enchafèd Flood* (New York: Random House, 1950), p. 6.

39. *Cape Cod* (New York: Bramhall House, 1951), p. 184.

40. *The Philosophy of Symbolic Forms*, Vol. II, p. 92.

41. The different qualities of rocky and vegetated places are discussed by Bachelard in Chapter 7 of *La Terre et les Rêveries de la Volonté* (Paris: Libraire José Corti, 1948).

42. *The Woodlanders* (1887; rpt. London: Macmillan, 1963), p. 59.

43. *The Naked and the Dead* (New York: Rinehart, 1941), pp. 456–57.

44. The imagery of America as a woman is the subject of Annette Kolodny, *The Lay of the Land: Metaphor as Experience and History in American Life and Letters* (Chapel Hill: University of North Carolina Press, 1975). For comments on the "eroticized landscape" of Huxley and Ford, see Robert S. Baker, "Spandrell's 'Lydian Heaven': Moral Masochism and the Centrality of Spandrell in Huxley's 'Point Counter Point,' " *Criticism* 17 (Spring 1974): 120–35.

45. Joseph Conrad, *The Heart of Darkness*, ed. Robert Kimbrough (New York: Norton, 1971), p. 34.

46. *The Mysteries of Udolpho*, ed. Dobree Bonamy (London: Oxford University Press, 1966), p. 344.

47. *Love in the Ruins* (New York: Dell, 1972), p. 61.

48. *The Tenants* (New York: Farrar Straus, 1971), p. 229.

49. *Ninety-Two in the Shade* (New York: Farrar Straus, 1972), p. 23–4.

50. "The Bear," *Go Down, Moses*, p. 209. Compare the sudden "miraculous" appearance of a hunted bear in Mitchell Jayne's *Old Fish Hawk* (Philadelphia: Lippincott, 1970), a novel that owes much to Faulkner: "As if caught in time, a slow-moving summer's dream that etched itself against the distant green of a grassy place, the dark hulk of the bear moved in and out of the willows that lined the creek bottom" (70). See also the appearance of the wild boar in William Humphrey, *Home from the Hill* (New York: Knopf, 1958).

51. Henry's story is based on a ritual enacted every year on the coast of Viriginia. Wild ponies are driven off the uninhabited island of Assateague and forced to swim over to a village on the adjacent island of Chincoteague. There the foals are separated from the herd and sold to buyers from the mainland; the adults and a few foals are then returned to Assateague to roam freely and breed. In Henry's charming story Phantom is the wild mare, who is eventually returned to the wilds, and Misty is her foal, who remains to be trained by an adoring boy and girl living on Chincoteague. Through the ritual of Pony Penning, a piece of the wild is domesticated to the delight of mankind yet the place where wildness originates is preserved. The theme is reinforced by geography: Assateague is the wilderness barrier island protecting Chincoteague from the destructive force of the sea, and Chincoteague is a border place between wilderness and the civilization of the mainland.

52. *Meditations on Hunting*, tr. Howard B. Wescott (New York: Scribner's, 1972).

53. *The Philosophy of Symbolic Forms*, Vol. II, 96.

54. *A God Within*, p. 125. Dubos is on much less certain ground when he tries to draw a relationship between light and philosophy: "Logic might not have flourished in Greece if the land had remained covered with an entangling opaque vegetation," "The Despairing Optimist," *The American Scholar* (Autumn 1978): 446.

55. The "mist motif" is collected by Howard Rollin Patch in *The Other World: According to Description in Medieval Literature* (Cambridge: Harvard University Press, 1950).

56. *Faulkner in the University,* pp. 74, 199.

57. *You Can't Go Home Again* (1940; rpt. New York: Sun Dial Press, 1942), p. 146; *Look Homeward Angel* (New York: Scribner's, 1929), p. 159.

58. *Paradise Lost as "Myth"* (Cambridge: Harvard University Press, 1959), pp. 76–7.

59. *Jane Eyre,* ed. Robert J. Dunn (New York: Norton, 1971), p. 372.

60. *L'espace Proustien* (Paris: Gallimard, 1963), p. 19.

61. *The Country of the Pointed Firs and Other Stories* (1896; rpt. New York: Doubleday, 1956), p. 56.

62. See especially the discussions on *Bleak House* and *Our Mutual Friend* in J. Hillis Miller, *Charles Dickens: The World of His Novels* (Cambridge: Harvard University Press, 1958).

63. *Henderson the Rain King* (New York: Viking, 1958), p. 46.

64. For my discussion of the Urvelt in general and of Melville's use of it, I am indebted to James Baird, *Ishmael* (Baltimore: Johns Hopkins Press, 1956), Chapter 13.

65. *Piazza Tales,* ed. Egbert S. Oliver (New York: Hendricks House, 1948), p. 149.

66. "Lived Space," *Readings in Existential Phenomenology,* ed. Nathaniel Lawrence and Daniel O'Connor (Englewood Cliffs, N.J.: Prentice-Hall, 1967), p. 184.

67. Gabriel Oak's relation to the landscape is discussed by Michael Squires, *The Pastoral Novel: Studies in George Eliot, Thomas Hardy, and D. H. Lawrence* (Charlottesville: University Press of Virginia, 1974), p. 135–37. Squires calls attention to another earth-orientation walk made by the Poysers in *Adam Bede* (pp. 73–7). Journeying characters in Hardy are discussed by J. Hillis Miller, *Thomas Hardy: Distance and Desire* (Cambridge: Harvard University Press, 1970); also by Tony Tanner, "Colour and Movement in Hardy's *Tess of the D'Urbervilles,*" *The Victorian Novel,* ed. Ian Watt (New York: Oxford University Press, 1971), pp. 407–31.

68. *Perspectives by Incongruity,* ed. Stanley Edgar Hyman (Bloomington: Indiana University Press, 1964), p. 84.

69. Moby-Dick, ed. Charles Feidelson, Jr. (New York: Bobbs-Merrill, 1964), pp. 227, 499.

70. The "vertical spatial organization" of the poem is carefully demonstrated by Jackson Cope, *The Metaphoric Structure of Paradise Lost* (Baltimore: Johns Hopkins Press, 1962).

71. See especially Leo Marx, *The Machine in the Garden* (New York: Oxford University Press, 1964) and Tanner, *City of Words.*

72. *The Sorrows of Young Werther* (New York: Holt, Rinehart and Winston, 1960), p. 107.

73. *Light in August* (1932; rpt. New York: Modern Library, 1959), p. 226.

74. *The Guermantes Way* (New York: Modern Library, 1925), II, p. 57.

75. *Swann's Way* (New York: Modern Library, 1956), pp. 196–97.

76. Compare Whitman in "Song of the Broad-Axe":

> The shape of the shamed and angry stairs trod by sneaking footsteps,
> The shape of the sly settee, and the adulterous unwholesome couple.

77. Welty's splendid essay "Place in Fiction" first appeared in *South Atlantic Quarterly* 55 (Jan. 1956): 57–72. A convenient reprint, and the one cited here, is to be found in *Critical Approaches to Fiction,* ed. Shiv. K. Kunar and Keith McKean (New York: McGraw Hill, 1968), p. 251.

78. See Wilfred Stone, *The Cave and the Mountain: A Study of E. M. Forster*

(Stanford: Stanford University Press, 1966); Tindall, *The Literary Symbol,* pp. 142–44.

79. The relationship of three places to three loves in *Sons and Lovers* is discussed by Claude M. Sinzelle, *The Geographical Background of the Early Works of D. H. Lawrence* (Paris: Didier, 1964), p. 77. Julian Moynahan in *The Deed of Life* (Princeton: Princeton University Press, 1963), finds the meaning of *Lady Chatterley's Lover* is associated with the manor house, industrial village, and woods. The geographical divisions of Walker Percy's *Love in the Ruins*—town, swamp, and suburbia—are discussed by Martin Luschei, *The Sovereign Wayfarer* (Baton Rouge: Louisiana State University Press, 1972).

80. James, *The Art of the Novel,* p. 294; Martin Turnell, *The Novel in France* (1951; rpt. New York: Vintage, 1958), p. 354.

81. *Epic and Romance* (1896; rpt. London, 1926), p. 5.

82. For contrasted places in Spenser, see C. S. Lewis, *Studies in Medieval and Renaissance Literature* (Cambridge, 1966), p. 116; in Shakespeare, see Leech, Introduction, *Two Gentlemen of Verona;* in Milton, see McCaffrey, *Paradise Lost as "Myth,"* p. 169, and Bodkin, *Archetypal Patterns in Poetry,* pp. 90–152.

83. *Hemingway: The Writer as Artist* (1952; rpt. Princeton: Princeton University Press, 1963), pp. 109, 102.

84. See Inga-Stina Ewbank, *Their Proper Sphere: A Study of the Brontë Sisters* (Cambridge: Harvard University Press, 1966), pp. 128–41.

85. See the discussions of *Roderick Hudson, The American,* and *The Ambassadors* in Charles R. Anderson, *Person, Place, and Thing in Henry James's Novels* (Durham: Duke University Press, 1977).

86. Ralph Freeman, *The Lyrical Novel: Studies in Hermann Hesse, André Gide, and Virginia Woolf* (Princeton: Princeton University Press, 1963), p. 235.

87. Gustave Flaubert, *Emma Bovary,* tr. Francis Steegmuller (New York: Random House, 1957), p. 221.

88. *Death in Venice,* tr. H. T. Lowe-Porter (New York: Vintage, 1954), p. 49.

89. *The Writing of Fiction* (New York: Scribner's, 1925), p. 85.

90. See Peter Butter, *Shelley's Idols of the Cave* (Edinburgh, 1954), pp. 45–89. For a similar demonstration of "visionary" geography, see Richard Wilbur, Introduction, *Poe* (New York: Dell, 1959).

91. "Symbolic Landscape," *Four Quartets,* ed. Bernard Bergonzi (Nashville: Aurora, 1970), p. 239. This essay was first published in *Essays in Criticism,* 1 (1951).

92. *The House of Mirth* (Boston: Houghton Mifflin, 1963), p. xx.

93. *Henry James* (New York: William Sloane Associates, 1951), p. 128. For further discussion of transplantation in Gide, Mann, and James, see Joseph Gerard Brennan, "Three Novels of Dépaysment," *Comparative Literature* 22 (Summer 1970): 223–36.

94. J. A. Ward, *The Search for Form: Studies in the Structure of James's Fiction* (Chapel Hill: University of North Carolina Press, 1967), p. 88.

3—A RHETORIC OF PLACE II: *The Metaphor of Place and Body*

1. On *Volpone* see the edition of the play edited by Alvin B. Kernan (New Haven: Yale University Press, 1962), pp. 18–19; on Bellow's novel see Marcus Klein, *After Alienation: American Novels in Mid-Century* (Cleveland: World Publishing, 1964), pp. 66–69; on *Madame Bovary* see Martin Turnell, *The Novel in France,* p. 274.

2. For a discussion of the Renaissance "Geography of the Soul," see Gordon

O'Brien, *Renaissance Poetics and the Problem of Power* (Chicago: Institute of Elizabethan Studies, 1956), pp. 92–95.

3. Letter to De Quincey, March 6, 1804, *Letters of William and Dorothy Wordsworth,* ed. Ernest deSelincourt, Vol. 2 (Oxford: Clarendon Press, 1939), p. 454.

4. "The Aesthetic Moment in Landscape Poetry," *The Interior Landscape: The Literary Criticism of Marshall McLuhan,* ed. Eugene McNamara (New York: McGraw Hill, 1971), p. 158.

5. *The Incarnate Word,* p. 122.

6. *Of the Farm* (New York: Knopf, 1965), p. 133.

7. *The Works of Sir Philip Sidney,* ed. Albert Feuillerat, Vol 3 (Cambridge: Cambridge University Press, 1923), 264.

8. Quoted in O'Brien, *Renaissance Poetics,* pp. 97–98. For a discussion of Renaissance correspondence of body and cosmos, as well as O'Brien, pp. 57–127, see Leonard Barkan, *Nature's Work of Art: The Human Body as Image of the World* (New Haven: Yale University Press, 1975); Elizabeth Sewell, *The Human Metaphor* (South Bend: University of Notre Dame Press, 1964).

9. *The Philosophy of Symbolic Forms* Vol. 2:90 and 1:206.

10. *The Devil's Race-Track: Mark Twain's Great Dark Writings,* ed. John S. Tuckey (Berkeley: University of California Press, 1980), p. 164. While working on *Huckleberry Finn,* Twain wrote in his notebook: "I think we are only the microscopic trichina concealed in the blood of some vast creature's veins, and it is that vast creature whom God concerns Himself about and not us," *Mark Twain's Notebooks,* ed. Albert Bigelow Paine (New York: Cooper Square, 1972), p. 170.

11. "Spring" *Walden* (New York: Rinehart, 1948), p. 257.

12. Chapter 119 in *Mardi* (New York: Capricorn Books, 1964), p. 317. Glauco Cambon has good reason to call this chapter Melville's "Song of Myself" (*The Inclusive Flame,* p. 251). The ship-man image occurs in Jean Genet's *Querelle,* a book that owes much to *Billy Budd.* The sailor Querelle imagines himself to be "A giant destroyer, warlord of the seas . . . carrying a cargo of explosives" (32–33).

13. Frank Bugden, *James Joyce and the Making of Ulysses* (1934; rpt. Bloomington: Indiana University Press, 1960), p. 21.

14. *James Joyce's Ulysses* (1930; rpt. New York: Vintage, 1960), p. 399.

15. *Ulysses* (New York: Modern Library, 1934), p. 721.

16. *Falconer* (New York: Ballantine, 1978), p. 203.

17. *Sons and Lovers* (New York: Viking, 1913), p.; 262.

18. *The Great Mother,* tr. Ralph Manheim (Princeton: Princeton University Press, 1970), p. 44.

19. *Man in the Landscape* (New York: Knopf, 1967), p. 98.

20. Jung: "Agriculture did in fact arise, though not exclusively, from the formation of sexual analogies," *The Structure and Dynamics of the Psyche,* tr. F. C. Hull (New York: Pantheon Books, 1960), p. 43. Freud: "the whole conception of agriculture was determined" by the symbolism of Mother Earth, "Tenth Lecture," in *A General Introduction to Psychoanalysis,* tr. Joan Rivière (New York: Washington Square Press, 1952), p. 170.

21. For the feminist point of view, see Kolodny, *The Lay of the Land;* for the agrarian's see Wendell Berry, *The Unsettling of America: Culture and Agriculture* (San Francisco: Sierra Club Books, 1977), p. 132.

22. *Symbols of Transformation,* Vol. 1, tr. R. F. C. Hull (New York: Harper and Brothers, 1962), 150n, 151.

23. "River Symbolism," *Psychoanalytical Quarterly* 26 (1957): 69.

24. *Love's Body* (New York: Random House, 1966), p. 48.

25. *The Castle*, tr. Willa and Edwin Muir (New York: Modern Library, 1969), p. 54.

26. *Select Letters of Christopher Columbus*, tr. R. H. Major (London: 1870), p. 136.

27. *The American Scene*, ed. Leon Edel (Bloomington: Indiana University Press, 1968), p. 20.

28. *Goethe's Faust*, tr. Walter Kaufmann (New York: Doubleday, 1962), p. 315.

29. *The Sot-Weed Factor* (1960; rpt. New York: Grosset and Dunlap, 1964), p. 348.

30. *The Rainbow* (New York: Modern Library, 1915), p. 2.

31. *The Octopus*, ed. Kenneth Lynn (Boston: Houghton Mifflin, 1958), p. 122.

32. *The Grapes of Wrath* (New York: Viking, 1939), p. 32.

33. *To A God Unknown* (1933; rpt. New York: Bantam, 1960), p. 8.

34. *On Poetic Imagination and Reverie: Selections from the Works of Gaston Bachelard*, tr. and ed. Colette Gaudin (New York: Bobbs-Merrill, 1971), p. 61.

35. *Apocalypse* (1931; rpt. New York: Viking, 1973), pp. 41–42, 200.

36. *St. Mawr and the Man Who Died* (1925; rpt. New York: Vintage, n.d.), p. 159.

37. *A World Elsewhere: The Place of Style in American Literature* (New York: Oxford University Press, 1966), pp. 42–43.

38. *Women in Love* (1920; rpt. New York: Bantam, 1969), p. 420.

39. *Ladders to Fire* (New York: Dutton, 1946), p. 89.

40. *Confessions of Nat Turner* (New York: Random House, 1967), p. 347.

41. *The Immoralist*, tr. Dorothy Bussy (New York: Knopf, 1930), p. 67.

42. *A Happy Death*, tr. Richard Howard (New York: Knopf, 1972), p. 136.

43. *The Stranger*, tr. Stuart Gilbert (New York: Vintage, 1946), p. 154.

44. *Landscape into Art* (1949; rpt. Boston: Beacon Press, 1961), p. 4.

45. This and the next two passages are cited by Stanley Stewart, *The Enclosed Garden: The Tradition and the Image in Seventeeth-Century Poetry* (Madison: University of Wisconsin Press, 1966), pp. 41–43.

46. See Frederick Crews, *The Sins of the Fathers: Hawthorne's Psychological Themes* (New York: Oxford University Press, 1966), pp. 121–23.

47. For a full discussion of the sexual imagery in "Kubla Khan," see Chapter 2 in Gerald Enscoe, *Eros and the Romantics* (The Hague: Mouton, 1967).

48. E. C. Pettet, *On the Poetry of Keats* (Cambridge: Cambridge University Press, 1957), p. 125, uses this phrase to describe Robert Bridges's comments on the poem in "A Critical Introduction to Keats," *Collected Essays of Robert Bridges*, Vol. 4 (London: Oxford University Press, 1929), 88–89.Pettet also discusses the eroticism of *Endymion* (pp. 171–74).

49. D. H. Lawrence, *Lady Chatterley's Lover* (1928; rpt. New York: Modern Library, 1959), p. 95.

50. *John Thomas and Lady Jane* (New York: Viking, 1972), p. 367. Lawrence's forest energy is discussed by Julian Moynahan, *The Deed of Life: Novels and Tales of D. H. Lawrence* (Princeton: Princeton University Press, 1963).

51. For a discussion of this aspect of Lawrence's sexuality, see *Novel*, Vols. 4 and 5 (1971), and Frank Kermode, *D. H. Lawrence* (New York: Viking, 1973), pp. 140–41.

52. See Barbara Lefcowitz, "The Inviolate Grove: Metamorphosis of a Symbol in *Oedipus at Colonus*," *Literature and Psychology* 17 (1967): 78–86.

53. *The Secular Scripture: A Study of the Structure of Romance* (Cambridge: Harvard University Press, 1976), p. 104.

54. *The Deerslayer* (Garden City, N.Y.: Doubleday, 1953), p. 128.

55. *The Writings of Henry David Thoreau: Journal*, ed. Bradford Torrey, Vol. 9 (Boston: Houghton Mifflin, 1906), 337. For a discussion of Thoreau's "chaste intercourse

with nature," see Richard Slotkin, *Regeneration Through Violence: The Mythology of the American Frontier, 1600–1860* (Middletown: Wesleyan University Press, 1973), pp. 531–33.

56. *The Lay of the Land*, pp. 112–13.

57. *The Short Stories of Ernest Hemingway* (New York: Scribner's, 1953). p. 231.

58. For a challenge of the accuracy of this stereotype, see Dawn Lander, "Eve Among the Indians," *The Authority of Experience: Essays in Feminist Criticism,* ed. Arlyn Diamond and Lee R. Edwards (Amherst: University of Massachusetts Press, 1977), pp. 194–211.

59. *Introduction to Psychoanalysis*, p. 160.

60. *Delta Wedding* (New York: Harcourt Brace, 1946), p. 34.

61. *Within A Budding Grove* (New York: Modern Library, 1924), Part I, p. 296.

62. See Stewart, *The Enclosed Garden*, pp. 37–38.

63. *The Metamorphoses of the Circle*, tr. Carlay Dawson and Elliott Coleman (Baltimore: Johns Hopkins University Press, 1966), p. xx.

64. *Mont-Saint-Michel and Chartres* (1905; rpt. Boston: Houghton Mifflin, 1933), pp. 34, 127.

65. See Kathleen Raine, *Blake and Tradition* (Princeton: Princeton University Press, 1968).

66. Mailer's echoing of Blake is called "purloining" by Kate Millett in *Sexual Politics* (New York: Doubleday, 1970), p. 14. Mailer's short story "The Time of Her Life" has a similar love scene but without the religious imagery.

67. *Finnegans Wake* (1939; rpt. New York: Viking, 1958), p. 571.

68. See Warren Hunting Smith, *Architecture in English Fiction* (New Haven: Yale University Press, 1934; Gill, *Happy Rural Seat,* pp. 227–52.

69. *The Improvement of the Estate* (Baltimore: Johns Hopkins University Press, 1971), p. ix.

70. Peter K. Garrett, *Scene and Symbol from George Eliot to Henry James* (New Haven: Yale University Press, 1969), p. 84. Considerable work has been done documenting the significance of houses in James. See R. W. Stallman, *The Houses that James Built and Other Literary Studies* (East Lansing: Michigan State University Press, 1964); Gill, "The Great Good Place: Henry James and the Country House," *Happy Rural Seat.*

71. See Woolf, *A Room of One's Own* (1929; rpt. New York: Harcourt Brace, 1957), p. 71; Chapter 18, *Oliver Twist.* Zora Hurston writes in her autobiography a passage very much like the one in *Jane Eyre:* "I used to climb to the top of one of the huge chinaberry trees which guarded our front gate, and look out over the world. The most interesting thing that I saw was the horizon. Every way I turned, it was there, and the same distance away. Our house, then, was in the center of the world. It grew upon me that I ought to walk out to the horizon and see what the end of the world was like," *Dust Tracks on a Road* (Philadelphia: Lippincott, 1942), p. 36.

72. George Eliot, *Middlemarch*, ed. Gordon S. Haight (Boston: Houghton Mifflin, 1956), p. 145.

4—THE WRITER AND PLACE: *The Case of Herman Melville.*

1. The importance of place in the life and works of Keats is discussed by Timothy Hilton, *Keats and His World* (London: Thames and Hudson, 1971); Guy Murchie, *The Spirit of Place in Keats* (London: Newman Neame, 1955). Other similar studies are

Vivian C. Hopkins, "The Houses of Robert Frost," *Centennial Essays,* ed. Jac L. Thorpe, *et al.* (Jackson: University of Mississippi Press, 1974), pp. 182–90; John J. Mood, " 'Silence Within': A Study of the Residences of Samuel Beckett," *Studies in Short Fiction* 7 (1970).

2. Troy, *William Troy: Selected Essays,* ed. Stanley Edgar Hyman (New Brunswick: Rutgers University Press, 1967), p. 30; Gass, "Gertrude Stein: Geographer," *New York Review* (May 3, 1973), p. 7.

3. Quentin Bell, *Virginia Woolf: A Biography* (London: Hogarth Press, 1972), p. 31.

4. *If It Lie,* tr. Dorothy Bussy (1935; rpt. New York: Vintage, 1963), p. 13.

5. Claude Bonnefoy, *Conversations with Eugene Ionesco,* tr. Jan Dawson (New York: Holt, Rinehart and Winston, 1970), p. 16.

6. Maynard Mack, *The Garden and the City: Retirement and Politics in the Later Poetry of Pope, 1731–1743* (Toronto: University of Toronto Press, 1969), p. 8.

7. "Why I Am So Clever," *Ecce Homo.*

8. Sinzelle, *Geographical Background of the Early Works of D. H. Lawrence.*

9. *"Lawrence and the Spirit of Place," A D. H. Lawrence Miscellany,* ed. Harry T. Moore (Carbondale: Southern Illinois University Press, 1959), p. 286.

10. Letter to Jonathan Spence, cited in Stone, *The Cave and the Mountain,* p. 12.

11. *Mosaic* 8 (Spring 1975); Malcolm Cowley, *Exile's Return* (1934; rev. ed. New York: Viking, 1951); Terry Eagleton,*Exiles and Émigrés* (New York: Schocken, 1970).

12. Considerable attention has been given to the effects of Lawrence's living abroad by David Cavitch, *D. H. Lawrence and the New World* (New York: Oxford University Press, 1969); James C. Cowan, *D. H. Lawrence's American Journey: A Study in Literature and Myth* (Cleveland: Case Western Reserve University Press, 1970); Mark Schorer, "Lawrence and the Spirit of Place"; Thomas R. Whitaker, "Lawrence's Western Path: *Mornings in Mexico," Criticism* 3 (1961): 219–21. See also Philip Thody, *Albert Camus: A Study of His Works* (New York: Grove Press, 1959).

13. A. Dwight Culler, *Imaginative Reason: The Poetry of Matthew Arnold* (New Haven: Yale University Press, 1966), p. 4. See also Alan Roper, *Arnold's Poetic Landscapes* (Baltimore: Johns Hopkins University Press, 1969).

14. See further, John M. Ditsky, "Music from a Dark Cave: Organic Form in Steinbeck's Fiction," *The Journal of Narrative Technique* 1 (Jan. 1971): 59–67.

15. *For Whom The Bell Tolls* (New York: Scribner's 1940), p. 471.

16. *On Poetic Imagination and Reverie,* pp. 42, 45.

17. *Of a Fire on the Moon* (New York: New American Library, 1971), pp. 55–56.

18. See Ludwig Binswanger, "Ibsen's *The Master Builder," European Literary Theory and Practice,* ed. Vernon W. Grass (New York: Dell 1973), pp. 185–216.

19. Book 4, lines 513–23. See letter to Benjamin Bailey, Oct. 8, 1817, *The Letters of John Keats,* ed. Hyder Edward Rollins, vol. 1 (Cambridge: Harvard University Press, 1958), p. 170.

20. *A Room of One's Own,* p. 74.

21. *Specimen Days,* ed. Floyd Stovall, *The Collected Writings of Walt Whitman, Prose Works* 1892, vol. 1 (New York: New York University Press, 1963), p. 210.

22. See Justin O'Brien, Introduction, *La Symphonie pastorale* (Boston: Heath, 1954), pp. xiv-xv; Gabriel Michaud, *Gide et L'Afrique* (Paris: Scorpion, 1961); Thomas R. Knip, "Gide and Greene: Africa and the Literary Imagination," *The Serif* 6 (June 1969); Gwen Boardman, *Graham Greene: The Aesthetics of Exploration* (Gainsville: University of Florida Press, 1971).

23. Benjamin F. Bart, *Flaubert's Landscape Descriptions* (Ann Arbor: University of Michigan Press, 1957), p. v.

24. "Travel and Writing," *Mosaic* 8 (Fall 1974): 2.

25. Jay M. Semel, "Pennsylvania Dutch Country: Stevens' World as Meditation," *Contemporary Literature* 14 (Summer 1973): 33.

26. *The American Adam: Innocence, Tragedy and Tradition in the Nineteenth Century* (Chicago: University of Chicago Press, 1955), p. 130.

27. Richard Chase, *Herman Melville: A Critical Study* (New York: Macmillan, 1949), first pointed this out: "The topography of the island had merged symbolically with the form of the human body" (126). Topographical details are interpreted as symbols in a wish-dream by Helen B. Petrullo, "The Neurotic Hero of *Typee*," *American Imago* 12 (1955): 317–23.

28. *Typee*, ed. Harrison Hayford et al. (Evanston Ill.: Northwestern University Press and The Newberry Library, 1968), p. 45.

29. *Omoo* (New York: Russell and Russell, 1963), pp. 367–68.

30. *Mardi* (New York: Capricorn Books, 1964), p. 191.

31. *Redburn* (New York: Doubleday, 1957), p. 173.

32. *Pierre* (New York: Grove Press, 1957), p. 46.

33. *The Wake of the Gods: Melville's Mythology* (Stanford: Stanford University Press, 1963), p. 125.

34. Blake's reaction to industrialism in England is discussed by Jacob Bronowski, *William Blake: A Man Without a Mask* (London: Secker and Warburg, 1947). Blake's figuration of America as a woman being violated is pointed out by David V. Erdman, *Blake: Prophet Against Empire* (1954: rev. ed. New York: Doubleday, 1969), p. 227.

35. See A. Sandberg, "Erotic Patterns in 'Paradise of Bachelors and The Tartarus of Maids," *Literature and Psychology* 18 (1968): 2–8.

36. *Israel Potter* (New York: Warren, 1974), p. 208.

37. *The Voyage of the Beagle*, ed. Leonard Engel (New York: Doubleday, 1962), p. 375. That Melville knew Darwin's account of the island is argued by H. Bruce Franklin, "The Island Worlds of Darwin and Melville," *Centennial Review* 11 (Summer 1967): 353–70.

38. "The Encantadas," *Piazza Tales* (New York: Hendricks House, 1948), p. 149. Compare Thoreau on Cape Cod: "It was the dreariest scenery imaginable. The only animals which we saw on the sand at that time were spiders . . . and a venomous-looking, long, narrow worm, one of the myriapods, or thousand-legs. . . . In June this sand was scored with the tracks of turtles both large and small, which had been out in the night, leading to and from the swamps," *Cape Cod*, p. 195.

Hart Crane, having read "The Encantadas" was struck by the "huge terrapin" of Cayman Island and in "O Carib Isle" associates them with death: "—Spiked, overturned; such thunder in their strain! And clenched beaks coughing for the surge again!"

39. *Clarel*, ed. Walter Bezanson (New York: Hendricks House, 1960), p. lxxvii.

40. Newton Arvin, *Herman Melville* (1950; rpt. New York: Viking Press, 1957), p. 273.

41. *Melville: The Ironic Diagram* (Evansville: Northwestern University Press, 1970), p. 5.

42. See David Charles Leonard, "The Cartesian Vortex in *Moby-Dick*," *American Literature* 51 (March 1979): 105–09.

5—PLACE AND NATIONAL LITERATURE: *The American and His Land*

1. See Benjamin T. Spencer, *The Quest for Nationality* (Syracuse: Syracuse University Press, 1957), pp. 48–49.

2. "Nationality in Literature," *Literary Criticism of James Russell Lowell,* ed. Herbert F. Smith (Lincoln: University of Nebraska Press, 1969), p. 118. The essay first appeared in *North American Review* (July 1849).

3. Olson, *Call Me Ishmael* (New York: Reynal and Hitchcock, 1947); Allen, "The Influence of Space on the American Imagination," *Essays in Honor of Jay B. Hubbell,* ed. Clarence Gohdes (Durham: Duke University Press, 1967), pp. 329–42. Allen's paper was not well received when it was delivered at the Conference on American Studies at the Newberry Library in 1961. The responses of participants are reported by Jules Zanger, "Whitman and the Influence of Space on American Literature," *Newberry Library Bulletin* (Dec. 1961): 299–414. Perhaps the best corrective to allegations of American space consciousness is to bear in mind that the most decisive influence on the modern conception of space was European and occurred as early as the sixteenth century with the activity of world explorers, cartographers, and astronomers. Marjorie Nicolson detects the influence on *Paradise Lost,* "a remarkable example of the extent to which telescopic astronomy effected in an imaginative mind a vast expansion of the idea of space," *Science and Imagination* (Ithaca: Great Seal Books, 1956), p. 108.

4. Cambon, *The Inclusive Flame,* p. 3.

5. Remarks on the influence of climate on the character of nations are to be found in the Introduction of Taine's *History of English Literature,* as well as in Chapter 1: "cold, moist lands, deep in black marshy forests" account for German melancholy and violence; the strong-willed, lawless English "live solitary, each one near the spring or the wood which has taken his fancy." In *The Philosophy of Art and Greece* (1869) Taine sees a relationship between clear ideas and the "clearness of relief and transparency of the atmosphere" (p. 93) in Greek landscape.

6. *Studies in Classic American Literature* (New York: Thomas Seltzer, 1923), pp. 8–9.

7. *The Symbolic Meaning: The Uncollected Version of Studies in Classic American Literature,* ed. Armin Arnold (New York: Viking, 1962), p. 16.

8. "Mind and Earth," *Civilization in Transition,* tr. R. F. C. Hull (Princeton: Princeton University Press, 1970), p. 49.

9. See Francis G. Townsend, *Ruskin and the Landscape Feeling* (Urbana: University of Illinois Press, 1951).

10. *Siren Land* (1911; rpt. London: Secker and Warburg, 1957), p. 26.

11. *Spirit of Place: Letters and Essays on Travel,* ed. Alan G. Thomas (New York: Dutton, 1969), pp. 157–58. The essay was first published with the title "Landscape and Character," New York *Times,* Magazine Section, June 12, 1960.

12. *A God Within,* p. 90.

13. *America and Cosmic Man* (New York: Doubleday, 1949), p. 27.

14. "A Description of New England," *Travels and Works of Captain John Smith,* vol. 1, ed. E. Arber and A. Bradley (Edinburgh: 1910), p. 187.

15. *Decades of the New World,* Third Decade, Eighth Book, tr. Richard Eden (1555); reprinted in *The American Landscape,* ed. John Conron (New York: Oxford University Press, 1973), p. 102.

16. See Evelyn Page, *American Genesis: Pre-colonial Writing in the North* (Boston: Gambit, 1973), p. 4.

17. Drayton, "To the Virginian voyage" (1606); see Hugh Honour, *The New Golden Land: European Images of America* (New York: Random House, 1975), p. 93.

18. *The Prose Works of William Byrd of Westover,* ed. Louis B. Wright (Cambridge: Harvard University Press, 1966), p. 408.

19. *The Holy Earth* (New York: Scribner's, 1915), p. 22.

20. "The Ponds," *Walden.*

21. *Where the Wasteland Ends* (New York: Doubleday, 1972), pp. 118–19.

22. *Letters from an American Farmer* (New York: Dutton, 1957), p. 41.

23. *Notes on the State of Virginia,* ed. Thomas Abernethy (New York: Harper and Row, 1964), pp. 157–58.

24. Meeker, *The Comedy of Survival,* p. 87.

25. *The American Scene,* p. 21.

26. Allan G. Bogue, "Farming in the Prairie Peninsula, 1830–1890," *The Old Northwest: Studies in Regional History, 1787–1910,* ed. Harry N. Scheiber (Lincoln: University of Nebraska Press, 1969), pp. 168–97.

27. *Complete Works of Ralph Waldo Emerson,* vol. 12 (Boston: Riverside Press, 1904), pp. 358–64. This is from an essay, "Agriculture of Massachusetts," published in vol. 13 of the *Dial.*

28. Richard Hofstadter, *The Age of Reform* (New York: Vintage, 1955), p. 30. Agrarianism in the South was stronger after the Civil War than before, according to Lucinda Hardwick MacKethan, *The Dream of Arcady: Place and Time in Southern Literature* (Baton Rouge: Louisiana State University Press, 1980), p. 8.

29. *Virgin Land* (New York: Vintage, 1950), p. 246.

30. *The Blithedale Romance,* Centenary Edition (Columbus: Ohio State University Press, 1965), p. 66.

31. *Literary Friends and Acquaintance* (New York: Harper and Brothers, 1901), p. 54.

32. *The American Notebooks of Nathaniel Hawthorne,* ed. Claude Simpson, Centenary Edition (Columbus: Ohio State University Press, 1972), p. 337.

33. *The Melville Log: A Documentary Life of Herman Melville,* ed. Jay Leyda, Vol. 1 (New York: Harcourt Brace, 1951), p. 396.

34. See further Philip L. Gerber, "Willa Cather and the Big Red Rock," *College English* (Jan. 1958).

35. *Death Comes for the Archbishop* (New York: Modern Library, 1926), p. 132.

36. *Phoenix: The Posthumous Papers of D. H. Lawrence,* ed. Edward D. McDonald (New York: Viking, 1968), p. 142.

37. *The Last of the Provincials* (London: Secker and Warburg, 1947), p. 196.

38. The same process of being weaned from dependence on the land to social revolution is to be found in Lewis Grassic Gibbon's trilogy *Scots Quair.* See Raymond Williams, *The Country and the City* (New York: Oxford University Press, 1973), pp. 268–71.

39. *East of Eden* (1952; rpt. New York: Bantam, 1955), p. 127.

40. *Tragic Ground* (1944; rpt. New York: New American Library, 1952), p. 138.

41. *A Garden of Earthly Delights* (Greenwich, Conn.: Fawcett, 1967), p. 365.

42. *Faulkner in the University,* p. 277.

43. John Alcorn, *The Nature Novel from Hardy to Lawrence* (New York: Columbia University Press, 1977), p. 116.

44. The natural law of land possession is traced from Locke, the Physiocrats, and Henry George to Faulkner in Dale G. Breaden, "William Faulkner and the Land," *American Quarterly* 10 (Fall 1958): 344–57. The influence of Rousseau in this matter is established by Lewis M. Dabney, *The Indians of Yoknapatawpha* (Baton Rouge: Louisiana State University Press, 1974), pp. 139–40.

45. *O Pioneers!* (1913; rpt. Cambridge: Houghton Mifflin, 1941), p. 308.

46. *The Sojourners* (Chicago: People's Book Club, 1953), p. 66.

47. Cotton Mather, *The Wonders of the Invisible World* (London: Russell and Russell, 1862), p. 13.

48. Leslie Fiedler, *Love and Death in the American Novel* (New York: World, 1962), p. 148.

49. See Richard Vitzthum, *The American Compromise: Theme and Method in the Histories of Bancroft, Parkman, and Adams* (Norman: University of Oklahoma Press, 1974), Chapter 4.

50. See Donald A. Ringe, *The Pictorial Mode: Space and Time in the Art of Bryant, Irving, and Cooper* (Lexington: University Press of Kentucky, 1971).

51. *Piazza Tales*, pp. 3–4.

52. "Baptism in the Forest: Wisdom and Initiation in William Faulkner," Introductory Essay, *Mansions of the Spirit: Essays in Literature and Religion*, ed. George Panichas (New York: Hawthorn Books, 1967), pp. 17–44.

53. *Requiem for a Nun* (New York: Random House, 1951), p. 94.

54. *Hawthorne's Tragic Vision* (1957; rpt. New York: Norton, 1964), p. 112.

55. *The Maine Woods*, pp. 83–84.

56. *Zen and the Art of Motorcycle Maintenance* (1974; rpt. New York: Bantam Books, 1975), p. 219.

57. *Why Are We in Vietnam?* (New York: Putnam, 1968), pp. 217–19.

58. *From Death to Morning* (New York: Scribner's, 1955), p. 203.

59. *Studies in Classic American Literature*, p. 44; *Phoenix*, p. 91.

60. See Nicholas Karolides, *The Pioneer in the American Novel* (Norman: University of Oklahoma Press, 1967), pp. 73–74.

61. *The Valley of the Moon* (New York: Grosset and Dunlap, 1913), p. 293.

62. "Some Green Thoughts on a Green Theme," *TriQuarterly* 23–24 (Winter-Spring 1972): 584.

63. See H. Daniel Peck, *A World by Itself: The Pastoral Moment in Cooper's Fiction* (New Haven: Yale University Press, 1977), Chapter 4; *The Writings of Henry David Thoreau: Journal*, Vol. 9, pp. 310–11.

64. "The Domesticated Stroke of John Cheever," *New England Quarterly* 4 (Dec. 1971): 547.

65. *Complete Works*, Vol. 7, 130.

6—PLACELESSNESS: *The Concern of Twentieth-Century Literature*

1. *Future Shock* (1970; rpt. New York: Bantam, 1971), p. 75.

2. *Where the Wasteland Ends*, p. 20. See especially Chapter 1, "The Artificial Environment."

3. *Place and Placelessness* (London: Pion, 1976), p. 143.

4. Of *Paradise Regained* Gary Hamilton writes: "The poet's new song celebrates the Paradise which Christ creates within himself, and it records the process of that creation," "Creating the Garden Anew: The Dynamics of *Paradise Regained*," *Philological Quarterly* 50 (Oct. 1971): 569.

5. There are numerous studies of Eliot's gardens: Leonard Unger, "T. S. Eliot's Rose Garden," *Eliot: A Selected Critique*, ed. Leonard Unger (New York: Holt, Rinehart & Winston, 1948); Robert D. Wagner, "The Meaning of Eliot's Rose Garden," *PMLA* 69 (Mar. 1954): 22–33; Steffan Bergsten, *Time and Eternity: A Study of the Structure and Symbolism of T. S. Eliot's Four Quartets* (Stockholm: Studia Litterarium Upsaliensia, 1960); David Perkins, "Rose-Garden to Midwinter Spring; Achieved Faith in the *Four Quartets*," *T. S. Eliot: Four Quartets*, ed. Bernard Bergonzi (Nashville:

Aurora, 1970); J. M. Reibetanz, "*Four Quartets* as Poetry of Place," *Dalhousie Review* 56 (1976): 526–41.

6. Robert F. Gleckner, *Byron and the Ruins of Paradise* (Baltimore: Johns Hopkins University Press, 1967).

7. *Sesame and Lilies* (1863). See Charles T. Dougherty, "Of Ruskin's Gardens," *Myth and Symbol*, ed. Bernice Slote (Lincoln: University of Nebraska Press, 1963).

8. *The Return of the Native* (London: Macmillan, 1975), p. 34. Hardy's prediction has turned out to be true. In England today there is a movement to preserve barren heaths from the encroachment of developers.

9. *Jude the Obscure,* ed. Robert C. Slack (New York: Modern Library, 1967), p. 119.

10. "Autobiographical Fragment," *Phoenix*, p. 829.

11. Drownings often bring an end to idyllic action and places: the drowning of Charlotte's child in Goethe's *Elective Affinities* spoils the love affairs of the two couples and the building of the projected summer house; Zenobia's suicide by drowning is the last episode in the pastoral experiment at Brook Farm in Hawthorne's *The Blithedale Romance;* the beauty of Esthwaite Lake is momentarily palled for Wordsworth when a man is drowned there in the *Prelude* (5.445).

12. The division of father and son over mining is seen also in Conrad's *Nostromo,* in which Gould implores his son never to become interested in the San Tome silver mine.

13. The insufficiency of eighteenth-century order for Lawrence is discussed by Keith Aldritt, *The Visual Imagination of D. H. Lawrence* (Evanston, Ill.: Northwestern University Press, 1971), p. 178ff.

14. "Lawrence and the Spirit of Place," p. 286.

15. *V* (1963; pt. New York: Bantam, 1968), pp. 189–90.

16. *Under the Volcano* (1947; rpt. New York: New American Library, 1971), p. 14.

17. A similar walk in Eden is to be found in Lowry's short story "The Forest Path."

18. See Karl E. Zink, "Faulkner's Garden: Woman and the Immemorial Earth," *Modern Fiction Studies* 21 (Autumn 1956): 139–49; Richard P. Adams, *The Apprenticeship of William Faulkner,* Vol. 12, Tulane Studies in English (1962); John Michael Ditsky, "Land-Nostalgia in the Novels of Faulkner, Cather, and Steinbeck," dissertation, New York University, 1967, p. 165.

19. *Sanctuary* (1931; rpt. New York: Penguin, 1947), p. 188.

20. *Brideshead Revisited* (1945; rpt. New York: Dell, 1972), pp. 208–09.

21. *Howards End* (New York: Vintage, 1921), p. 323.

22. A year after *Howards End* was published, Virginia Woolf made the same kind of observation in a letter to Gerald Brenan: "My eyes are entirely grey with England," *Atlantic Monthly* (Oct. 1976): 65. A character in Norman Douglas's *South Wind* (1917) "cannot endure England" because "the country is full of half-tones" (60).

23. *The Cave and the Mountain,* p. 265. See also Lionel Trilling, *E. M. Forster* (1943; rpt. New York: New Directions, 1964), pp. 134–35.

24. *A World Elsewhere,* p. 17.

25. *I'll Take My Stand* (New York: Harper and Brothers, 1930), p. 9. All through the years of the Great Depression there was a good deal of "back-to-the-soil" agitation. A convenient short history of the movement may be found in Warren French, *The Social Novel at the End of an Era* (Carbondale: Southern Illinois University Press, 1966), p. 50ff. For special emphasis on the Southern Agrarians, see John L. Stewart, *The Burden of Time: The Fugitives and Agrarians* (Princeton: Princeton University Press, 1965) and Alexander Karanakis, *Tillers of a Myth: Southern Agrarians as Social and Literary Critics* (Milwaukee: University of Wisconsin Press, 1969).

26. See Robyn Davidson, "Alone Across the Outback," *National Geographic* (May 1978): 581–611. On May 1, 1978, the Japanese explorer Naomi Uemura reached the North Pole after travelling 500 miles in 57 days by dogsled. Airplane drops were used in both journeys, however.

27. *The Tender Carnivore and the Sacred Game* (New York: Scribner's, 1973).

28. *The Indians of Yoknapatawpha*, pp. 156–57.

29. *Meditations On Hunting*, p. 140.

30. *Lord of the Flies* (1955; rpt. New York: Capricorn, 1959), p. 71.

31. *Faulkner in the University*, p. 59.

32. *The Need for Roots*, tr. A. F. Wills (London: Routledge and Kegan Paul, 1952), p. 41.

33. *Uprooted Children* is reprinted in *Migrants, Sharecroppers, Mountaineers* (Boston: Little, Brown, 1972), p. 208.

34. *Philosophy in a New Key* (1942; rpt. New York: New American Library, 1962), p. 245.

35. *Mechanization Takes Command* (New York: Oxford University Press, 1948), p. 721.

36. "Mind and Earth," *Civilization in Transition*, p. 49. In the same collection, see also "The Role of the Unconscious," in which Jung writes: "I would not speak ill of our relation to good Mother Earth. . . . He who is rooted in the soil endures."

37. *The Greening of America* (1970; rpt. New York: Bantam, 1971), pp. 188–89.

38. *Cannibals and Christians*, p. 235.

39. *The Sacred and the Profane*, p. 212.

40. *New York Review of Books* (May 3, 1973), p. 7.

41. Irving Babbitt, *The New Laokoön* (Boston, 1910), p. 185.

42. A close examination of Welty's own fiction by Bessie Chronkai, "Eudora Welty's Theory of Place and Human Relationships," *South Atlantic Bulletin* (May 1978), reveals that commonly shared places are thought to be essential in the "happy equilibrium" of individuals, families, and communities.

43. *Exile's Return*, p. 214.

44. *All the King's Men* (New York: Harcourt Brace, 1946), p. 330.

45. *You Can't Go Home Again* (New York: Sun Dial Press, 1940), p. 704.

46. *Hemingway*, p. 49.

47. See the discussion of the setting of "Big Two-Hearted River" in Richard Hovey, *Hemingway: The Inner Terrain* (Seattle: University of Washington Press, 1968), p. 34.

48. *The Great Gatsby* (New York: Scribner's, 1925), p. 3.

49. *Tono-Bungay* (1908; rpt. New York: Modern Library, 1935), pp. 276–78.

50. *Tender Is the Night* (1933; rpt. New York, Scribner's, 1962), p. 312.

51. *Lion in the Garden: Interviews with William Faulkner*, eds. James B. Merriwether and Michael Millgate (New York: Random House, 1968), p. 131.

52. Francois L. Pitavy, "The Landscape in *Light in August*," *Mississippi Quarterly*, 23 (1970), 265–72.

53. A number of commentators have addressed themselves to the use of motion in Faulkner: Karl E. Zink, "Flux and the Frozen Moment; The Imagery of Stasis in Faulkner's Prose," *PMLA* 71 (June 1956): 285–301; Darrel Abel, "Frozen Movement in *Light in August*," *Boston University Studies in English* 3 (1957): 32–44; Warren Beck, *Man in Motion: Faulkner's Trilogy* (Madison: University of Wisconsin, 1961); Richard P. Adams, *Faulkner: Myth and Motion* (Princeton: Princeton University Press, 1968); Mary Sue Carlock, "Kaleidoscopic Views of Motion," *William Faulkner: Prevailing Verities*

and World Literature, eds. Wolodymyr T. Zyla and Wendell M. Aycock (Lubbock: Texas Technical University, 1973), pp. 95–113.

54. Introduction, *Brave New World* (New York: Harper Brothers, 1950), p. xiii.

55. *Antic Hay* (1923; rpt. New York: Modern Library, 1932), p. 332.

56. Siegfried Giedion, *Space, Time, and Architecture* (1941; rpt. Cambridge: Harvard University Press, 1954), pp. 430–50.

57. "The Diamond Lane Slowdown," *Esquire* (August 1976): 36.

58. *Play It as It Lays* (New York: Farrar, Straus, 1970), p. 16.

59. *Los Angeles: The Architecture of Four Ecologies* (New York: Harper and Row, 1971), p. 213.

60. *Slouching Towards Bethlehem* (New York: Farrar, Straus, 1968), p. 165.

61. *Space and Place,* p. 138.

62. *The Last Gentleman* (1966; rpt. New York: Farrar, Straus, 1975), p. 153. Michel Butor, in taking note of the contemporary "multiplication of secondary residences" and the use of vehicles as domiciles, speaks of "a higher form of nomadism, the union of residency and wandering," "Travel and Writing," p. 11.

63. For discussions of hallucinatory landscapes, see Jonathan Baumbach, *The Landscape of Nightmare: Studies in the Contemporary American Novel* (New York: New York University Press, 1965); Freedman, *The Lyrical Novel,* pp. 38–40.

64. *Earth House Hold,* pp. 107–08, 116.

65. *Let It Come Down* (New York: Random House, 1952), p. 266.

66. *Dog Soldiers* (1973; rpt. New York: Ballantine, 1975), pp. 170–71.

67. For a fine discussion of dissolution in a single Faulkner work, see André Bleikasten, *Faulkner's "As I Lay Dying,"* tr. Roger Little (Bloomington: Indiana University Press, 1973), pp. 107–44.

68. See Patricia Hernlund, "Author's Intent: *In Watermelon Sugar,*" *Critique* 16 (1974): 5–17. For an opposite view of the novel, however, see Harvey Leavitt, "The Regained Paradise of Brautigan's *In Watermelon Sugar,*" *Critique* 16 (1974): 18–24. Brautigan's Forgotten Works resembles the "prole" neighborhoods in Orwell's *1984* where remnants of the old world could still be found. Also, there is a trout stream in the patch of golden country where Winston Smith and Julia make love.

69. For Ellison's and Bellow's treatment of New York as an underground see my *Heroic Fiction: The Epic Tradition and American Novels of the Twentieth Century* (Carbondale: Southern Illinois University Press, 1971). Good discussions of Bellow's city are: Mark M. Christhilf, "Death and Deliverance in Saul Bellow's Symbolic City," *Ball State University Forum* 18 (Spring 1977): 9–23; Robert Joseph Nadon, "Urban Values in Recent American Fiction," dissertation, University of Minnesota, 1969.

70. *America and Cosmic Man,* p. 184. See the geographer David E. Sopher's distinction between the "domicentric view" of home and the "domifuge questing myth" in "The Landscape of Home: Myth, Experience, Social Meaning," *The Interpretation of Ordinary Landscape,* ed. D. W. Meinig (New York: Oxford University Press, 1979), pp. 129–49.

71. *The Gutenberg Galaxy* (1962; rpt. New York: Signet, 1969), pp. 43–44.

72. *Human Geography in a Shrinking World,* ed. Ronald Ahler (North Scituate, Mass.: Duxbury Press, 1975), p. 33.

73. *The Art of the Novel,* p. 292.

74. *L'espace Proustien,* pp. 19, 40.

75. "Henry James and the Trapped Spectator," *Explorations* (1947; rpt. New York: New York University Press, 1964), pp. 181, 189.

76. The restrictiveness of space in Dostoevsky's city world is discussed by George Panichas, "The World of Dostoevsky," *Modern Age* 22 (Fall 1978): 346–57.

77. "Enclosure, the Adversary Culture and the Nature of the Novel," *Mosaic* 7 (1974): 11. The most extended treatment of "spatial reduction" in twentieth-century literature is to be found in Frederick Hoffman, *The Mortal No* (Princeton: Princeton University Press, 1964).

78. *Franny and Zooey* (Boston: Little, Brown, 1961), p. 93. Bathrooms in Salinger have drawn comment from a number of his readers: Ihab Hassan, "J. D. Salinger: Rare Quixotic Gesture," *Salinger: A Critical and Personal Portrait,* ed. Henry Anatole Grunwald (New York: Harper and Row, 1962), pp. 138–63; Carl F. Strauch, "Kings in the Back Row: Meaning Through Structure, A Reading of Salinger's *Catcher in the Rye*," *J. D. Salinger and the Critics,* eds. William F. Belcher and James W. Lee (Belmont, Ca.: Wadsworth, 1962), pp. 76–98.

INDEX

THE ROLE OF PLACE IN LITERATURE

was composed in 10-point Linotron 202 Times Roman and leaded two points
by Coghill Book Typesetting Co.,
with display type in Parisian by Dix Typesetting Co., Inc.;
printed by sheet-fed offset on 50-pound, acid-free Glatfelter Offset,
Smythe-sewn and bound over binder's boards in Joanna Arrestox B,
by Maple-Vail Book Manufacturing Group, Inc.;
and published by

SYRACUSE UNIVERSITY PRESS

SYRACUSE, NEW YORK 13210